Robert E. Slavin
Johns Hopkins University

Research Methods
in Education:
A Practical Guide

Prentice-Hall, Inc. Englewood Cliffs, New Jersey 07632

Library of Congress Cataloging in Publication Data

Slavin, Robert E.
  Research methods in education.

  Bibliography: p. 291
  Includes index.
  1. Education—Research. I. Title.
LB1028.S526 1984   370'.7'8   83-16073
ISBN 0-13-774364-5

Editorial/production supervision and interior design: Barbara Kelly Kittle
Cover design: George Cornell
Manufacturing buyer: Ron Chapman

Printed in the United States of America

10 9 8 7 6 5 4 3 2 1

ISBN   0-13-774364-5

Prentice-Hall International, Inc., *London*
Prentice-Hall of Australia Pty. Limited, *Sydney*
Editora Prentice-Hall do Brasil, Ltda., *Rio de Janeiro*
Prentice-Hall Canada Inc., *Toronto*
Prentice-Hall of India Private Limited, *New Delhi*
Prentice-Hall of Japan, Inc., *Tokyo*
Prentice-Hall of Southeast Asia Pte. Ltd., *Singapore*
Whitehall Books Limited, *Wellington, New Zealand*

To Nancy

Contents

chapter five

Measures and Sampling   75

chapter six

Internal and External Validity: Is This a Good Research Design?   107

chapter ten

Statistics by Computer   217

chapter eleven

Writing up the Project: Dissertations and Articles   253

Preface

This book is designed for use by students or others who are planning to do research in schools. Its primary purpose is to serve as a basic text for a course on research methods in education, but it could be used by anyone who expects to conduct educational research.

In writing this book, I have tried to communicate a flavor of what research in schools is really like, and how to use research designs and procedures to get the best possible answers to the best possible questions. I have avoided giving pat formulas for research designs, as I believe that researchers must think through the purposes of their research and then adapt methods to these purposes, rather than adapting their purposes to rigid formulas.

In addition to the material usually seen in books on research design in education, I have attempted to describe the real-life choices and pitfalls that face the educational researcher. I have provided guides (from my own experience) to getting into schools, clearing human subjects review panels, implementing projects in schools, and maintaining the integrity and impartiality of the research. Throughout the book I have tried to discuss research design issues in the light of the limitations and realities of the school setting. I wrote the book as though I were advising a student or colleague about to do his or her first educational research. My hope is that this book will increase both the quality and the quantity of school research by reassuring potential researchers that high-quality research can be done in the school setting.

Many individuals have helped make this book a reality. Nancy Madden is responsible for most of the exercises, and gave valuable advice and support at every stage of the writing process. Mary Rohrkemper made important contributions to the sections on interviews and ethnography, and made useful comments on other sections as well. Noreen Webb and William Zangwill also made many important criticisms on earlier drafts, as did Nancy Karweit (on Chapter 10) and Michael Cook (on the Glossary). Kathy Glyshaw edited several drafts, and Barbara Hucksoll and Hazel Kennedy typed them. Without the moral and substantive support of these people and others, I doubt that this book would have been completed.

Preparation of this book was supported in part by a grant from the National Institute of Education, No. NIE-G-80-0113. However, the opinions expressed are mine and do not represent NIE policy.

—Robert E. Slavin

chapter 1

The Purpose
of Research Design:
The Best Possible Answer

WHY RESEARCH?

Even though almost everyone criticizes the way it is done, no one denies the importance of education in our society. For at least twelve of their first eighteen years, most children in America spend half of their waking hours in school. Their experiences in school shape the character and intellectual resources of the next generation. More than a fifth of the entire U.S. population is in school on any given school day.

Thus, it is only natural to expect that what goes on in schools is of critical interest to the nation as a whole, and it is true that few issues of local government are more hotly debated than education. Yet much of the constant debate about how best to educate students, both within the education community and in society at large, is based on passion rather than facts, ideology rather than data.

The primary antidote to educational change (or failure to change) based on the passions of the moment is well-designed, unbiased research. Such research can be used, for example, to understand the teaching-learning process, to evaluate new instructional programs, or to see how various aspects of schools and classrooms affect learning and other outcomes. Results of educational research cannot be used by themselves to guide educational decisions; our values and laws must also be involved. But only research can provide the kind of objective information needed to intelligently make educational decisions on which so much depends.

THE LOGIC
OF RESEARCH DESIGN

Research design. These words send chills down the spines of many graduate students in education and other fields. Research design is too often seen as a complex, arcane subject that only methodologists or statisticians can possibly understand, so that the experts' prescriptions must be slavishly followed.

Actually, the basic logic of research design is quite simple. Let's say you have reason to believe that two things are related. For example, you might think that asking students more questions increases their math achievement, or that students who are liked by their classmates are likely to be more tolerant toward handicapped children than students who are less well-liked, or that the more experience teachers have, the better behaved their students will be. If you collect data on these pairs of variables (questions and math performance, popularity and attitudes toward the handicapped, teacher experience and student behavior), you can use statistics to try to find out whether or not you were correct in guessing that they are related. If your statistics say that the relationship *does* exist, your research design must enable you to say confidently that the relationship exists in *fact*, and that your observation of it is not limited to the particular group of students or teachers from whom you collected the data. If your statistics do *not* show any relationship, you want to be as sure as you can be (you can never be certain) that your failure to find a relationship is due to the fact that there really is no relationship, rather than to problems in your design, measures, or other aspects of your study.

The best research design is one that will add to knowledge *no matter what the results are.*

SCIENTIFIC METHOD:
RULING OUT
ALTERNATIVE EXPLANATIONS

Any scientific investigation begins with a *hypothesis*. A hypothesis is a formalized "hunch" about the relationship between two or more variables. A clearly stated hypothesis gives a fairly accurate idea of what we would have to do to provide evidence to confirm or disconfirm the hypothesis. A few hypotheses are listed below:

1. Use of daily mental arithmetic drills will increase the mathematics performance of fifth graders more than daily written drills.
2. Eighth-grade students who have brothers and/or sisters will be more popular among their peers than only children.

3. Teachers who belong to unions will be more highly rated by their supervisors than teachers who do not belong to unions.
4. A program in which students, based on their behavior in class, are given points exchangeable for comic books, will improve their behavior.

The purpose of research design is to determine as unambiguously as possible whether or not hypotheses such as these are true. Good research design simply rules out the greatest possible number of alternative explanations for a particular outcome.

Take the hypothesis above concerning disruptive students. Let's say we want to evaluate a method of giving points to disruptive students every two minutes if they are in their seat working on assigned material. Students may turn in their points for comic books or other rewards at the end of each day. Does this program improve the behavior of these students?

Let's say we start the program with a single student and observe his behavior. After a week we find that he is on-task (in his seat doing assigned work) 88% of the time. Because 88% of the time seems like a high figure, we conclude that the program worked. This is Experiment 1 in Figure 1–1. But how much of the time was he on-task before the program began? Since we don't know, we can't tell whether or not the program changed the student's behavior.

Now let's assume that we had measured the student's behavior the day before the program began. He was on-task 70% of the time on that day, and since he was on-task 88% of the time during the treatment, we conclude that the program was effective (see Experiment 2 in Figure 1–1). But this one day might have been unusual, so we still can't be sure that the program worked.

As a third alternative, we might have observed the student for two weeks before the beginning of treatment to get a baseline (an average level of behavior in the absence of treatment). During this time he was on-task only 75% of the time. Since his time on-task increased to 88% during the treatment, the program seems to be effective (Experiment 3 in Figure 1–1). However, it is still possible that other factors, such as changes at home, changes in other classes, or even the effect of being observed every day, made the student decide to be on-task during the week of the treatment.

To rule out this last possibility, we remove the points and rewards at the end of the week and observe for one more week. The student's on-task behavior drops back to an average of 76% (Experiment 4 in Figure 1–1). *Now* we can have some confidence that the program was what made the difference, at least for this student. Since the changes in the student's behavior correspond to the introduction and withdrawal of the treatment so directly, it is highly unlikely that factors other than the treatment could

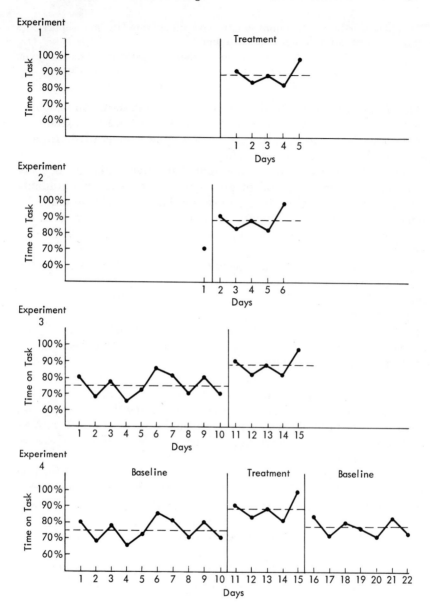

FIGURE 1–1   Ruling out Alternative Explanations

explain the changes. To rule out the possibility that this is the *only* student for whom the program would work, we would have to replicate the same experiment on several disruptive students.

As you can see, each step in this process of building a good research design ruled out one or more explanations for the student's behavior other than the explanation in which we were interested—that the program made the difference. At each step it seemed that the program was working, but a skeptic could easily point to other explanations. However, the results of Experiment 4 (illustrated in Figure 1–1) make other explanations so unlikely as to be negligible.* Experiment 4 is an example of an ABA or reversal design, described in detail in Chapter 3. However, similar logic would apply to other kinds of designs, such as experimental (Chapter 2) and correlational (Chapter 4) designs; their purpose is to isolate particular factors and rule out alternative explanations.

Theory

A *theory* is essentially an explanation of how one or more variables are related to other variables. In the experiment described above, we might have had a theory that explained *why* we expected the treatment to influence the behavior of the disruptive student. In this case, the theory might have gone something like this:

1. All organisms act to seek pleasure and avoid pain.
2. Students are organisms, so they seek pleasure and avoid pain.
3. Comic books give students pleasure.
4. If we make the acquisition of comic books dependent on a student's on-task behavior, the student's on-task behavior will increase, because increased on-task behavior will earn him or her comic books and thus pleasure.

Each of these statements is separately testable, but they are all very sensible, and the first two (on which the others rest) are quite firmly established. A theory gives a study meaning beyond the particulars of the procedures and subjects used. In the case of this study, we have found out that if points exchangeable for comic books were given as a reward for on-task behavior, the student's on-task behavior increased. But our theory would imply that if candy bars gave students pleasure, they might work just as well as comic books, or that giving points based on smiling behavior might increase smiling behavior, and so on. If we conducted similar experiments using different rewards and different behaviors and the results came out the same way, we might find a general principle of behavior that would have considerable explanatory power.

Incidentally, it is possible for an experiment's underlying *theory* to be wrong, while the data nonetheless prove the *hypothesis* to be correct. In the present example, it might turn out that some or all disruptive students don't like to read comic books at all, but the program works anyway because the points themselves give them pleasure.

*It should be noted that Experiment 4 shows the effect of the treatment on the student's behavior only if the effect is not long lasting. If the student's behavior stayed at 88% on task or continued to increase, we could not rule out the possibility that something other than the treatment caused the change. See Chapter 3 for more on this.

Science is a process of gradually refining theories, making them more general while illuminating conditions under which they may or may not apply. The experiment described above might be one small step toward a theory that would go like this:

> Given any organism, the frequency of the occurrence of any existing behavior can be increased by providing pleasurable stimuli contingent on exhibition of the behavior (that is, behaviors that are rewarded increase in frequency).

Disproving the Null Hypothesis

The hypotheses listed earlier in this chapter were stated in the form, "A is related to B." This is the hypothesis with which a researcher usually sets out. However, the logic of scientific method actually demands that we begin each experiment with the hypothesis that "A is *not* related to B." This is called the *null hypothesis* (H_o). Our task is to demonstrate *beyond any reasonable doubt* that the null hypothesis is incorrect. If we leave any significant possibility that the null hypothesis is correct, then we must continue to believe it. In the case of the experiment evaluating the point system for on-task behavior, Experiments 1, 2, and 3 left open the possibility that the null hypothesis (that is, the treatment does *not* affect student behavior) is true. Only Experiment 4 made the null hypothesis untenable.

In any study, the researcher's task is to build an argument ruling out explanations for any findings *other* than the explanation implied in the theory on which the hypothesis is based. Certain features of the research may buttress that argument considerably, but no matter how sound the design is, the researcher must always justify his or her explanation of what happened, by providing overwhelming evidence that the null hypothesis is false. The null hypothesis can never be proved to be true; it is logically impossible to prove that A is *not* related to B (because it is always possible that there is a relationship that our methods failed to detect). However, with a strong research design, if the data indicate that A and B are not related, we can establish that it is unlikely that A and B are in fact related, or if they are, that the size of the relationship is negligible.

Statistical Significance

One key concept involved in disproving the null hypothesis is *statistical significance*. Statistics can be used to test the null hypothesis. To see how this works, consider the following example.

Let's say a researcher wants to study the effects of watching a violent movie on subsequent aggressive behavior in preschoolers. She takes a group of thirty children and randomly assigns them to a "violent movie" group or a "Mary Poppins" group by putting them in pairs and then flipping a coin to see which movie each child will see. Following the movie, she lets the children play with a number of toys and records the number of aggressive acts. Two possible sets of outcome data are depicted in Figure 1–2.

In Figure 1–2, each "X" represents the number of aggressive acts for a single child. Note that in both sets of outcomes, the average number of aggressive acts for the "violent movie" group is 7 and for the "Mary Poppins" group is 5. In both cases, the "violent movie" appears to have created more aggressive behavior. But are 7 and 5 different enough from each other to indicate that their difference is due to effects of the different movies, or could this difference be due to random, meaningless variation? In other words, do we have sufficient evidence to reject the null hypothesis?

In Outcome B, we cannot reject the null hypothesis. The number of aggressive acts varies from zero to 14 in one group, and zero to 13 in the other; one third (5) of the children in the "Mary Poppins" group have scores higher than the average in the "violent movie" group. There is no clear pattern, even though the means are different. However, in Outcome

FIGURE 1–2   Example of Statistical Significance

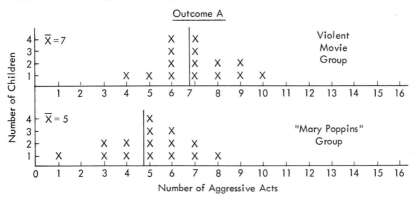

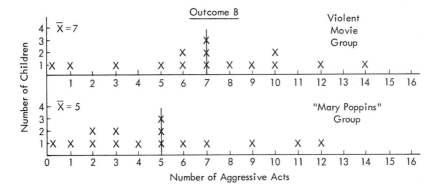

A, the "violent movie" group clearly shows more aggressive behavior than the "Mary Poppins" group. The two groups hardly overlap at all; only one child from the "Mary Poppins" group has a score above the mean of the "violent movie" group. The null hypothesis is untenable in this case, so we can reject it.

Of course, Outcome A and Outcome B are extreme cases; ordinarily, we cannot just look at a graph to see whether or not two groups differ. To make this comparison, we would use statistics that essentially test whether the difference between the two means is large compared to the amount of dispersion in the scores. If the amount of dispersion of scores around the mean is small (as in Outcome A), a small difference between means can be judged to be "statistically significant" (that is, reliably different), while a much larger difference is needed when the dispersion is greater. The statistics themselves are presented in Chapter 9, but the concept of statistical criteria for rejecting the null hypothesis is what is important here.

Types of Error

In testing a hypothesis about the relationship between two or more variables, there are two ways to be wrong. One can be called *false positive error* (related to the statistical concept of Type I or Alpha error). This type of error occurs when a relationship does not really exist, but your analysis claims that it does. The second, *false negative error* (related to Type II or Beta error) occurs when the relationship *does* exist, but your analysis fails to show that it does.

Statistics and other aspects of research design are directed primarily at minimizing the possibility of false positive error. That is, we want to be conservative about rejecting the null hypothesis. The risk of missing some true relationships is preferable to the risk of cluttering up our understanding of important variables with false relationships. We reject the null hypothesis only when the evidence against it is overwhelming. Statistical conventions generally demand that there be less than one chance in twenty (5%) that a difference between two means could have happened by chance. In some instances, researchers are not satisfied unless there is less than one chance in a hundred (1%) that random variation could account for findings. The more stringent we are in setting criteria for rejecting the null hypothesis, the more we reduce the possibility of false positive error, but by doing so, we also increase the possibility of false negative error.

However, we can also reduce the possibility of false negative error without increasing the possibility of false positive error. One means of doing this is to use large numbers of subjects. If there had been 150 children instead of 15, and the pattern of scores had been the same, it would have been clear in Outcome A that there were reliably more aggressive acts in the "violent movie" group than in the "Mary Poppins" group. Another means of reducing the possibility of false negative error is to use more reliable measures. The wide dispersion depicted in Outcome A in Figure 1–2 might have been caused by observers having difficulties deciding whether certain behaviors were aggressive or not. If observers are unsure how to code the behaviors, the aggression measure would be unreliable; that is, the same behaviors might not be coded the same way by different observers, creating some degree of meaningless variation. The aggression measure might have been made more reliable by giving the observers more training or by defining aggression more concretely. Paper-and-pencil tests can also vary in reliability; for example, unspeeded mathematics tests are almost always very reliable, because students would mostly get the same items right or wrong no matter how many times they took the test. Measures of opinion or judgment, or such nonacademic measures as tests of creativity, tend to be less reliable.

Suppose a researcher hypothesizes that physically handicapped students are more creative than nonhandicapped students. To test this hypothesis, he gives a test of creativity to ten handicapped students from a school for the handicapped and to ten nonhandicapped students in a regular school. Let's say he finds no statistically significant difference between the goups. Having failed to reject the null hypothesis, can he safely conclude that there is in fact no difference between the two groups? Not at all. The small sample size (ten per group) makes statistical significance difficult to achieve. Inadequate measurement of creativity (which is difficult to define and measure) might account for the findings. The chances are thus very high that false negative error is responsible for the failure to find significant results.

What if the researcher *had* found a significant difference between the groups in the hypothesized direction? Since small sample size and unreliable measures work against finding statistical significance, they are less of a problem if significant findings are obtained. However, there are several potential sources of bias in this study. The central hypothesis concerned differences between handicapped and nonhandicapped students in general. There are thousands of handicapped students and millions of nonhandicapped students in the United States alone. The ten of each chosen for this study (from only two schools) are certainly not representative of all such students. They may not even be comparable to each other. The physically handicapped students might be drawn from better-educated families than the nonhandicapped students. They might have better teachers, or teachers who place greater emphasis on creativity. Any number of factors other than the fact they are handicapped might account for their higher scores. If the handicapped students were significantly lower in creativity, the same problems would make this result questionable. In either case, if we decided to believe that the finding of a statistically significant difference in measured creativity between handicapped and nonhandicapped students is due to the experience of being handicapped, we could have little confidence that we were not making a false positive error.

The researcher could have predicted in advance that the chances of finding statistically significant differences between the groups was small (even if true differences did exist) and that even if he found statistically significant differences, their origin would be unclear. In other words, he could have predicted in advance that his research would be inconclusive.

Internal Validity

Internal validity refers to the degree to which a study rules out any explanations for the study's findings other than the one claimed by the researcher. If a researcher wants to compare Treatment A with Treatment B, she wants to be sure that if her study shows Treatment A to be superior to Treatment B, the reason for this will be that Treatment A really is better than Treatment B. In other words, she wants to be sure that any difference observed is due to a true difference between the treatments, not to defects in the study. The same logic applies to a finding that Treatments A and B do not differ. In a study high in internal validity, we can be relatively confident that if no differences are found between the two treatments, none exist in fact. We can never be sure that a failure to find statistically significant differences means that two treatments do not differ, but in a well-designed study high in internal validity we can make that argument more confidently than in a poorly designed study. In the fictitious example mentioned above, we learned little or nothing about handicaps and creativity as a result of the study that was done to investigate this relationship, because the study was too low in internal validity; any number of factors other than a true difference between handicapped and non-handicapped students could have explained the results.

Determining whether or not a study is high in internal validity is largely a matter of common sense, aided by experience with reading and interpreting research. For example, let's say a researcher measures students' attitudes toward school in January and then introduces a program in which students receive colorful stickers for doing well on their classwork. In May he gives the students the same attitude scale again, and he reports that students' attitudes have significantly improved. Is the sticker program effective? We have no idea, because we don't know what would have happened to student attitudes had we *not* used the stickers. Perhaps students are happier in May. Perhaps something else changed to improve their attitudes. Perhaps students wanted to help their teacher look good by responding positively on the attitude scale. On the other hand, it is possible that attitudes did improve because of the sticker program. However, if we cannot rule out all of the alternative "perhapses" beyond a reasonable doubt, our study has little internal validity, and it therefore has little informative value. The burden of proof is always on the researcher to argue that his or her explanation for the study results in the only explanation that has any real chance of being true. Common threats to internal validity in educational research are discussed in Chapter 6.

External Validity

In social science research, it is never enough to say that, for a particular sample, variable A and variable B are related, or that group A is different from group B. The next question is "So what?" If, for example, we find that in Ms. Jackson's twelfth-grade physics class, students' heights are correlated with their physics grades, we know very little. Would that relationship hold up in other physics classes? In other subjects? At other grade levels? Is it due to that fact that twelfth-grade boys tend to be taller than girls, and that Ms. Jackson favors boys in her grading, or to some other explanation?

As scientists, we have very little interest in Ms. Jackson's physics class unless we can learn something in it that has meaning for some larger class of individuals, such as all physics students, all science students, all twelfth graders, or all high school students. The degree to which the results of a study can be generalized or applied to a population in which we are interested is called *external validity* or *generalizability*. External validity is not as cut-and-dried as internal validity, because we never know for certain that a finding has external validity until we assess it on the entire population in which we are interested. If the population we wish to understand is that of a small Pacific island, we might be able to study the entire population. However, even when anthropologists study such populations, they are really trying to learn principles that will have some application to understanding other Pacific islanders, or even to understanding human society in general. In research in schools, we almost always intend our research to have meaning for a much larger population and under a much wider range of conditions than the particular sample and conditions we study. For this reason, external validity is a major concern. Threats to external validity which are common in educational research are discussed in Chapter 6.

TYPES OF RESEARCH
IN EDUCATION

All research can be subsumed under two large categories: experimental and nonexperimental. In *experimental* research, a researcher manipulates one or more *independent* variables to observe the effect on one or more *dependent* variables. For example, a researcher might study the effect of the use of reading groups in the fifth grade by randomly assigning some teachers to use reading groups and others to use whole-class instruction, and then measuring the reading achievement of the students. What makes this an experiment is that the researcher assigned the teachers to use reading groups or whole-class instruction, perhaps by flipping a coin to decide which method each teacher should use. The independent variable manipulated by the researcher is teaching method (reading groups versus whole-class instruction); the dependent variable (so called because its values may *depend* on the value of the independent variables) is reading achievement.

In *nonexperimental* research, the researcher usually observes relationships between two or more variables *as they exist*, without trying to manipulate them. For example, a researcher could have attempted to answer the question about reading groups and achievement by locating a group of teachers who already use reading groups or whole-class instruction and then measuring their students' achievement. In other nonexperimental research, the researcher simply seeks to describe a certain group in terms of one or more variables, as in an opinion poll designed to discover how many teachers favor open space classroom construction.

Experimental Comparison Designs

There are two primary kinds of experimental research. The most common is the *experimental comparison* (see Chapter 2), in which different groups are assigned by the researcher to receive different treatments, after which the groups are compared on one or more dependent measures. The comparison between teachers assigned to use reading groups and those assigned to use whole-class instruction is an example of an experimental comparison design, as is the study of the effects of watching violent movies discussed earlier. Of course, an experimental comparison can involve more than two treatments; for example, we might compare the achievement of students who receive homework assignments every day, three times per week, once per week, or never. Experimental comparisons always involve comparisons of *groups* that have received different treatments.

Single Case Experiments

The second primary experimental design is the *single-case experimental design* (see Chapter 3). In this type of design, the same subject or subjects are given different treatments in a planned sequence, and the subjects' behaviors are observed under the different treatments. If these behaviors change when the treatments change, then it can be demonstrated that the behaviors (the dependent variable) are under the control of the treatments (the independent variables). The study of in-seat behavior described earlier (and depicted in Figure 1-1) is an example of a single-case experiment. Sometimes a group is treated as a "single case." For example, a teacher might record the number of "naughty words" used each day by his class as a whole. Then he might announce that for each "naughty word" he hears, the entire class will lose one minute of recess. After two weeks of this program, he might stop the "naughty word" program. The dependent variable in this study is the average number of "naughty words" used by the class as a whole, so the class is treated as the "single case." If the number of "naughty words" drops sharply during the treatment period but goes up again when the treatment is removed, we can say with confidence that class "naughty word" behavior was affected by the treatment.

Correlational Designs

The most common nonexperimental design is the *correlational design* (see Chapter 4), in which the researcher measures two or more variables to determine whether or not there is a relationship between them. A correlation coefficient can range from -1.0 to $+1.0$. If one variable is high when another is high but low when the other is low, the two variables are *positively correlated*. For example, we know that student reading performance is positively correlated with mathematics performance. This does not mean that reading skill and math skill are the same; many good readers are poor in math, and vice versa. However, *on the average*, a good reader is usually better than average in math, and a student who is good in math is a better-than-average reader. For example, on the Stanford Achievement Test, the correlation between total reading and total mathematics scores is $+0.82$ for fourth graders, a high positive correlation (because it is close to $+1.0$). An example of a negative correlation is that between grades and days absent; students with high grades have fewer days absent than those with low grades. The strength of a correlation can be determined from its distance from zero, not its sign. A correlation of -0.7 is stronger than a correlation of $+0.2$. This can be easily understood if you consider that if the correlation between grades and days absent were -0.6, the correlation between grades and days *present* (really another measure of the same variable) would be $+0.6$.

Descriptive Research

Another type of nonexperimental research, *descriptive research* (see Chapter 4), simply seeks to describe particular phenomena as they are. Opinion polling is one kind of descriptive research. For example, we might ask teachers their attitudes toward teacher accountability. In most descriptive research, the principal consideration is *sampling*. If we want to be able to determine the attitudes of American teachers toward teacher accountability, we would have to give questionnaires to a large sample of teachers at all levels of education throughout the U.S. Obviously, the attitudes of teachers at any one school or in any one district do not represent the attitudes of all teachers.

Local, state, and national testing programs are another form of descriptive research. They yield information on such topics as the average grade equivalent or percentile scores of students in particular schools, districts, or larger units. When tests give information that compares students to other students or to norms established for a test, they are called *norm-referenced tests*. In contrast, we might want to know the percentage of students who can correctly answer certain questions or perform certain operations. For example, we might be interested to know specifically what percentage of all Missouri high school students can figure sales tax on purchases totaling $11.75. This type of test would be called a *criterion-referenced test*.

Evaluation research is descriptive research directed at determining whether or not a particular program has achieved its goals. For example, a school might decide to extend the number of hours it opens its school library for a trial period. The school administration might establish a 20% increase in library use as a criterion of success. Evaluation research might simply seek to find out whether this criterion was met.

Another type of descriptive research is called *ethnography*. In ethnographic research, the researcher obtains very detailed and elaborate descriptions of activities in a particular setting. For example, an ethnographer might observe teacher-student interactions in high, middle, and low reading groups to get a sense of how life in these different settings is different for teachers and students. Ethnographic research makes few claims regarding representativeness, concentrating instead on explaining social processes in great detail.

Finally, *historical research* examines evidence from the past in an attempt to describe past events or to draw principles from the past that may have continuing relevance. For example, an historical researcher might study the life of John Dewey to understand the role and experience of innovators in American education, an understanding that might help explain the experience of educational innovators today.

ESSENTIALS OF RESEARCH DESIGN

Research design is really quite simple, as it is based on logic and common sense. The critical skill in research design is to decide upon a question that is important, and then to choose research methods that will answer that question as unambiguously as possible, given limited resources. Letting research methods determine one's questions, or following research design formulas instead of thinking through what one is trying to learn, impairs the usefulness of research in informing us about the issues we want to understand. If a researcher can in all honesty answer the following questions in the affirmative, he or she knows all that is necessary about research design:

1. Is the problem I am planning to study an *important* one?
2. Do I have a sensible *theory* that links the variables I plan to study?
3. If the data *confirm* my hypotheses or expectations, can I be confident (a) that the relationship I hypothesized to exist does in fact exist, (b) that it exists for the reason I say it exists, and (c) that the finding has meaning beyond the particular group I studied?
4. If the data *fail to confirm* my hypotheses, can I be as confident as it is possible to be that the relationship I hypothesized does not in fact exist?
5. Is the study *feasible* given my resources?

The following chapters are guides to answering these questions.

EXERCISES

A researcher conducted a study to determine whether having football games improved students' attachment to the school. He stopped a group of 10 students in the hall and gave them a questionnaire involving one question about school spirit one day after a football game. He stopped another group of 10 students and gave them the same questionnaire on another day.

1) State the null hypothesis of this study.
2) How does the sample size affect the chances of false positive or false negative error?
3) How does the method of choosing students for the study affect the chances of false positive or false negative error?
4) How does the structure of the questionnaire chosen affect the chances of false positive or false negative error?
5) Suppose the researcher in this study found a statistically significant difference between the two groups of students given the questionnaire. The students given the questionnaire the day after the football game showed more school spirit. What alternative explanations for this can you supply?
6) Suppose the research found no differences between the groups given the questionnaire. What can you conclude from the study?
7) Comment on the internal and external validity of this study.

chapter 2

Experimental Comparison Designs

No single experimental design is best for all purposes. Each has its benefits and its problems, both in terms of interpretability of results and in terms of practicability. Designs must be suited to the questions the researcher is asking and the nature of the data. A true experiment, usually considered the "best" design, may be completely inappropriate for some kinds of investigations; single-case, correlational, or descriptive designs may be the most appropriate designs for some questions. However, the experiment—in which the researcher randomly assigns subjects to two or more groups, applies different treatments to the different groups, and compares results—is the design of choice for most educational research.

RANDOM ASSIGNMENT

One of the most important features of most experimental comparison designs is the use of *random assignment* of subjects to the various treatments. In an experimental comparison study, some subjects (students, for example) are assigned to receive one treatment, while others are assigned to receive a different treatment. Some students might be assigned to study mathematics using programmed instruction, while other students are assigned to receive mathematics instruction in the form of lectures. If students are randomly assigned to treatments, the experimenter determines which students will be in which treatments by a chance process, such as flipping a coin to determine whether each student will go into the programmed instruction class or the lecture class (for example, all "heads" might be assigned to the lecture class).

Random assignment solves one of the most critical problems of research design: *selection bias*. One of the biggest problems in learning from studies that do not use random assignment evidence is the difficulty in separating selection effects (preexisting differences between individuals or groups) from treatment effects. Does Jones Junior High really do the best job of teaching in the city, or does it simply have the best students? Do good coaches make good teams, or do good players make their coaches look good by winning? Does small class size increase student achievement, or do more able students tend to find themselves more often in small classes? Whenever we wish to compare the effect of one treatment to another, we must be sure that the subjects in each treatment are reasonably equal (on the average) on all important criteria. Otherwise, unequal selection effects, or selection bias, may make any differences we find between treatments uninterpretable.

Random assignment to different treatment conditions virtually rules out selection bias as an explanation for differences between treatments, making it one of the best ways to avoid false positive or false negative errors. The essence of random assignment is that there is no way to tell in advance who will receive each treatment. For example, a researcher might take a list of 100 children, put their names on slips of paper in a box, mix up the slips, and draw names at random, putting half of the slips in one pile and the other half in another. The children whose names are in the first pile will see a film designed to improve their attitudes toward Mexican-Americans; the other students will see a film unrelated to Mexican-Americans. At the end, all students will complete a questionnaire on their attitudes toward Mexican-Americans.

What is important about random assignment in this study is that picking students at random for the two conditions answers most questions about the equivalence of the two groups before they saw the movies. If the group that saw the film on Mexican-Americans does have more positive attitudes on the attitude scale given after the film, it is highly unlikely that this conclusion would be invalid because the selected students are brighter, more tolerant, more experienced with Mexican-Americans, or from more liberal families than the other students. All students had an equal chance to be chosen for either group, and the number of students in each condition (50) is large enough to make it almost certain that the groups will be very close to equal on these and other factors.

Random Assignment of Individuals

There are many ways random assignment can be done. We might use a table of random numbers (one appears in the back of most statistics texts). To do this, we would first give a number to each student, from 00 to 99. We would then flip a coin to decide whether to start with the experimental group or the control group, and we would choose a random starting place in the random numbers table. Let's say our coin flip indicated that we would start with the control group, and the random numbers table began as follows:

7628213143295835...

To do the random assignment, we would assign student #76 to the control group, student #28 to the experimental group, #21 to control, #31 to experimental, and so on. When we ran into a number for the second time, we would skip over it. We would continue this process until all 100 students had been assigned.

Stratified Random Assignment

Although random assignment usually produces functionally equivalent groups, there is no guarantee that the groups will in fact be equal on every relevant factor. By chance, it is possible that the groups will be different in some important way, especially if the number of subjects in each group is smaller than thirty or so. Whenever it is possible to obtain data on each subject on variables that could be related to the outcomes we are studying, particularly when the number of students in each group is small, random assignment should be stratified on these variables. Stratified random assignment means that students are randomly assigned *within* a particular category, or stratum. In our example regarding the Mexican-American film, we might want to make sure that there were equal numbers of boys and girls in each treatment group, because we suspect that boys and girls might have different attitudes or that they might be affected differently by the film. Let's assume that there were 56 boys and 44 girls. We might have randomly assigned the boys (28 boys to each treatment group) and then the girls (22 to each group), guaranteeing that the two groups would have equal numbers of boys and girls. If there were blacks and whites in the sample, we might have randomly assigned students within the subsamples of black boys, black girls, white boys, and white girls, thereby stratifying on two variables, sex and race.

In research on student achievement, the most important variable we need to be sure is equal in different treatment groups is prior academic achievement level. Because students' learning rates depend to a large degree on how much they have learned in the past, even small group differences on prior achievement tests (or similar measures) can make meaningful interpretation of differences in posttest measures difficult.

Figure 2–1 shows how a class of 31 students might be randomly assigned to two treatment groups, stratifying on academic achievement level and sex.

FIGURE 2-1   Example of Random Assignment Stratifying
on Achievement Level and Sex

	Boys	Girls
(Highest) Achievement Rank	1. Sam 2. Tyrone ✓	1. Amanda ✓ 2. Sylvia
	3. Raoul ✓ 4. Alan	3. Stephanie ✓ 4. Isabel
	5. Todd ✓ 6. Ivan	5. Gwynn 6. Natalie ✓
	7. Frank ✓ 8. Isaac	7. Maria ✓ 8. Evelyn
	9. Eric 10. David ✓	9. Noreen ✓ 10. Teresa
	11. Richard 12. Antonio ✓	11. Ellen ✓ 12. Xanda ✓
	13. Nathan ✓ 14. Dan	13. Melissa 14. Paula
(Lowest)	15. Otto 16. Mack ✓	15. Laura ✓

Note: A check (✓) indicates that the student was randomly assigned to the experimental group.

The boys and girls were separately ranked, based on their most recent grades (achievement test scores or teacher judgment could also have been used). Then they were placed in matched pairs for random assignment (for example, Sam and Tyrone are the highest scoring boys, Paula and Laura are the lowest scoring girls). To assign the students to the experimental (checked) or control (unchecked) group, a coin was flipped for each pair. If the coin came up heads, the top student in the pair was assigned to the experimental group; if tails, the bottom student. Note that one student, Maria, was left over in the matching. We made sure that the leftover student was average in past achievement, so that it would make no difference to which group she was assigned. We flipped our coin and assigned her to the experimental group.

Stratifying on sex and achievement makes it certain that the experimental and control groups will have very nearly equal numbers of boys and girls and of high and low achievers, but the groups are still randomly assigned because there was no way to predict who would be in each group.

Not using random assignment increases the chance that we will make either a false positive or a false negative error. For example, let's say that instead of randomly assigning students to treatments, we had shown the attitude-improvement film to Ms. Jackson's first-period class and the neutral film to her fifth-period class. If attitude differences favoring the students who saw the attitude-change film are found, they could well be due to the fact that the students in the first-period class already had more positive attitudes than those in the fifth-period class. This would produce a false positive error. If differences are not found, it could be that the film (which was, let's assume, effective in improving attitudes) had the effect of making the class with poor attitudes resemble the one with good attitudes, so the failure to find statistically significant differences would be a false negative error.

Unfortunately, random assignment is often impossible in social science research. In a study about differences in creativity between handicapped and nonhandicapped students, it is of course impossible to randomly assign students to be handicapped or nonhandicapped. School administrators are usually reluctant to randomly assign students to classes for any substantial period of time, and it is almost impossible to randomly assign students to schools. On the other hand, it is often relatively easy to randomly assign classes or teachers to different treatments in educational research, and there are ways to deal with the problems of nonrandom assignment. These are discussed below. However, whenever there is a deviation from true random assignment of individuals, the burden of proof is on the researcher to demonstrate that groups being compared can truly be considered equivalent.

RANDOMIZED
EXPERIMENTAL COMPARISONS

The ideal experimental design is the true experiment, or *randomized experimental comparison*, in which individuals are randomly assigned to one or more treatment conditions, the treatments are applied, and the results are compared. A pretest may be given at the beginning of the study. This is not absolutely necessary, however, since the random assignment is likely to produce equal groups, especially if the number of subjects in each group is large and/or the randomization was stratified on characteristics that must be equal across treatments (such as achievement level, sex, or race, depending on what the research is about).

As an example of a randomized experimental comparison, consider the case of a researcher who wants to find out whether students learn better from text if they are allowed to talk about the text with a classmate (classmate discussion) than if the teacher conducts a class discussion on the text (teacher-led discussion). The researcher locates four fifth-grade classes in an elementary school and randomly assigns students to four new classes, stratifying on reading achievement test scores to be sure that the groups are equal on this critical variable. Two classes are assigned to receive the classmate discussion treatment, and two to receive the teacher-led discussion treatment. Each day the students spend twenty minutes reading short stories, and twenty minutes either discussing the stories with partners or participating in a whole-class discussion, depending on the treatment. To rule out possible differences due to teacher abilities or styles, teachers are rotated each day across the four classes, alternating classmate discussion and teacher-led discussion treatment groups. After four days, all students are tested on their recall of the main ideas from the stories.

In terms of internal validity, this is a good study. The groups can be definitely considered equivalent, because students were randomly assigned to groups stratifying on reading achievement. If the groups turn out to differ significantly on the posttest, we can be relatively confident that it was the difference in treatments, not preexisting differences between students or other external factors, that accounts for the difference in outcomes. This is the beauty of the true experiment; the design of the study rules out most explanations for findings other than that the treatments made the difference (although it should be noted that we may not know what aspect of the treatment made the difference.)

While there is no better experimental design than a randomized experimental comparison (all other things being equal), this is not to say that use of such a design is a *guarantee* of internal validity.

Consider the above example, a true experiment. What if the researcher had used only two classes instead of four, and had not rotated teachers? In this case, it would have been impossible to separate teacher effects (for example, the ability of the teacher to organize the class and present material) from true treatment effects. Since we are interested in the treatments and not in the qualities of individual teachers, teacher effects are pure nuisance.

On the other hand, rotating teachers across classes has its problems too. Although this procedure reduces the chance that teacher effects will be confounded with treatment effects, it could be argued that the rotation itself becomes part of both treatments, and might impact the two treatments differently. For example, the classmate discussion group did not rely very much on the teachers, as students spent their time either reading independently or working with partners. In the teacher-led discussion treatment, the teachers' abilities to lead a class discussion was very important. It could be argued that the experiment was biased against the teacher-led discussion treatment because the rotating teachers would not have enough time to build rapport with their classes and would thus be less effective then they would have been if they had had a longer time to work with a class. On the other hand, if there were no differences between the classmate discussion and teacher-led discussion groups, it could be argued that the experiment did not give the students in the classmate discussion group enough time to learn how to discuss effectively with each other, while the students in the teacher-led discussion group were doing something more familiar that would not require any start-up time. The brevity of the study might have been dictated by the use of random assignment of students, as teachers might well be unwilling to have their students in randomly assigned groups (and to rotate among them) for more than a week or two.

What this discussion is meant to convey is that in field research, there is no way to guarantee an unassailable design. The classmate discussion study described above is a good study. Its design rules out the objections (sample differences and teacher effects) most common in educational research. Because it is an experiment with random assignment, there would be little possibility that factors other than the treatments caused any differences between the groups. The topic is important and builds on prior literature. This does not mean that the criticisms discussed above are invalid; it does mean that the study itself is strong enough to be a basis for further research (perhaps involving a large number of classes, so that teachers need not be rotated) that might answer the criticisms. However, these criticisms illustrate that while randomized experimental comparisons have important strengths, by themselves they are in no way a guarantee of adequate internal validity. Only educated common sense can tell us when a study adequately answers the questions it poses.

Pretesting

Donald Campbell and Julian Stanley's *Experimental and Quasi-Experimental Designs for Research* (1963), which for two decades has been the most widely read book on experimental design in education research, advocates the use of experimental designs in which groups are randomly assigned to experimental and control groups, the experimental group receives the treatment, and then both groups are posttested, (as in the Mexican-American film example discussed above). They feel that this design may be superior to pretest-posttest experimental designs, where randomly assigned groups are pretested, the treatment is applied to one group, and both groups are posttested. As noted earlier, pretests are not absolutely necessary when subjects are randomly assigned to treatments, but are they harmful or helpful?

Campbell and Stanley argue that giving a pretest leaves open the possiblity that the pretest may differentially sensitize the subjects in the different treatments, leading to a false appearance that the treatment made a difference, when in fact the treatment would not have worked unless the pretest was also given. This might occur in the study of the film designed to change attitudes toward Mexican-Americans discussed earlier in this chapter; filling out a survey on their attitudes toward Mexican-Americans just prior to seeing the film might make students especially sensitive to the film. However, the problem of sensitizing students to experimental treatments is rare in educational research, especially research on achievement. It is hard to see why a spelling pretest would sensitize students to one form of spelling instruction or another. In the case of the Mexican-American attitude film, the students were not told that the purpose of the film was to change their attitudes, but a pretest might tip them off. It would be difficult to teach spelling, however, without students being aware of your primary objective.

While the dangers of pretesting in educational research are minimal except in unusual circumstances, the dangers of not doing so are great. What if the experimental and control groups are initially equal, but three students leave school before the end of the project or refuse to fill out a valid posttest? Getting a 100% return rate is rare in educational research. If any students are lost we no longer know whether or not we have equivalent groups, and we have no way to do anything about it; such data are of limited usefulness.

Even more important, when pretests are given, they make it possible to use analysis of covariance (see Chapter 9) to compare group means. In analysis of covariance (or equivalent multiple regression procedures), scores on an outcome measure are adjusted for scores on some number of covariates, such as pretests. Analysis of covariance can make groups that are somewhat different on a pretest approximately equivalent for statistical analysis. For example, let's say that in an experiment with two treatments, we find that despite random assignment, students in Treatment A have a pretest mean of 6.4 grade equivalents, while students in Treatment B have a pretest mean of 6.0 grade equivalents. Of course, even if the treatments had no effect, we would expect students in Treatment A to score higher than those in Treatment B on the posttest, because they started higher. Analysis of covariance would adjust the posttest scores to correct for this. The adjustment would diminish the posttest scores for Treatment A and increase the posttest scores for Treatment B. The magnitude of this adjustment would depend on the correlation between the pretest and the posttest. The higher the correlation, the greater the adjustment (see Chapter 4 for definitions of correlation).

Analysis of covariance also usually increases statistical power (the ability of a statistic to avoid false negative error) by diminishing the effect of student-to-student differences on the dependent measure (see Chapter 9). This advantage of analysis of covariance and related statistical procedures makes pretesting highly desirable in most educational research, particularly research on academic achievement and other variables likely to be correlated with achievement. So much of the variance in any test score is explained by student ability or past achievement that treatment effects are almost always small in relation to student-to-student differences. If these differences are not controlled for using analysis of covariance or a similar procedure, treatments that are in fact effective will often appear ineffective—a serious and common false negative error.

EXPERIMENTS WITH MORE THAN TWO TREATMENTS

Of course, comparing one group to another is not the only possible experimental comparison. For example, a researcher might randomly assign 90 students to three mathematics classes, one that takes weekly tests and gets daily homework, one that gets daily homework but no tests, and one that gets neither homework nor tests. In this design, we might pretest all students on their mathematics achievement, implement the treatments for several weeks, and posttest. We would then perform a 3 x 1 analysis of covariance, with the pretests as covariates (see Chapter 9).

FIGURE 2-2 Hypothetical 3 x 1 Experimental Comparison

Homework + Tests	Homework Only	Control
N = 30	N = 30	N = 30

Factorial Designs

Factorial designs are another type of experimental comparison design involving more than two treatments. In a factorial design, treatments may be organized in such a way that they share common factors with other treatments. A "factor" is a variable that may take on a small number of values or categories. Examples of factors might include sex (male versus female), race (black versus white versus Oriental), or type of school (private school versus public school). Continuous variables such as achievement, age, or attitudes (which can take on many values) can be made into factors by establishing ranges of values for each level of the factor. For example, IQ could be a factor with three levels—low (for example, below 85), average (85-115), or high (above 115). Other variables could be dichotomized (reduced to two levels) by splitting subjects into a high group (above the median) and a low group (below the median).

Experimental treatments may be seen as factors. For example, if the Homework and Tests study could have had four groups, it might have used a 2 x 2 factorial design, as depicted in Figure 2-3.

	Tests	No Tests
Homework	Homework + Tests	Homework Only
No Homework	Tests Only	Control

FIGURE 2-3
Hypothetical 2 x 2
Experimental Comparison

The factors in the experiment depicted in Figure 2-3 are "homework" (homework versus no homework) and "tests" (tests versus no tests). The factorial design has more statistical power (that is, smaller differences between means will be statistically significant) and produces more information than would a comparison of the same four treatments in a 4 x 1 analysis. A 2 x 2 analysis of variance or analysis of covariance for the study diagrammed in Figure 2-3 would produce a statistic for a homework factor, one for a test factor, and one for a homework by tests interaction. Some of the possible outcomes of this factorial study are shown in Figure 2-4.

Interactions in Factorial Experiments. An interaction describes a relationship between two factors in which a certain combination of the factors produces a result that is not simply the sum of the factors' effects. For example, if we gave a rat food but no water, he would survive a little longer than if we gave him nothing. If we gave the rat water but no food, he would also survive a little longer than if we gave him nothing. However, if we gave the rat food *and* water, he would survive much longer than we would expect based on the increases in survival time we saw for food alone or water alone.*

Figure 2-4 depicts some of the main effects and interactions that could have been seen in the 2 × 2 factorial experiment on homework and tests. A "main effect" indicates that on the average, subjects who were at one level of a factor (e.g. homework vs. no homework) scored differently than subjects at another level of the same factor, regardless of their scores on other factors (e.g. tests vs. no tests). In Figure 2-4, a "homework" main effect would be observed if, on the average, the students in the homework + tests group and the homework only group learned more than students in the tests only group and the no homework, no tests group.

Interactions are usually seen in factorial studies when subjects in one cell score much better (or much worse) than they would have been expected to score based on their respective factors. For example, in the

---

*This is an extreme example of an interaction, but illustrates one way in which a certain combination of two factors might produce an effect greater than the sum of the effects of each factor.

	Homework	No Homework
Tests	Hi	Lo
No Tests	Hi	Lo

Homework Main Effect
No Effect of Tests
No Interactions

	Homework	No Homework
Tests	Hi	Hi
No Tests	Lo	Lo

Tests Main Effect
No Effect of Homework
No Interactions

	Homework	No Homework
Tests	Hi	Lo
No Tests	Lo	Hi

No Main Effects
Homework by Tests Interaction

	Homework	No Homework
Tests	Very Hi	Hi
No Tests	Hi	Lo

Two Main Effects
Homework by Tests Interaction

FIGURE 2-4   Some Possible Outcomes of a 2 x 2 Factorial Experiment

homework and tests study, it is possible that either daily homework or regular tests would have a small positive effect on achievement, but a combination of the two would have a strong positive effect on achievement. That is, homework and tests would have an "interactive" effect on achievement; they work better together than they work separately (analogous to the joint effect of food and water in the example discussed above).

Interactions may take many forms, and their forms have considerable bearing on their interpretations. Let's say we compared traditional instruction to an individualized instruction program in fifth-and eighth-grade classes, and found that traditional instruction was better than individualized instruction in the fifth grade but the opposite was true at the eighth-grade level. This is called a *disordinal interaction* because the *order* of the treatments depend on values of the other variable. In this case, opposite results are obtained for type of instruction depending on the grade level involved. Another possible outcome might have been that the individualized instruction program was a little better than traditional instruction for fifth graders, but much better than traditional instruction for eighth graders. This is called an *ordinal interaction*; the results are larger at one grade level than at the other, but the order of the treatments is the same at each grade level (that is, the individualized treatment is higher at both grade levels). Ordinal and disordinal interactions are diagrammed in Figure 2-5.

The meaning of an interaction depends to a considerable degree on whether the interaction is ordinal or disordinal. In a disordinal interaction, main effects for one factor depend completely on the other factor. In the disordinal interaction depicted in Figure 2-5, we cannot talk about the effects of individualized versus traditional instruction in general, because the effects depend totally on grade level. In contrast, in a case of an ordinal interaction, main effects are interpretable. In the example discussed above, individualized instruction is better than traditional instruction at both grade levels. However, the interaction does require caution about assuming that individualized instruction will be more effective than traditional instruction for, say, third graders, because they fall outside the range we studied. In fact, in the graph of the ordinal interaction presented in Figure 2-5, if the lines were extended down to third grade, they would show an advantage of traditional instruction over individualized instruction. However, we could make no assumptions about third graders until we had replicated the study including a third grade sample.

For more on interactions, see Campbell and Stanley (1963) and Winer (1971). Also see Chapter 9 for statistics for factorial designs.

Factorial Designs with More than Two Factors.   Factorial designs may have any number of factors, including a mix of treatments (to which subjects are randomly assigned by the experimenter) and factors over which the researcher has no experimental control. For example, a researcher might hypothesize different effects of homework for boys and girls and for blacks and whites. She might set up a 2 x 2 x 2 factorial design, as in Figure 2-6.

FIGURE 2-5   Ordinal and Disordinal Interactions

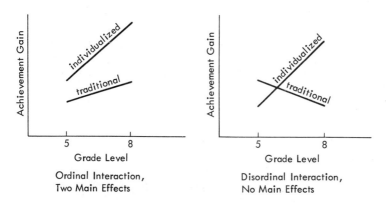

Ordinal Interaction,
Two Main Effects

Disordinal Interaction,
No Main Effects

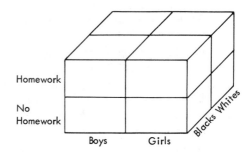

FIGURE 2-6
Hypothetical 2 x 2 x 2 Experimental
Comparison

If such a design were used, the researcher would probably stratify on sex and race in making her random assignments to treatments (homework versus no homework) to make sure that boys, girls, blacks, and whites are approximately equally distributed among the various cells. A three-factor experiment of this type would produce three main effects, three two-way interactions (homework by sex, homework by race, race by sex), and one three-way interaction (homework by sex by race).

Chapter 9 describes statistical procedures for factorial design as well as for analysis of variance and analysis of covariance.

ALTERNATIVES TO RANDOM ASSIGNMENT OF INDIVIDUALS

In school research, random assignment of individual students is very difficult to achieve. Because the purpose of schooling is to educate and socialize students, not to provide a laboratory for researchers, schools are often less than enthusiastic about disrupting class assignments during the school year, and are no more positively inclined toward making permanent class assignments on a random basis. When random assignment can be made, it is often for a short time or with a small group. For example, it may not be difficult to get a teacher to divide his or her class into two randomly assigned groups for a week or two, but for many kinds of research these groups would be too small and the time period too brief for a meaningful study. Furthermore, a randomly assigned group is itself an innovation in schools, where tracking, student course selection, or other systematic assignments are the norm. A randomly chosen group of students who do not know one another may be so different from the typical classroom setting that research with such a group may have limited generalizability; in fact, any situation that allows for random assignment may already be so unusual that results from that situation may be difficult to apply to other settings.

Random Assignment of Classes, Schools, or Teachers

Random assignment of individual students is not an absolute requirement for a valid study. All other things being equal, it is still the best way to be sure that groups are functionally equivalent, but as noted above, all other things are *not* typically equal, as individual random assignment has its own problems in school settings.

A more practical procedure for much educational research is random assignment of classes (or schools) instead of students. Consider the study of the effects of homework and weekly tests on student achievement, described above. In the example, three classes were mixed up and randomly assigned to the three conditions. In this design, teacher effects would be completely confounded with treatment effects unless the teacher were rotated across classes, but the rotation itself would introduce practical as well as experimental design problems. The rotation could be avoided by having several teachers in each treatment, but to find a large number of teachers willing to have their classes randomly assigned is extremely difficult.

As an alternative to this procedure, classes could be randomly assigned to the three treatments. For example, the researcher might solicit three fourth-, fifth- and sixth-grade teachers at each of two schools (a total of eighteen classes). She might assign classes to each condition within grades and within schools, so that one intact class is assigned to each treatment at each grade level in each school. All classes are pretested, the treatments are implemented, and the students are posttested. Analysis of covariance is used.

This study has many advantages over the three-class version with individual random assignment. The larger number of teachers (six per experimental treatment group) makes it highly unlikely that teacher effects would be confounded with treatment effects; rotation is unnecessary, and potential school effects are neutralized because there are three teachers in each school in each treatment. Random assignment of classes makes substantial pretest differences unlikely, but the analysis of covariance is capable of adjusting for any small differences that do exist. There are six times as many subjects in each group, making a false negative error less likely. The only real drawback to this design is that there is six times as much data to deal with and six times as many teachers and classes to monitor. When random assignment is done at the class level, at least three classes (preferably five or more) should be included in each treatment, to reduce the chance of false treatment effects because of a peculiar class or teacher (see Slavin, 1983).

Of course, the benefits of random assignment at the class level are simply benefits of large sample size and larger numbers of teachers. These are not impossible to achieve with random assignment at the individual level. However, studies with random assignment of individual students rarely involve more than two or three classes, making teacher and class effects a serious problem.

Within-Teacher Random Assignment.   In schools with departmentalization, where teachers have more than one class in the same subject, it is often possible to have teachers serve as their own controls by randomly assigning two or more of their classes to experimental and control (treatment 1 and treatment 2) conditions. A very good study can be done in such circumstances with as few as two teachers, where each teaches at least two experimental and two control classes. A smaller number of teachers can be used because in this design we need not be very concerned about teacher effects. We do still want at least three classes in each treatment condition, to reduce the chances that treatment effects are due to peculiarities of a single class.

When randomly assigning teachers' classes to different treatments, especially when classes are tracked, stratifying is critical. To do this, we would assign classes to treatments stratifying on teacher and on average class achievement, in the same way we assigned students to treatments stratifying on sex and achievement level. Consider a study in which the researcher wants to find out if weekly certificates for the most improved student will improve the motivation and achievement of all students. The researcher obtains the cooperation of three eighth-grade mathematics teachers in a junior high school. One teacher, Ms. Wilson, volunteers all five of her classes. Mr. Clark has two classes for the talented and gifted that he does not want to be involved in the study, so he volunteers three classes. Ms. Gonzales teaches only three eighth-grade classes, which she volunteers for the study. Classes are tracked in this school. Based on the class averages on a standardized test, the classes are ranked from 8-1 (the highest-scoring eighth-grade class) to 8-11 (the lowest-scoring class). Each teacher's classes are listed in Figure 2-7. The researcher puts the classes into comparable pairs for random assignment, so that no matter how the coin flips go, the two groups will be about equal. Figure 2-7 illustrates the random assignment. The pairs are circled. Note that the

FIGURE 2-7   Example of Random Assignment of Classes

Ms. Wilson	Mr. Clark	Ms. Gonzales	Experimental	Control
8 - 5	8 - 1	8 - 3	8-5 (Wilson)	8-7 (Wilson)
8 - 7	8 - 2	8 - 4	8-11 (Wilson)	8-8 (Wilson)
8 - 8	8 - 9	8 - 6	8-9 (Clark)	8-10 (Wilson)
8 - 10			8-2 (Clark)	8-1 (Clark)
8 - 11			8-4 (Gonzales)	8-3 (Gonzales)
				8-6 (Gonzales)

middle-scoring class, 8-6, is left out at first. Because it is the middle class, it will make no difference to which group it is assigned.

To assign the classes, the researcher flips a coin to decide which class gets the experimental treatment and which the control. That is, he flips a coin between 8-5 and 8-7, 8-8 and 8-9, 8-10 and 8-11, and so on. There need not be an even number of classes to assign. Note that Ms. Gonzales's 8-6 class, which was not initially paired because there are an odd number of classes, was assigned to the control group on the basis of a coin flip. Again, this will not upset the comparability of the experimental and control groups, because 8-6 is an average-achieving class. The results of the coin flips and assignments to conditions are shown in Figure 2-7.

This random assignment makes the two groups comparable and ensures that each teacher has some experimental and some control classes, as evenly balanced as possible. By the vagaries of random assignment, the average rank of the experimental group (6.2) is somewhat lower than that of the control group (5.8). If the actual pretest scores reflect this difference, this will be well within the range where use of analysis of covariance can make the groups statistically equivalent (see the section on unequal pretests, below). Once the groups are assigned, the study would proceed in the same way as any experimental comparison.

There are some limitations to the use of within-teacher random assignment of classes. This design cannot be used when there is a chance that the teachers will have trouble keeping the experimental and control treatments separate. In the two examples discussed in this section, this was not a problem; teachers could easily and reliably give homework and/or tests in some classes but not others, or certificates in some classes but not others. However, consider a study in which the experimental treatment involves having teachers trained to ask questions that require students to think. It might be difficult for the same teachers to reliably ask mostly "thinking" questions in one class and mostly factual questions in another. If no differences were found between the treatments, it would be unclear whether or not the failure to find differences is due to the fact that the skills the teachers learned were also used in the "control" classes. In any study in which teachers serve as their own controls, it is particularly important to systematically observe the classes in order to verify that the treatments were reliably implemented (see Chapter 8).

Within-teacher random assignment can create another, more general problem. If teachers guess the researcher's hypothesis about which treatment is best, they may help that treatment to be best in ways other than simply implementing the prescribed procedures, such as by giving favored treatment to the experimental class. The researcher can reduce this unwanted "help" by being very clear with the teachers that the purpose of the experiment is not to prove a hypothesis but to give it a fair test, by refraining from making his or her hopes too obvious, and by carefully monitoring the classes, both during project implementation and during testing. This problem is greater when there is a control group that is obviously a control group than when there are two treatments being compared. In some research, researchers write teacher's manuals for the control group that essentially formalize what the teachers were already doing. By presenting this method as an alternative treatment rather than an untreated control group, and by presenting the study as a comparison of two interesting methods, the researcher can be more confident that each treatment will get the teachers' best efforts.

Another limitation of within-teacher random assignment is that it is hard to use experimental designs that involve more than two treatments. It is usually too much to expect a teacher to implement three or four different treatments in different classes.

While the problems and limitations of within-teacher random assignment should be carefully considered, this design does largely solve the very serious problem of confounding of teacher effects and treatment effects. This makes it a very useful design in departmentalized schools.

Experiments without Random Assignment

Random assignment generally satisfies the most important prerequisite for a valid experiment: that the groups can be considered equal at the beginning of the experiment, so that any differences seen on the posttest can be assumed to be due to treatment effects. While random assignment (especially stratified random assignment of individuals) is the best guarantee of initial equality, some assurance that groups do not differ markedly can be achieved in a study without random assignment. However, when there is no random assignment, the conditions of sample selection and sample characteristics become critically important.

Consider a study in which a researcher wants to evaluate the effects of a common staff planning period and staff participation in school decision making on staff attitudes and cohesiveness. The researcher approaches four schools. Two refuse to participate, but agree to be tested as part of a control group. The other two schools are delighted to participate. The researcher determines from state testing results that the four schools are similar in student achievement, and he learns that they are also similar in terms of the number of students receiving free lunch (a measure of socioeconomic status), school racial composition, and general student characteristics. Teachers in the schools have similar numbers of years of experience and an approximately equal number of postgraduate credits.

Despite the appearance that the experimental and control groups for this study are equivalent, they are not. For a measure such as staff cohesiveness, it is highly consequential that the "experimental" schools volunteered for the study while the control schools asked not to be included. The fact that the experimental schools had the courage and self-confidence to invite a researcher into the school with a new program may indicate that the staff is already cohesive and already has positive attitudes. On the other hand, it could be that a principal would go for the program because of a hopeless staff-relations situation, and the experimental group could be at a disadvantage. Whichever way the inequality goes, the fact of deciding to participate is so important for the research that it would be difficult to interpret the results, whatever they were.

The problems of self-selection in experimental comparison studies using nonrandom designs are often serious, but they can be reduced. The best procedure is to allow some number of schools or teachers to volunteer to be in the experimental group, and then to approach similar schools or teachers and allow them to volunteer to receive the same treatment at a later time, on the condition that they must first serve as a control group for the first group of schools or teachers. For example, consider a study in which a researcher wants to evaluate a new elementary mathematics program. The researcher wants whole schools to participate or not participate, because the treatment involves cooperative planning among all teachers in the school. She approaches a school district research committee, which identifies four schools in which they would like to have the project implemented. The principals in the four schools all enthusiastically agree to participate.

The research committee's decision makes random assignment impossible. However, there are many schools like the four chosen schools that the researcher could use as control schools. If she simply convinced four more principals to allow their classes to be pre- and posttested, she would run the risk of having the experimental schools be different from the control schools because of the enthusiasm of their principals toward the new mathematics program. Instead, she approaches schools similar to the four chosen ones and offers to implement the mathematics program in their schools at the end of the study. If principals agree to this, it can be assumed that they are about as favorably inclined toward the mathematics program as the experimental schools are, removing one source of bias. Use of such a "delayed treatment" control group has practical advantages, too. If the experimental program sounds attractive to principals, offering it to the principals of the control schools may make them eager to participate in the study, and may make them more helpful in collecting clean and complete data. The only real drawback to the "delayed treatment" plan is that the treatments must be given to twice as many subjects.

At the very least, when random assignment is impossible, similar control schools should be chosen from among schools that never had a chance to volunteer for the treatment. If schools refuse to participate, that is a strong statement that they are different from schools that do volunteer to participate. However, if schools that never had a chance to participate are solicited to serve as a control group, this problem is diminished. Such schools might have agreed to participate in the experimental group, and their agreeing to be in the control group is some assurance that they are at least willing to be examined.

Of course, the same principles would apply to teachers as apply to schools. If half of the teachers in a school agree to implement an experimental treatment, the half that did not should certainly not be used as a control group; instead, teachers in a similar school or schools elsewhere should be given a chance to volunteer to be in a delayed treatment group or in a control group.

The more exceptional, difficult, or controversial the experimental treatment is, the more self-selection bias is a problem. For example, in a study of the effects of homework on student achievement, it might be expected that most schools would be reasonably receptive to the treatment and the research, and the fact that teachers are more or less motivated may be of limited importance. On the other hand, a study of a new form of open schooling might take such extraordinary teacher dedication and commitment to certain philosophical precepts that we would want to be more certain that whatever effects were observed would not be due to the teachers' dedication and philosophies themselves, rather than to the treatment. In such a study, random assignment or at least a delayed treatment control group would be critical.

As in the case of semirandomized experimental comparisons, pretests or other covariates are essential. Again, any number of covariates may be used to be sure that the groups can be considered equal. In the study of common planning time and teacher participation in school decision making, covariates could include the following: teacher experience in general; teacher experience at the experimental school; teacher subject matter certification; teacher postgraduate education; teacher sex and race; average school achievement; average school socioeconomic status (for example, the number of students receiving free lunch); and all staff attitude and staff cohesiveness pretests. The more covariates used, the more it is possible to answer specific objections about possible differences between the experimental and control groups before the study began.

What If Pretests Are Not Equal in Different Treatment Groups?

There is seldom any point in comparing apples and oranges in educational research, although it is frequently done. For example, it is really useless to try to compare how much students learn in ninth-grade general math to how much students learn in ninth-grade algebra. No matter how the groups are matched (unless students can somehow be randomly assigned to algebra or general math), and no matter what statistics are used, there are too many systematic reasons why a student would be assigned to general math or algebra that make the groups fundamentally different. Similarly, studies comparing students in special education to students in regular classes are difficult to interpret; even if two students are equal in achievement, the fact that one was assigned to special education and the other to a regular class means that the two students are likely to be different (perhaps in behavior, attitudes, or whatever goes into a screening committee's decision making).

When groups are very different on a pretest or some other covariate, matching (selecting a subset of similar individuals) is *not* a solution. Take the comparison between students in special education and students in regular classes. We could choose a group of students from the regular classes whose level of academic performance is similar to that of the special education students. However, if students were initially selected into special or regular classes on the basis of an achievement test score, we would expect that they would regress toward the population mean on a second test. To understand this, imagine that we selected students scoring below 250 on the SAT (200 is the minimum). If we tested the same group the next day, their scores would increase, because to get such a low score, a student would have to have everything going against him or her—bad luck (for example, poor guessing, a headache, nervousness) as well as low skill. Although most of the students would still score below 250, many would do much better the second time, because it is unlikely that bad luck would strike twice. If we selected students scoring above 750 (800 is the maximum), we would see a reduction in scores the next day, because to get such a high score, everything must be going right for a student, and this is unlikely to happen twice. For the same reason, if students were initially selected into special or regular education on the basis of a test score alone, we would expect the special education group to appear to "increase" on a second test. If we gave the special education students a special treatment and used the regular students as a control group, the special education group might appear to do better, but this would simply be due to the statistical regression described above. More typically, attributes other than achievement are used to assign students to special education. For example, if two students have the same low test scores, the one who also has behavior problems will be more likely to be assigned to special education than the one who is well-behaved. If we tried to "match" special education and regular class students on test scores, we would thus find students with more behavior problems (or other problems that would not show up on an achievement test) in the special education group. These other factors would work against the special education students, making treatments applied to the special education students appear to be ineffective when they are, in fact, effective.

These examples would apply equally well to any situation in which systematic selection into different groups makes comparison of the groups fundamentally impossible. For example, if we matched public school students with private school students on their parents' incomes, the public and private school students could still not be considered equivalent, because (among other reasons) the private school students' parents chose to send their children to private school while the public school students' parents did not.

There are times when two or more groups are significantly different on an important pretest despite random assignment. This occurs particularly frequently when random assignment takes place at the class or school level, but it can happen with individual random assignment too. If the differences between groups are very large (for example, more than half a standard deviation), there may be no way to adjust. If they are statistically significant but smaller, there will still be some problems of interpretation. Analysis of covariance never controls completely for pretest differences; the larger the differences, the less well the covariate will work. (For more on this, see Chapter 9.) Analysis of variance using gain scores (postscore minus prescore for each individual) is sometimes used in this situation, but there are problems with this procedure. On some tests, students who score high on a pretest will also gain more than those who score low. This phenomenon is called *fan spread.* On others, there is a *ceiling effect;* students who score high have nowhere to go, and they gain less than students who initially scored low. Use of gain scores thus does not completely solve the problem of pretest differences.

Again, note that this discussion of statistical procedures for differences in pretests or other covariates applies *only* to situations in which the differences appear despite random assignment from among relatively similar groups. When the groups are systematically different on variables important to the research (such as special versus regular class placement), no comparison can be legitimately made. This is not to say that we cannot study differences between these groups using correlational or descriptive designs (see Chapter 4), although results from such studies must be interpreted cautiously. However, it is never appropriate to use one group as a control group for another quite dissimilar group in an experimental study without random assignments to treatments.

EXERCISES

1) A researcher proposed to test two 3-week social studies modules with three teachers, each of whom had three classes. Two teachers volunteered to participate. Each teacher was randomly assigned to implement one of the modules. The classes taught by the third

teacher, who had declined to participate, served as a control group. What are the problems with this method of assignment?

2) Describe three alternative means of assigning students and teachers to treatments in a study such as the one described above.

3) A researcher wanted to assess the impact of a physical education game on arm strength with a group of 70 boys and girls aged 5 to 10. Describe a method of stratified random assignment for this study.

4) A researcher found the following results in a randomized factorial experiment regarding the impact of teacher recognition and higher salary on teacher morale.

   How would you describe this result in terms of main effects and interactions? How would you describe the meaning of this result to the teachers involved?

   Group 1 Teacher recognition and high salary
            —teacher morale very high
   Group 2 High salary, no teacher recognition
            —teacher morale low
   Group 3 Teacher recognition, low salary
            —teacher morale low
   Group 4 No teacher recognition, low salary
            —teacher morale low

chapter 3

Single-Case

Experimental Designs

Use of an experimental comparison design is not the only means of demonstrating that a treatment has a reliable effect on a dependent measure. This chapter presents the second major category of experimental designs, called *single-case experiments*. In a single-case experiment, one or more subjects are observed many times over several days or weeks. These observations establish a "baseline" on the variable or variables being observed. Then, some treatment is begun. If there is an abrupt change from baseline in the variables we have measured, there is some likelihood that the treatment is what caused the change. However, this is not enough, because it is still possible that some other factor caused the change. To rule out this possibility, we may do several things. We might remove the treatment. If the variable(s) return to their previous level, we can be relatively sure that the treatment was responsible for the initial change. This is called a *reversal design*. We might apply the treatment at different times to other subjects, other variables, or other settings. If the treatment has similar abrupt effects in two or more situations, this makes it more likely that the treatment is what caused the changes. This is called a *multiple-baseline design*. Finally, if neither of these designs is possible, we might demonstrate statistically that such an abrupt change would be extremely unlikely to occur by chance. These statistics are called *time series analyses*. Each of these single-case designs is described in the following sections.

Reversal (ABA) Designs

The most common single case experimental design in social science is the reversal design. Consider a program to increase the in-seat behavior of a retarded boy who has trouble staying in his seat. At first, the boy's in-seat behavior is observed for ten consecutive days. The boy is found to be in his seat only 30% of class time, and there is no trend toward improvement. Then the treatment is applied. The teacher brings in a egg timer and sets it to go off at various intervals averaging about two minutes. If the boy is in his seat when the timer rings, he receives a coupon. He may exchange coupons for toys at the end of the day. The treatment is implemented for 13 days, until the boy's in-seat behavior has stabilized at a new level, around 80% of class time. Then the timer and coupon system is withdrawn, and the boy's behavior returns to its previous level. This experiment is diagrammed in Figure 3-1.

The experiment described in Figure 3.1 is called a reversal, or ABA design, so called because it alternates baseline (A) with treatment (B) and then returns to baseline (A). It is commonly used in behavior modification studies. Note that in this study, there is virtually no doubt that the treatment was effective. The boy was in his seat far more consistently under the experimental treatment than he was at baseline. It is hard to imagine how these changes could have occurred for any reason other than the experimental treatment.

This is very efficient and powerful design. Note that only one subject was required to demonstrate the effect. Had we replicated the study with four or five similar students, we could have been even more confident that the treatment would work on many retarded students similar to the students who served as subjects in this study under similar circumstances.

FIGURE 3-1: Example of a Reversal (ABA) Design

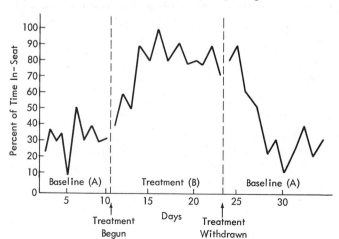

One important issue in reversal designs is how long to observe to establish a baseline, how long to keep the treatment in place, and how long to observe during the second baseline period. Unfortunately, there are no simple rules for these decisions. In general, it is best to continue to observe in each condition until "stability" is achieved. Stability means that you have a clear pattern of scores that are neither increasing nor decreasing, but vary around some mean value. For example, in Figure 3-1, the treatment was begun when it was clear that the subject's in-seat behavior had stabilized at around 30% to 35%, which is where the observations fell in periods 7 to 10. Had we begun the treatment after observation 5 (an exceptionally low point) or observation 6 (an exceptionally high point), the treatment effects would have been more difficult to identify. The same logic applies to the treatment period; the treatment was continued until a relatively stable pattern around 80% was established. Sometimes it is easier to see stable patterns if you average every two or three consecutive observations (for example, 1-2, 3-4, 5-6) instead of including a point on the graph for each observation period.

Multiple-Baseline Designs

In many cases, a reversal is impossible, undesirable, or even unethical. The reversal in the study described above was needed to demonstrate that the behavior change observed was due to the treatment, not to the passage of time or some other factor. It could be considered ethical because out-of-seat behavior is not damaging to the student, and it is highly probable that the good behavior can be reinstated by reinstating the treatment. However, consider a study in which the target behavior is fighting. Once we reduced a student's fighting behavior, it would be unethical to withdraw a presumably effective treatment to bring fighting back. In this case, we might use a design called a multiple baseline. In a multiple-baseline design, we establish that the change in behavior is due to the experimental treatment (not just to passage of time or other factors) by beginning the treatment at different times in different settings, with different subjects, or for different behaviors.

Consider a study in which the experimental treatment is a program to reduce the fighting behavior of a girl who constantly gets into fights in school. A researcher observed her behavior for two weeks, and found that she got into an average of two fights per day during recess, and three fights per day waiting for the school bus. He then began the treatment, which consisted of having the bus monitor give the girl a card if she got into no fights at the bus stop. The researcher arranged to have the girl's parents give her a special privilege if she came home with a card. The procedure reduced the girl's fighting behavior at the bus stop to near zero in two weeks. However, her fighting during recess did not change. As soon as the girl's behavior stabilized at the bus stop, the researcher began a similar treatment during recess, where the girl could earn a different card if she could get through recess without fighting. If she got this card, her father would play Parcheesi with her in the evening. After a short time, the girl's fighting during recess also diminished to near zero. The results of the study are depicted in Figure 3-2. It shows that the improvement in behavior closely follows the beginning of the treatments, making it highly improbable that the changes in behavior are due to factors other than the treatments themselves, such as unrelated changes in the girl's situation at home or school. However, had the experiment taken place only at the bus stop with neither a multiple baseline nor a reversal, we would not be able to say that it was the treatment that made the difference.

The multiple-baseline design, like the reversal design, can demonstrate unequivocally that the experimental treatments control the behavior in question. In this case, the effect of the treatment on the student's fighting behavior was demonstrated by showing that the same treatment could be initiated at different times in different settings, and behavior change would closely follow the introduction of the treatment. In the fighting example, the same purpose might have been served by locating two or more students who have problems with fighting at the bus stop. The treatment could have been implemented with the first student; then, after that student's behavior stabilized at a new level, the same treatment could have been applied to a second student, and so on. Again, if improvements in each student's behavior occurred closely following the imposition of

FIGURE 3-2   Example of a Multiple-Baseline Design

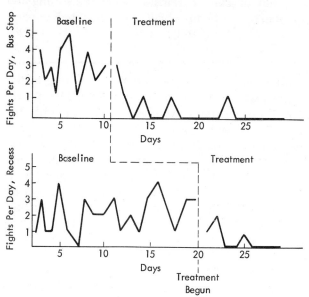

the experimental treatment, we could be confident that the treatment accounted for the behavior change. This would be a multiple baseline across subjects. We might also have started by reducing the girl's fighting behavior at the bus stop, and then reducing her swearing behavior using a similar treatment. This would be a multiple baseline across a behaviors.

Single-case experiments can be more complicated than the ABA design and the multiple baseline. We can compare different treatments using, for example, ABCBA designs, where "C" is an experimental treatment different from the "B" treatment. We can establish still more certainty that our treatment is effective by using an ABAB design, in which the experimental treatment is reintroduced following return to baseline.

Groups as "Single Cases"

Single-case experimental designs used in social science research are typically "single-subject" designs. That is, only one subject is studied at a time. If more than one subject is involved, the results from the additional subjects are considered replications of the experiment; data on different subjects are rarely combined. However, in some cases the relevant "case" is a group, not individuals. Consider a study in which a decibel meter is put into the classroom to monitor classroom noise. After a week of baseline readings, the class is told that if it can keep its noise level below a certain point on the decibel meter, the students will get an additional 15 minutes of recess. In this study, the "case" is the class as a whole, and the average decibel readings for the class would be the important data. In educational research, we are usually concerned with treatments applied to the whole class, and therefore class means may be appropriately used as the data for "single-case" research designs.

Statistics are rarely used in single-case designs. Many researchers in the behavior modification tradition (who most often use single-case designs) argue against the use of statistics, on the basis that in applied research if a treatment is not so effective that its effects can be easily seen on a graph, it is not worth considering. Also, the use of statistics requires combining subjects or data points, which may obscure important patterns. In general, the graph itself is the test of treatment effects.

However, failure to use statistics requires the use of very powerful treatments, and may not permit examination of more subtle differences. Take the example of the decibel meter study discussed above. A decibel meter is expensive, and few teachers have access to one. Would the reward-for-less-noise system work as well with teacher judgments of noise as with a decibel meter? To assess this, we could use an ABCBA design, where the treatments are baseline (A), teacher judgment (B), decibel meter (C), teacher judgment (B), baseline (A). Both teacher judgment and the decibel meter are likely to reduce class noise more than in the baseline periods. However, to determine which of these two treatments is more effective, we might have to use statistics. For statistics in single-case designs, see Kazdin (1976).

Time Series Analysis

There has been increasing attention among methodologists in the past few years to statistical procedures that enable researchers to determine that an abrupt change in a dependent variable following introduction of an experimental treatment is extremely unlikely to have occurred by chance. In "single-case" terminology, this would be called an "AB" design, considered nonscientific (see Hersen and Barlow 1976). However, such designs may have considerable utility with large samples or when long, stable baselines have been established, when control groups are unfeasible, and neither reversal designs nor multiple-baseline designs are appropriate. For example, if we have several years of daily data on student attendance as a baseline, we might implement an attendance-improvement program and compare the new pattern of attendance to the baseline. See McCleary and Hay (1980) for more on statistical analysis for single case experimental designs without reversals or multiple baselines.

Limitations of Single-Case Designs

While the efficiency and power of single-case experimental designs recommend their use in certain kinds of research, there are some limitations to the applicability of these strategies. The most important limitation is that use of these designs requires that the behavior in which we are interested occur frequently and be observable at many points in time. This is why the majority of single-case experiments involve observable behavior, such as time in seat, fighting, and other measures of conduct, rather than the paper-and-pencil measures of achievement and attitudes characteristic of experimental comparison studies in schools. Obviously, we cannot measure student self-esteem every day for four weeks and look for a sharp change following the introduction of a treatment. Daily quiz scores can be taken and we can see how they change following a treatment, or we can measure the number of items or units students complete each day under different motivational conditions, but these measures would not tell us how much students had actually retained as a consequence of the experimental treatments; a retention test could not be given every day. The difficulty of measuring affective outcomes using single-case designs means that it may be hard to study affective "side effects" of experimental treatments. For example, referring again to the decibel-meter study, what if the experimental treatment worked but made students hate school, or feel hostile toward their noisier classmates? Unless there were specific observable behaviors that we could consider as indicators of hating school (such as frequency of negative comments), we might never know what "side effects" the treatment had except in an impressionistic way. In an experimental comparison study, we could have given a "liking-of-school" scale and an "attitude-toward-classmates" scale to more scientifically assess any possible side effects of the treatment.

Single-case designs are also difficult to use for low-rate behaviors that do not occur often enough to establish a stable baseline. For example, if the girl in the fighting study only fought once or twice per week, but these fights were very serious, we would have to observe for many weeks to get a baseline, and even then it might be hard to see the treatment effects unless her fighting fell to zero for a month or more. If she got into serious fights only once or twice a month, it could take a year to do the study, and we might still not know whether or not the treatment was effective. Obviously, behaviors that cannot be regularly observed, such as stealing or other delinquent acts, are very difficult to study using single-case designs.

Another limitation of single-case experimental designs is that while they usually avoid false positive errors, they are highly subject to false negative errors, or situations in which we have no idea whether or not the treatment was effective. For example, take the problem of generalization. A teacher or therapist would be pleased if he applied an experimental treatment, saw an improvement in behavior, then removed the treatment and found that the behavior continued at its improved level. However, this outcome would make the results of an ABA design uninterpretable, as the reversal did not take place. We would then be unsure whether the experimental treatment caused the improvement or whether the behavior would have improved on its own.

Recall the example of the retarded boy who had trouble staying in his seat. The experimental treatment might have given the boy his first opportunity to find out how satisfying it is to experience success at academic tasks and to receive informal teacher praise for that success as well as for staying in his seat. By the time the point and reward system is withdrawn, the boy's positive in-seat behavior might be maintained by these more subtle rewards, and his behavior might not return to baseline. This situation is depicted in Figure 3-3. Clinically, we have a success story, but the failure to demonstrate the reversal might make the study inconclusive, because we cannot rule out the possibility that something other than the treatment made the boy's behavior improve.

This distressing outcome could have been averted by the use of multiple-baseline design, where a reversal is not needed. For example, we could have applied the experimental treatment in math class first and then in reading class to see if the behavior improved in each setting following the implementation of the treatment. However, generalization can also interfere with the interpretation of multiple baselines across

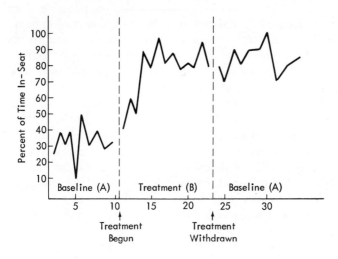

FIGURE 3-3   Example of an Inconclusive ABA Experiment

settings and across behaviors (and even across subjects if the subjects are in the same classroom or have some other connection). For example, what if the boy finds that being in his seat is rewarding in math and spontaneously improves his in-seat behavior in reading? Again, we cannot be sure that the effect observed was not due to some other event that happened to occur at the same time the treatment was begun. We might cover our bets by doing a reversal *and* a multiple baseline, but there are still no guarantees that the design will not be ruined by success (that is, by generalization to other settings or time periods).

False negative errors can also be made in single-case designs when, as noted above, two effective treatments are being compared, or in any other situation in which the effects are consistent and important but small relative to observation-to-observation variance. For example, if we applied a program to reduce school vandalism and obtained a 10% reduction, we might consider this a worthwhile reduction. However, this true effect might be hard to detect with a graph because there is considerable week-to-week variation in vandalism. We might falsely conclude that the experiment has failed. Results of single-case designs may also be difficult to interpret when the baseline is already rising or falling. For example, attendance rates drop in most secondary schools in late spring. If we implemented an attendance improvement program in March and continued it through June, maintaining March levels of attendance could in fact be a success, but the graph might not show it.

Despite these limitations, whenever a study involves a behavior that can be easily and frequently observed, a single-case experiment is likely to be the appropriate experimental method. The small numbers of subjects required and the precision of the conclusions that can be drawn in many cases makes these designs powerful and practical.

For more on single-case experimental designs and their interpretation, see Hersen and Barlow (1976).

EXERCISES

1) A researcher used a single-case design to study the effectiveness of a program designed to increase cooperative play between preschool children. He conducted baseline observations for ten days, began the treatment and observed for ten more days, then withdrew the treatment for ten days. The results are shown below.

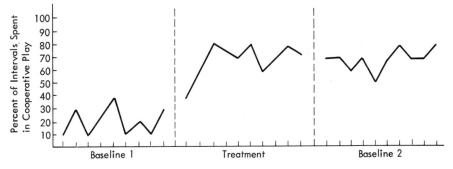

a) What kind of design is this?
b) Can the researcher make any conclusions? Why or why not?
c) What are two hypotheses that could explain the increase in cooperative behavior?
d) What are two hypotheses that could explain the sustained high level of cooperative behavior during Baseline 2?
e) Suggest a multiple-baseline design that might have been used in this study.

2) A researcher wishes to study the effects of a new period-by-period attendance record-keeping system on attendance in a departmentalized middle school (students in grades 6 to 8 go to different English, math, social studies, science, and physical education teachers). Describe two different multiple-baseline designs that could be used to conduct this study.

chapter 4

Nonexperimental Designs

CORRELATIONAL DESIGNS

The previous chapters discussed experimental designs, in which the researcher manipulated one or more independent variables to observe the effect on one or more dependent variables. For example, in an experiment, a researcher might randomly assign some teachers to use programmed instruction to teach science while others are randomly assigned to use more traditional methods. The random assignment to teaching methods constitutes the independent variable manipulated by the experimenter. The effect of the independent variable on one or more dependent variables (for example, science achievement, attitudes toward science) would be assessed.

However, the same variables could be studied in another way. The researcher might have located a school district in which many teachers use programmed instruction in science and many do not. She might collect science achievement and science attitude data in a sample of these classrooms, and compare the differences by computing a correlation between use/nonuse of programmed instruction and science achievement, and use/nonuse of programmed instruction and science attitudes.

This would be an example of a *correlational study*. In a correlational study, the researcher obtains data on two or more variables *as they are*, without attempting to manipulate them. The researcher then attempts to determine whether or not the variables are *correlated*. Correlation refers to the degree to which two variables consistently vary in the same direction (positive correlation) or in opposite directions (negative correlation). If two variables are *positively correlated*, one tends to be high when the other is high and low when the other is low. For example, students' high school grades and SAT scores tend to be positively correlated: Students who have high grades usually have high SAT scores and vice versa. However, note that this is only true on the average. The fact that grades and SAT scores are positively correlated does not mean that there are no students with high grades and low SAT scores or low grades and high SAT scores. It does mean that these students are rare relative to the number of students with high grades and high SATs or low grades and low SATs.

A *negative correlation* exists when one variable tends to be high when the other is low, and vice versa. For example, there is usually a negative correlation between grades and days absent, because students with high grades are rarely absent a great deal, while those who are absent much of the time usually get low grades. Again, there are exceptions. Many students who get low grades are rarely absent, and a student who is sick or injured and is therefore absent for many days can still get high grades. But as a general rule, high grades and low absenteeism go together.

Correlation Coefficients

The degree to which two variables are related is indicated by a statistic called a *correlation coefficient*. Correlation coefficients can take on values from -1.00 to $+1.00$. The "strength" of a correlation is indicated by the distance of the correlation coefficient from zero, not by its sign ($+$ or $-$). That is, there is a stronger relationship between two variables correlated $-.70$ than $+.40$. This can be easily seen in the example of grades and absenteeism. If grades and days absent were correlated $-.60$, grades and days present would be correlated $+.60$. That is, the same variable (absent/present) expressed in different ways could be positively or negatively correlated with another variable.

What the strength of a correlation does depends on is how consistently the variables go together. For example, date of birth and age would be correlated -1.0; there is a perfect negative correlation between these two variables, because if you know one, you can predict the other with certainty, and the earlier ("lower") the date of birth, the higher the age. However, *day* of birth and age would be uncorrelated; knowing a person's birthday (but not birth year) tells us nothing about his or her age, so the correlation between birthday and age would be zero.

In actual research, there are few correlations of $+1.00$ or -1.00. Date of birth and age are perfectly correlated because they are really the same variable, and because they can be reliably measured. For the same reason, this is an uninteresting correlation. The correlations we care about are less perfect. For example, grades and SAT scores are highly correlated because many of the factors that would increase one would increase the other (for example, learning ability, motivation, a family background supportive of achievement). However, other factors might affect grades and SAT scores differently. A student who is terrified by timed tests might do poorly on the SAT but still get good grades. An intelligent student who is frequently late and hands in sloppy work might get low grades but do well on the SAT, and so on. Measurement error (low reliability) also reduces correlations (see Chapter 5 for more on reliability).

Table 4-1 lists a few correlations reported in recent research to give an idea of the relative sizes of various correlations.

Note that in Table 4-1, the highest correlations are for different measures of the same thing—instructors' and students' evaluations of the instructors' enthusiasm (+.54) and the same reading vocabulary test given to the same students four weeks apart (+.90). Correlations between variables we know to be related but not the same tend to be somewhat lower. Time spent on homework and grades (+.32) and parent education and mathematics achievement (+.31) are examples of these. The very small negative correlation between time spent watching television and grades and the small positive correlation between mathematics achievement and attitudes are not statistically different from zero (no relationship). It should be noted that the correlations presented in Table 4-1 are not necessarily representative of all correlations between the variables involved; other studies using different samples or measures find different correlations.

There are tests of significance for correlations, testing the null hypothesis that the correlation is not different from zero (that is, there is no relationship between the two variables). The larger the number of indi-

TABLE 4-1   Examples of Correlation Coefficients from Assorted Research

Correlation Between:	Correlation Coefficient
Instructors' evaluations of their own enthusiasm and students' evaluations of the instructors' enthusiasm (Marsh 1982)	+.54
Time students say they spent on homework and high school grades (Keith 1982)	+.32
Time spent watching television and grades (Childers and Ross 1973)	−.08
Seventeen-year-olds' parents' education and their mathematics achievement (Welch and others 1982)	+.31
Scores of fifth graders on the Comprehensive Test of Basic Skills Reading Vocabulary scale and their scores on the same test given four weeks later (CTBS Technical Bulletin No. 2, 1977)	+.90
Students' reports that their teachers encourage participation in class and their enjoyment of science lessons (Fraser and Fisher 1982)	+.32
Mathematics basic concepts test (STEP) and attitude toward mathematics (Peterson and others 1982)	+.12

viduals on whom variables are measured, the smaller the correlation needed to be statistically significant. For example, with 20 subjects, a correlation of .44 would be needed to be statistically significant (with a 5% chance of making a false positive error). With 100 subjects, a correlation of only .20 would be statistically significant (see Chapter 9).

Correlational Designs with Multiple Measures

One advantage of correlational research is that relationships between many variables can be studied at the same time. For example, a researcher might design a questionnaire asking teachers for their opinions on busing, their attitudes toward mainstreaming, their own sex and race, and whether or not they are union members. Attitude scores could consist of the number of items (for example, "Do you believe in busing students to improve racial balance?") with which teachers agreed or disagreed. Race, sex, and union membership would be scored dichotomously (yes-no).* That is, teachers would be assigned scores of 2 if they are black, 1 if white on the race variable; 2 if female, 1 if male on the sex variable; and 2 if union members and 1 if nonmembers on the union variable. These values (2s and 1s) are arbitrary. Any values would do just as well. The correlation matrix that might have resulted from this study appears in Figure 4-1.

To read a correlation matrix, simply look across for one variable and down for another. The number at the intersection is the correlation coefficient. For example, the correlation between teacher sex and attitude

*It should be noted that correlations involving dichotomous variables have somewhat different properties than correlations between two continuous variables (see Chapter 9).

FIGURE 4-1 Example of a Correlational Study

	Attitude toward Busing	Attitude toward Mainstreaming	Race	Sex	Union
Attitude toward Busing	——	.46	.32	.03	−.34
Attitude toward Mainstreaming		——	.11	−.10	−.06
Race (Black = 2, White = 1)			——	.00	.22
Sex (Female = 2, Male = 1)				——	−.18
Union (Member = 2, Nonmember = 1)					——

toward mainstreaming is −.10 (that is, females have slightly less favorable attitudes than males). Note that only half of the correlation matrix is shown in Figure 4-1; the other half would simply be a mirror image. Also note that no correlation coefficients are presented for each variable with itself, because this correlation would always be 1.00.

Let's say that the criterion for a statistically significant correlation in this study was .30. We could then conclude that there is a positive correlation between attitudes toward busing and attitudes toward mainstreaming (.46), and that black teachers and nonunion members are more favorably disposed toward busing than are white teachers and union members. None of the other correlations are significantly different from zero. We can tell from the correlation matrix that blacks are more pro-busing than whites because of the positive correlation between race and attitude toward busing (+.32) and the fact that race was coded black = 2, white = 1. That is, when race is "high" (2), attitudes toward busing are high, producing a positive correlation. If whites had been coded 2 and blacks 1, this correlation would have been −.32. The correlation between "union" and "attitudes toward busing" is negative only because union members were coded higher than union nonmembers, and nonmembers had more positive attitudes.

This study reported correlations between ten different pairs of variables. Some of these comparisons are not interesting (for example, race and sex), but most are useful. This kind of correlational research usually produces information on many relationships. If data are collected on V variables, $V(V\text{-}1)/2$ correlations will be computed; 50 variables would produce 1,225 different correlation coefficients!

Advantages of Correlational Designs

In addition to the fact that correlational analyses can provide information on many relationships between variables at the same time, there are several advantages of correlational designs over experiments. First, correlational designs allow for study of independent variables over which the researcher cannot have any control. For example, if we wanted to study the relationship between gender and mathematics achievement, we obviously could not randomly assign students to be boys or girls and then observe the effect on achievement. Other examples of variables whose effects we might wish to study but which could not be experimentally manipulated are race, socioeconomic status, place of residence, and so on. Other variables could be experimentally manipulated in theory, but are very difficult to alter in practice. For example, theoretically we might randomly assign students to one school or another, but this is rarely feasible. In these cases, correlational designs would have to be used. There are other types of variables that cannot be altered directly and must be studied correlationally. For example, we might want to know if there is a relationship between attitudes toward mainstreaming and attitudes toward busing (as in the above example). Because we could not directly manipulate attitudes toward mainstreaming to observe the effects on attitudes toward busing, a correlational design would be most appropriate to study this issue.

Experiments must use *discrete variables* as independent variables. Discrete variables can take on a finite number of values, such as male versus female, black versus white, treatment versus control, high versus moderate versus low frequency of quizzes, etc. Correlational studies may use either continuous or discrete variables. Continuous variables can take on any value in a given range. Examples of continuous variables are parental income, achievement test scores, and attitudes toward school.

Finally, many researchers prefer correlational designs because they allow them to study phenomena as they exist, without artificial alteration. For example, in a study of teacher emotional warmth, we might randomly assign some teachers to be "warm" and others to be "cold," but the artificiality of such an experiment might confuse the meaning of the research.

Large Correlation Matrices

While it is an advantage of correlational research that many variables can be studied at the same time, this can also lead to serious errors of interpretation. For example, it would be easy to collect data on 50 different variables on a questionnaire. As noted earlier, if we then made a correlation matrix with these 50 variables, we would have 1,225 different correlations. Statistical significance of a correlation coefficient at $p < .05$ (the most widely accepted standard of statistical significance) means that there is a 5% chance that a statistically significant correlation coefficient occurred at random. That is, if we computed 100 correlations between random lists of telephone numbers, about five of the correlations would be statistically significant entirely by chance. These correlations would of course be meaningless. In the case of 50 variables, we would expect about 61 ($1,225 \times 0.05 = 61.25$) to be statistically significant even if there were in fact no relationships between any of the variables. If we rejected the null hypothesis of a zero correlation on the basis of these statistics, we would be making a serious false positive error. Obviously, isolated correlations in large correlation matrices should be interpreted with extreme caution. To diminish this problem, some researchers dealing with large samples randomly break their sample into two subsamples and compute separate correlations on each. Only correlations that are statistically significant in both subsamples are considered to be reliable.

The Problem of Causation
in Correlational Research

The most serious problem in interpreting the results of correlational research is determining *causation*. Assume that variables *A* and *B* are correlated. Does *A* cause *B*? Does *B* cause *A*? Do *A* and *B* cause each other? Are both caused by some other factor? The fact of a statistically significant correlation between two variables tells us nothing about any of these possibilities by itself. Determination of *direction of causality* (which variable causes the other) can be accomplished by logic or by statistics. For example, there is a correlation between gender and grades in elementary school (girls do better). Obviously, grades do not cause gender, so gender must affect grades. When one variable occurs earlier than another, it can usually be assumed that either the earlier variable causes the later, or that both are caused by a third variable. However, time order may still not clarify the *process* by which one variable influences another. Even though gender is determined long before grades, it obviously does not have a *direct* effect on grades; several other variables that correlate with gender (perhaps developmental rate, socialization practices, or teacher bias) must be involved. Logic can be used to determine direction of causality even when both variables occur at the same time. For example, there is a correlation between the unemployment rate and the suicide rate. Obviously, the suicide rate has a minimal impact on the unemployment rate, so direction of causality must run from the unemployment rate to the suicide rate, unless a third variable (perhaps general disaffection in society) causes both.

Mutual Causation.   It is easy to make errors in attributing direction of causality. For example, a researcher might find a correlation between a measure of students' beliefs that schoolwork is important and their grades, and conclude that this belief *causes* high grades, because students who believe schoolwork is important will work harder. However, it is just about as likely that a student who gets high grades comes to believe that schoolwork is important (that is, high grades cause the belief that schoolwork is important). In fact, this could be a case of *mutual causation*, where both variables cause each other. Another example of mutual causality is the vicious cycle. For example, success breeds confidence which breeds success; failure breeds resignation which breeds failure.

Self-Selection Bias.   Another common mistake in attributing causation occurs when correlational methods are used to compare different treatments. In contrast to the experimental comparison, in which the researcher decides (randomly) who will receive each treatment, the individuals involved in a correlational study select themselves into different treatments depending on their own preferences, resources, abilities, and situations. Consider a study conducted to determine what effect giving essay tests has on social studies achievement. A researcher might locate a sample of 30 teachers, test their students' social studies knowledge in the fall and again in the spring, and compute a correlation between the number of essay tests the teacher gave the students over the course of the school year and student achievement gains. If we think of "giving essay tests versus not giving essay tests" as a treatment, such a study could be seen as an "experiment" without random assignment in which teachers selected themselves into the "essay test" or "no essay test" conditions. Such an "experiment" might say little or nothing about the effects of essay tests on social studies achievement, because many other factors might go along with a teacher's decision to use essay tests. Let's say we found that students who are given essay tests achieve more than students who are given objective tests only. This might occur because teachers who give (and score) essay tests are more conscientious, harder working, and more committed to achievement goals than are teachers who do not give essay tests. These teacher qualities (rather than the essay tests themselves) could explain the increased achievement. Teachers who give essay tests could be in schools in which students tend to be from middle-class families. Such students are usually more motivated, better behaved, and higher in verbal skills than students from lower-class homes. Teachers who give essay tests might have smaller classes than those who do not, and so on. In a correlational study, it is impossible in principle to rule out all alternative hypotheses to account for a correlation, although there are both statistical and logical means (discussed in this chapter) of arguing that a correlation has meaning.

Spurious Correlations.   When a correlation between two variables is in fact due to correlations between the variables and one or more other variables, it is called a *spurious correlation.* For example, we might observe a correlation between membership in the biology club and success at getting into a high-quality college (as measured by the average SAT scores of students who go there). We might conclude that students should therefore join the biology club to improve their chances of getting into a good college. However, students who belong to the biology club and students who get into high-quality colleges are also students who tend to be high in academic ability and motivation. Since neither membership in the biology club nor getting into good colleges is likely to have much of an effect on students' overall academic ability and motivation, we can assume that ability and motivation lead to increased chances of joining the biology club *and* getting into a good college. Deciding what causes what in a correlational study involves justifying a *causal model.* The two causal models discussed above, one spurious and one correct, are diagrammed in Figure 4-2.

Serious problems of confused direction of causality are, unfortunately, common in correlational research in education. Do harmonious relations between teachers and principals produce higher student achievement, or is it easier to have harmonious staff relations in a school with high-achieving students? Do private school students score higher on standardized tests because private schools have better teachers and programs or because they select motivated, high-achieving students from relatively well-off families and expel low achievers and troublemakers? Does high time on-task lead to increased student achievement, or are more able students simply more likely than less able students to spend most of their class time on-task? Many of the social science debates in the news turn on just this question; the correlation is clear, but what causes what?

The main point illustrated in the above examples is that *correlation does not necessarily imply causation.* That is, the fact that two variables are correlated does not mean that either causes the other.

The Role of Theory in Correlational Research

All research must be guided by some idea of how the variables being studied are related. That is, you must have a plausible theory before beginning a research project. The theory plays a major role in determining what variables will be measured on what samples.

FIGURE 4-2   Examples of Spurious and Correct Causal Models

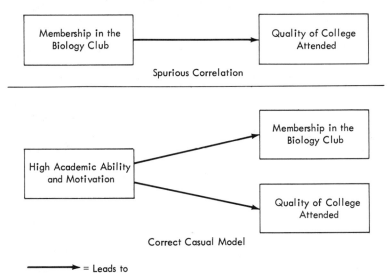

The role of theory is especially important in correlational research. A simple correlation between two variables rarely has much meaning or importance by itself. A correlation takes on importance when we understand which variable influences the other, how or why it does so, and what other variables may influence the relationship. The examples discussed in this chapter illustrate this. Simply observing a correlation between gender and grades, frequency of essay tests and social studies achievement, or biology club membership and college acceptance, says little about what is really going on.

Control Variables

When we find a correlation between two variables that our theory predicts are causally linked (i.e., one causes the other), we have only begun our task. The next step is to attempt to rule out explanations for this correlation other than the one predicted by our theory.

Think back to the biology club study. We might hypothesize that *even after taking academic ability into account*, membership in the biology club increases students' chances of acceptance at a selective college, because admissions committees are impressed by it. Let's say we know students' ninth-grade mathematics and language scores on the standardized Comprehensive Test of Basic Skills (CTBS). We could use these scores as control variables to take the influence of ability out of the correlation between biology club membership and quality of college attended. For the sake of simplicity, we'll add together the mathematics and language scores to get a total academic ability measure. Figure 4-3 shows a possible correlation matrix for this study.

Note that in Figure 4–3, biology club membership and quality of college attended are positively correlated (.42). However, there is an even higher correlation between quality of college attended and academic ability (.68), and there is a positive correlation between biology club mem-

FIGURE 4-3   Example of a Correlation Matrix for a Study with a Control Variable

	Biology Club	Academic Ability	Quality of College
Biology Club membership (2 = member, 1 = nonmember)	——	.48	.42
Academic Ability (Total CTBS Score)		——	.68
Quality of College			——

bership and academic ability (.48). This is essentially the situation depicted in Figure 4-2; the simplest theory would state that both biology club membership and quality of college attended are caused by academic ability.

To find the correlation between biology club membership and quality of college attended (controlling for academic ability), we could compute a *partial correlation*. The statistics for this are presented in Chapter 9. However, the basic idea is that a correlation between variables A and B is computed with the effects of variable C on A and on B removed. In the present example, the partial correlation (controlling for academic ability) between biology club membership and quality of college attended would be .12, a very small correlation that would not be statistically significant. If this partial correlation had been larger, we might have been able to claim that after controlling for ability, biology club membership still has a positive effect on the quality of the college students attend. However, the small partial correlation would imply that joining the biology club would have little or no direct effect on a student's chances of getting into a good college.

Multiple Regression.   Partial correlations are rarely used when there is more than one control variable. In such cases *multiple regression* is more commonly used. In the biology club example, we might want to control for both academic ability *and* parents' income, on the basis that students with wealthier parents might be more likely both to join the biology club and to be able to go to selective colleges. For statistical procedures for multiple regression, see any of the statistics texts listed at the end of Chapter 9, especially Pedhazur (1982).

Use of a multiple regression approach to correlational data requires a careful specification of the causal model we have in mind (that is, what causes what and why?). We must decide which is the dependent variable, which are the independent variables, and which variables are to be used as control variables. These decisions must be guided by a well-thought-out theory linking the different variables, not by throwing the data into the computer to see what comes out. For these reasons, multiple regression analysis is a much more sophisticated and powerful method than simple correlational analysis, but its results must be interpreted equally cautiously.

Limitations of Control Variables.   It is important to note that statistically controlling for certain variables does not rule out the possibility that these variables explain an observed correlation. For example, let's say a researcher wanted to compare achievement of students who take advanced placement (AP) chemistry with those who take regular chemistry. Using a standardized chemistry test, she might test students in several of each kind of class in the fall and spring, intending to use fall scores as a control variable for the correlation between spring score (the dependent variable) and type of chemistry class, AP or regular (the independent variable). However, the AP students would surely have higher fall test scores than the regular class students, which is to say that fall scores will strongly correlate with type of class (and of course with spring scores). In this case, the fall scores will fail to control adequately for student ability, making the AP class appear more effective than it is. It is both statistically and conceptually impossible to compare very different groups by controlling for the variables on which they are different. As noted in Chapter 2, we must be extremely cautious in interpreting the results of comparisons such as those between children in special education and regular education, private schools and public schools, math nine and algebra I, or high reading groups and low reading groups. Controlling for prior achievement level or other background factors can never change the fact that these populations are fundamentally different.

Path Analysis

A useful extension of multiple regression analysis is *path analysis*, in which the researcher specifies variables to be considered background factors (such as sex, race, age, IQ, and other variables likely to influence other variables but unlikely to be influenced by them), mediating variables (such as attitudes or perceptions), and outcome variables (such as achievement or other attitudes). A path model shows to what degree each background variable affects each mediating variable, how much mediating variables affect each other, how much mediating variables affect outcome variables, and how much background variables directly affect outcome variables. In a path model, arrows are drawn to indicate statistically significant effects of each variable on any others, controlling for all variables entered earlier in the model. These arrows portray causal mechanisms by which certain outcomes come about. A typical path model is shown in Figure 4-4.

The path model depicted in Figure 4-4 (from Blau and Duncan 1967, 170) shows how, for men aged 20 or more, the respondent's father's occupation and education and the respondent's education and first job predict the job status of his current job. A straight arrow from any variable to another variable implies that the first variable directly causes the second. The curved arrow shows that the background variables are correlated. For example, the respondent's level of education, which is largely predicted by his father's education and occupation, has a direct effect on his ultimate job status. The respondent's educational level also has an indirect effect on the job status of his current job through its influence on the status of the respondent's first full-time job. This path model thus

FIGURE 4-4   Example of a Path Model

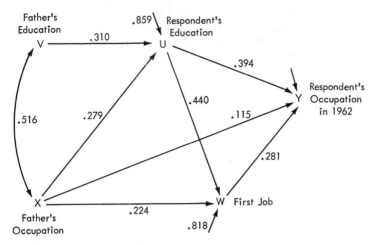

Adapted from *The American Occupational Structure* © 1967, by Peter Blau and Otis Dudley Duncan, Figure 5.1, page 170. Reprinted with permission of MacMillan Publishing Company.

shows how a set of variables influence each other, resulting (in this case) in a complex but very useful explanation of how and to what extent a man's occupational success is determined by his father's occupational and educational status. Path analysis is not just a statistical procedure; before conducting a path analysis, a research must have a well-thought-out theory linking the variables involved. The path analysis then tests and gives numerical weights to the individual relationships that make up the larger theory.

The complexities of multiple regression analysis, path analysis, and related methods are beyond the scope of this chapter. See Pedhazur (1982) for statistical procedures for multiple regression, and Duncan (1975) for a treatment of path analysis.

DESCRIPTIVE RESEARCH

Correlational research is the most common nonexperimental research in education. However, there are other types of nonexperimental research designs that do not involve correlations of two or more objectively measurable variables. These are subsumed under the category of *descriptive research*. Examples of descriptive research are discussed below.

Surveys

Sometimes we simply want to find out how many people agree with certain statements, intend to vote in a particular way, or have certain characteristics. For example, we might want to know what proportion of teachers in the Los Angeles Unified School District support busing, or what proportion of tenth-grade students in the Des Moines Public Schools own hand calculators. To investigate these questions, we would distribute a survey to some sample of the population we wanted to study. In survey research, the most important tasks are to be sure that the measures being used are reliable and valid, and to be sure that the individuals from whom we receive surveys are representative of all individuals to whom we wish the results to apply. Reliability, validity, and methods of sampling in survey research are described in Chapter 5.

Assessment Research

One form of descriptive research that is widely (and increasingly) used in schools is assessment research directed at determining how many students at a particular grade level know a particular set of facts or are proficient in a particular set of skills. Assessment research typically uses "criterion-referenced tests," which are constructed to measure skills that are believed by the test writers (in consultation with teachers, parents, experts, or other knowledgeable or interested individuals) to be important. This is in contrast to norm-referenced tests (such as standardized achievement tests), which are constructed to differentiate between students and relate student performance to that of a "normal sample." The National Assessment of Educational Progress collects criterion-referenced information on a national scale (sampling from all U.S. schools), assessing student knowledge in a wide variety of subject areas. Most states and school districts have their own assessment programs. The uses and problems of assessment research are essentially the same as those of survey research; representative sampling and reliable and valid measurement are critical (see Chapter 5).

Ethnography

One criticism of quantitative research is that it sacrifices meaning in the interests of obtaining reliable or generalizable data, that a few questions on a questionnaire or survey do not begin to get at the important dynamics in a social setting. For these reasons, there has been an increase over the past decade in the use in educational research of methods derived from anthropology, called *ethnography*. In ethnographic research, the researcher spends a great deal of time in one place (such as one school or one classroom) to get an understanding of what is really going on there. The researcher may interview participants in the activity at hand or key informants, and is sometimes actively involved in the activity under study.

In ethnographic investigations, the researcher typically enters a setting that is already intact and already has its own unique history. The researcher's task is to understand the meaning assigned to events or actions by the participants in the setting and to understand the roles and relationships of the participants. An ethnographer typically stays with a particular group for many weeks or months to get a sense of how these roles and relationships change in response to various events over extended time periods. In contrast to experimental and correlational researchers, for whom the first step in an investigation is to form a hypothesis, ethnographers try to enter the setting they are studying without any hypotheses at all. The critical task in ethnography is maintaining objectivity, not allowing preset ideas to cloud the interpretation of what is happening. As the ethnographer gains understanding of the dynamics of the social setting, he or she may form tentative hypotheses and then conduct additional observations to further explore them. The end result of an ethnographic investigation is a detailed description of the roles, expectations, relationships, events, physical attributes, and other features of a setting. Ethnographic writings usually strive to describe a setting *as it is*, not as it could be. Ethnographers tend to be very cautious about prescribing practice or speculating outside of the experiences they are describing.

For more on ethnographic methods, see Overholt and Stallings (1976) or Wilson (1977).

Historical Research

Research on the history of education is one type of descriptive research. The sources for historical research are typically documents rather than people, and the goal of historical research is to find connections between events in the past rather than between variables in the present.

Historical investigations seek to bring to light facts about certain events in the past or relationships between events in the past by means of critical reviews of documentary evidence, sometimes supplemented by interviews with "eyewitnesses" involved in the events. For example, suppose a researcher wished to study the statewide teachers' strike in Florida in the late 1960s. It would be possible to locate many of the individuals involved on both sides of that strike and to obtain their impressions of what took place. It would also be possible to locate documentary evidence, such as minutes of public meetings, state board of education meetings, and so on, as well as to locate newspaper and magazine accounts of the events. In historical research, it is always important to obtain evidence from sources as close to the actual events as possible. For example, eyewitness reports are better than documentary evidence, newspaper reports from the time of the events are better than later summaries of what happened, and so on. Firsthand accounts of events are called primary sources. Other documentary evidence, secondhand reports, or later articles or books about the events are called secondary sources. A large part of the task of the historical researcher is to weigh the credibility and objectivity of various sources of information. For example, statements made by strike leaders and the state superintendent of education to newspaper reporters in press releases would have to be critically examined, as such statements are usually carefully tailored to serve the purposes of those making them. In contrast, secret minutes of meetings of strike leaders or of the state board of education would give much more insight into the true opinions and plans of the central actors in the strike events.

Sources of historical documents are listed in the *Guide to Historical Literature*, published by the American Historical Association and available in most libraries. However, finding sources of information mostly requires good detective work, such as beginning with secondary sources and working backward to locate the primary sources on which they were based, interviewing eyewitnesses or experts for suggestions on information sources, visiting archives in the locations where events occurred, visiting the locations themselves, and so on.

For more on historical research, see Barzun and Graff (1977); Block (1953); Brickman (1973); Brickman and Cordasco (1975); Herbst (1973).

EXERCISES

1 A researcher found these correlations in a study of adults aged 30 to 50:

Sex and Income	.43
Educational Level and Income	.22
Educational Level and Sex	-.13
Years of Experience and Educational Level	.09
Years of Experience and Income	.49
Years of Experience and Sex	.37

(Female is coded 1, Male is coded 2)

   a) Make a correlation matrix showing these relationships.
   b) Given the size of the sample, a correlation of .30 is statistically significant. Discuss possible meanings of the correlations in light of this.

2) A researcher correlated 10 variables with each other, computing 45 correlation coefficients. She found that size of school was significantly correlated with attitude toward school, and authoritarian administrative structure was significantly correlated with number of extracurricular activities. All other correlations were nonsignificant. Comment on these findings.

3) a) Develop a correlation matrix using the following correlations:

Teacher Warmth and Student Achievement	.50
Teacher Warmth and Attitude toward Administrative Staff	.47

Achievement and Attitude toward Administrative Staff   .60
Sex of Teacher and Teacher Warmth   -.46
Sex of Teacher and Student Achievement   -.21
Sex of Teacher and Attitude Toward Administrative Staff   -.14
(Female coded 1, Male coded 2)

b) Assuming that the criterion for significance for a correlation in this study is .45, describe the findings.

c) The researcher concluded the following: "It seems clear that a supportive, responsive administrative staff can encourage the expression of warmth by a teacher which in turn can help increase academic achievement." Describe the flaw in this reasoning. Suggest at least one alternative interpretation.

chapter 5

Measures and Sampling

Obviously, a good design and an important problem do not automatically make a good study. Details of the research design and implementation (such as the character, reliability, and validity of measures, the nature of the individuals to whom the measures are given, the sample size, and the degree to which all procedures have been explicitly laid out in advance) may be more important to the success of a study than anything else. A poorly designed study with poorly designed measures or a study that is too small is unlikely to produce meaningful or reliable results. This leads to the statement seen in hundreds of forgotten research reports—"It is unclear why the experimental treatments failed to produce the hypothesized effects. . ."

MEASURES: RELIABILITY AND VALIDITY

There are two concepts that are of critical importance in understanding issues of measurement in social science research: *reliability* and *validity*. These are discussed below.

Reliability

The term reliability refers to the degree to which a measure is consistent in producing the same readings when measuring the same things. A 12-inch straight ruler is a reliable measure for short lines. If 50 people used the same ruler to measure a 3 1/4-inch line, they would all come very close to the same answer. The same ruler would be less reliable for measuring around corners or measuring the length of a football field. In these cases, different people would come up with different answers for the same dimensions. Thus, a 12-inch ruler could be considered a reliable measure for short, straight lines, but a less reliable measure for long or curved lines.

In the case of questionnaires, tests, and observations, the goal is to create measures that will consistently show differences between individuals who are really different, and will show the same scores for individuals who are the same (such as the same individual on two occasions). Reliability can range from zero (no reliability) to one (perfect reliability). In educational research, examples of relatively low reliability include such measures as judgments or formal observations of teachers or students on criteria that are hard to quantify (for example, warmth, originality, "withitness," rapport), or questionnaire scales attempting to measure hard-to-quantify variables. These measures would be low in reliability because scores on them tend to be inconsistent from day to day, from observer to observer, or from item to item. On the other end, well-designed achievement and aptitude tests tend to be high in reliability, because the same students who score high on a test would be likely to do so on the same test any day they take it, regardless of who administers the tests, and because each test item would tend to discriminate consistently between students high in ability or achievement and those low on these variables.

Forming Scales.   Test and questionnaire reliabilities are usually computed on "scales" composed of the sum of scores on two or more items. A single questionnaire may contain several scales; for example, an "Attitude toward School" questionnaire might have scales assessing attitudes toward teachers, attitudes toward administrators, and attitudes toward other students. Scores for each response to each item should be assigned by the researcher. For example, on an "Attitude toward Administrators" scale, there might be an item "Do you feel that your principal is fair to all students?" Responses might be coded: yes = 3, not sure = 2, no = 1. For a negatively phrased question such as, "Do you think your vice principal is too strict?", responses would be coded in the opposite direction: yes = 1, not sure = 2, no = 3. The scores for all such items would be added up to form the scale score, and it is this scale score that is examined for reliability.

Computing Reliability Coefficients.   Reliability can be computed in many ways. Some common methods for tests and questionnaires include "internal consistency" measures such as split half (for example, how well the even items correlate with the odd items across individuals), coefficient alpha (a statistic that approximates the mean of all possible split-half correlations), or KR 20 (coefficient alpha for tests on which there are only two response options, such as right-wrong, agree-disagree, and so on). Formulas for split-half reliability, coefficient alpha, and KR 20 are presented in Chapter 9. These internal consistency measures indicate how much random variation there is *within* a scale of several items in comparison with variation *between* total scores of individuals who take the scale. For example, if a student who answered Item 1 "yes" is no more likely than a student who answered "no" on Item 1 to agree with Item 2 or Item 3, the scale is low in internal consistency. In a scale high in internal consistency, a student who answers a certain way on any item is likely to answer the same way on other items in the same scale.

Reliability may also be estimated by correlating scores received by a set of individuals at two different times. This is called *test-retest reliability*. For example, we might give a questionnaire to a group of students in September and again in December, and compute a correlation between scores at these two times. If the correlation is high, we may conclude that the scale is reliable (see Chapter 9 for computation of correlation coefficients). Similarly, we might compute reliability by calculating a correlation between scores on a test and scores on a parallel form of the same test (standardized tests often have two very similar, or parallel, forms of the same test). Reliability coefficients for behavioral observation measures, which typically involve agreement between two or more observers, are discussed later in this chapter.

The Importance of Reliability. What is particularly important about reliability is that the reliability of a measure places an upper limit on the degree to which it can correlate with anything else. This is easy to see with test-retest reliability; how could anything correlate better with a measure than does the measure itself? For example, if the scores students obtain on Tuesday are correlated .70 with the scores they receive on the same test on Friday, it is difficult to imagine how some other variable could possibly correlate better than .70 with this measure.

The use of measures that are low in reliability increases the chance of making false negative errors. Let's say that we gave a test of creativity that had students name every use for a brick they could think of in two minutes. The reliability of this measure would probably be low, in part because such variable factors as speed and motivation might enter into the score. If we tried to correlate our creativity measure with student IQ, we might find no statistically significant relationship. However, this could be due to the low reliability of the creativity measure, not necessarily to the lack of a "true" relationship between IQ and creativity. A more reliable creativity measure might show the correlation. Obviously, if we tried to correlate two unreliable measures, the chance of finding a correlation would be remote, even if a true relationship existed between the variables supposedly measured.

When is Scale Reliability Adequate?   It is difficult to say what is an adequate reliability coefficient for a questionnaire or achievement scale. There are different standards for different measures and different methods of computing reliability. Helmstadter (1970) examined reliabilities in published articles, and found that while achievement and aptitude batteries had median reliabilities around .90, attitude and personality scales had median values close to .80. Internal consistency measures (e.g., coefficient alpha, KR 20) tend to show lower reliabilities than do correlational measures of reliability (for example, test-retest). Scales with few items usually have lower reliabilities than longer scales. Reliabilities tend to be lower with skewed distributions, such as tests that most students find very hard or tests that most students find very easy. Scales given to young or low-achieving students are usually lower in reliability than tests given to older or higher-achieving students, because these students tend to be more inconsistent in their responses. Thus, a 4-item scale administered to low-achieving second graders would not be expected to produce a reliability coefficient as high as a 20-item scale given to high-achieving sixth graders.

When no significant relationships are found between a moderately reliable scale and other variables, there is no way to know whether the failure to find a relationship is due to inadequate reliability or to a true lack of differences. For example, let's say we compute a correlation between teachers' expectations for their classes (measured at the beginning of the school year) and their classes' actual achievement over the course of the year. No significant correlation between expectations and achievement is found. However, we observe that the reliability of the expectation measure is only .40. Because the reliability of the expectation measure is relatively low, we cannot be confident that a true relationship between teacher expectations and class achievement does *not* exist; we may well be making a false negative error by concluding that there is no correlation.

If a significant relationship *were* found between expectations and achievement, the fact that the reliability of the expectation measure is only moderate would not automatically invalidate the finding, as long as the scale is a valid measure of teacher expectations (see below). Reliability is of great importance in reducing false negative errors, but has less relevance to reducing false positive errors.

For more on reliability, see Anastasi 1982; Cronbach 1970; Guilford and Fruchter 1978; Stanley 1971.

Validity

A measure's *validity* refers to the degree to which it actually measures the concept it is supposed to measure. The issue of validity is particularly important for research design. A measure may be reliable, but this does not mean that it measures what it is supposed to measure. It is not uncommon to see questionnaire scales with titles that imply one thing, but with items that clearly measure something else. Let's say a researcher wants to study the relationship of IQ to liking of school. He constructs a measure called "liking of school" that includes such agree-disagree items as "I get good grades in this school," "This school is preparing me for college," and "This school helps me get good test scores." Such a scale might be very reliable, but it is not a "liking of school" scale; it seems to be a "self-perception of ability" scale. In this case the researcher is biasing the study (intentionally or not) toward a conclusion that IQ does correlate with liking of school, when in fact he may simply be showing that students with high IQs perceive themselves as more able than do students with low IQs, a quite different claim.

Types of Validity.   There is no single numerical criterion of validity. A researcher creating a new scale must make an argument that the scale is valid. At minimum, the scale items should have "face validity." That is, the items should look as though they measure what they are supposed to measure. The "liking of school" measure discussed above was low in face validity, because its items appeared to measure something other than liking of school. Other types of validity are discussed below.

Content Validity.   Content validity is of particular importance in achievement and aptitude testing. It refers to the degree to which the content of a test matches some objective criterion, such as the content of a course or textbook, the skills required to do a certain job, or knowledge deemed to be important for some purpose. For example, a Spanish test would be high in content validity to the degree that it covered the skills identified in the course syllabus, taught in class, and/or presented in the class text. If three quarters of the test covered verb conjugations, but verb conjugations occupied only one quarter of the course content, the test would be low in content validity. There is no numerical criterion of content validity. Content validity is usually established by showing a comparison between the concepts tested by the test items and those covered in the text(s) used to teach a particular course. Sometimes groups of experts (such as teachers, curriculum supervisors, professionals, and so on) are consulted to determine the degree to which a test measures what a course is supposed to teach.

A very common error in educational research is to use a standardized achievement test as an assessment of school learning without examining it carefully to see that it corresponds to what is taught in school. For example, a standardized social studies test or science test is unlikely to have much overlap with what is taught in a particular seventh-grade history or life science class. Use of the standardized test as a measure of learning in those particular classes may be totally inappropriate, even though the standardized test is likely to be more reliable and more valid for other purposes (such as measuring *aptitude* for social studies or science) than any test made up by the researchers for a particular study. In studies of student achievement, it is particularly important that the achievement test used cover the content taught in all experimental conditions.

Predictive Validity.   Predictive validity refers to the degree to which scores on a scale or test predict later behavior (or other scores). For example, if an aptitude test given in September were highly correlated with students' grades, the test would be considered high in predictive validity. If we gave an "educational aspirations" scale measuring intentions about going to college, and found a low correspondence between scores on this scale and whether or not students actually went to college, the scale would be low in predictive validity. Predictive validity can be measured by means of a correlation coefficient between individuals' scores on the scale and their later behavior.

Concurrent Validity.   Concurrent validity refers to the correlation between scores on a scale and scores on another scale or measure of established validity given at about the same time. For example, we might give a group of students a sociometric measure asking them to list their "best friends in this class." We might then observe them on the playground. If there is a high degree of correspondence between the friends they named on the sociometric measure and the classmates with whom they actually play in a free-choice situation, the concurrent validity of the sociometric measure would be high. If we gave teachers a scale on which they were to judge their students in terms of learning problems, the correlation between student ratings by their teachers and their scores on established achievement tests administered by a school psychologist might be used as an indication of the validity of the judgment scale. The only difference between concurrent validity and predictive validity is that in concurrent validity, the criterion with which the new scale is correlated is a measure given at about the same time, while in predictive validity, the validating measure is a behavior or performance that occurs in the future. Concurrent and predictive validity are often referred to together as criterion-related validity.

Construct Validity.   Construct validity refers to the degree to which scores on a scale have a pattern of correlations with other scores or attributes that would be predicted by a well-established theory. For example, we would expect that a scale measuring antisocial attitudes would show strong differences between students in a training school for juvenile offenders and students in regular schools. Construct validity is high when we can demonstrate that a scale not only correlates with other measures with which it is supposed to correlate, but also fails to correlate with measures of concepts from which it is supposed to be different. For example, let's say we made a test of creativity, and found that it correlated with students' grades in art class. If the scale turned out to correlate equally well with students' grades in math, science, and social studies, as well as with students' scores on aptitude tests (such as IQ), we would have little reason to believe that the creativity test measured creativity, but would rather presume that it measures all-around aptitude or achievement. On the other hand, if the creativity test correlated with art grades, English composition scores, and ratings of students' science fair projects, but did not correlate highly with scores on English mechanics, mathematics, or science facts tests, we might have more confidence that the creativity test measured creativity rather than general intelligence or aptitude.

It is possible that the results of a study will help establish the construct validity of a measure not known beforehand to be valid. For example, if a study demonstrates that an experimental treatment designed to affect a particular outcome affects a scale of unknown validity that is supposed to measure that outcome, this lends support to an argument that the scale does measure the concept it is supposed to measure. If a program directed at improving attitudes toward the handicapped improved scores on a measure of attitudes toward the handicapped, this would provide important support for the construct validity of the scale.

TYPES OF MEASURES

There are four primary types of measures used in educational research: achievement/aptitude tests, paper-and-pencil questionnaires, interviews, and behavioral observations. These are discussed in the following sections.

Achievement/Aptitude Tests

Achievement and aptitude tests are the most commonly used measures in school research. There has been much debate for decades over the distinction between aptitude and achievement; clearly, any aptitude test (such as IQ) assesses achievement to some degree, and almost any achievement test has some aptitude component.

Achievement tests can be standardized, or specially made to assess a particular content domain. The most common achievement tests, such as the Iowa Test of Basic Skills, the Stanford Achievement Test, the California Achievement Test, and the Comprehensive Test of Basic Skills, cover broad topics in reading, mathematics, and other subjects. There also exist many more specific tests for particular subjects (for example, language usage, geometry, basic French). These tests, if published, can be located in Buros's *Mental Measurements Yearbook (1978)*. Many researchers make up their own tests when they want an assessment of achievement in a specific content area. These are called *content-specific tests*.

Standardized Tests.   There are several advantages to using standardized tests. First, they tend to be highly reliable, and they cover a wide range of student performance levels, making it unlikely that many students will get almost everything right (a ceiling effect) or almost everything wrong (a floor effect). Because the vast majority of school districts now use standardized tests, teachers and administrators are much more interested in treatment effects on standardized tests than in effects on content-specific tests. Standardized tests yield grade equivalents and percentile ranks for scores, which both give a sense of the magnitude of treatment effects and help locate individual or class performance levels. For example, a program that increases seventh graders' math achievement in one year from a grade equivalent of 4.0 to one of 5.0 is quite different from one that increases achievement from 7.0 to 8.0.

As attractive as standardized tests are, they also have several drawbacks. One is that almost all standardized tests use a multiple-choice format (to allow for machine scoring). This is appropriate for some content areas, but it allows guessing or "testwiseness" to play a part in student scores. For example, a student can usually pick up a few points by randomly guessing on items he or she does not know. More importantly, the links between the test and the content students have studied may be very indirect, making the tests insensitive to variations in instruction. Because standardized tests are constructed to reliably show differences between individuals rather than to sample all concepts taught in school, they often correlate better with student IQ than with what the student actually did in school.

Content-Specific Tests.   Content-specific tests made by the researcher are of course more likely than standardized tests to closely cover the content being taught. Question formats other than multiple choice can be used. This is particularly important for content in which higher-order understanding should be shown, as in essay questions or paragraph writing, or in mathematics, where a multiple-choice format alerts students that an attempted answer was wrong, or allows students to get the right answer by estimating rather than working out the problem.

There are several problems with content-specific tests. If the material being studied is new, a content-specific test will be of little use as a pretest because most students will get scores near zero. Such a test would be ineffective as a covariate or control variable, because it would not correlate well with the posttest (or anything else). Also, unless a test is very carefully constructed and tried out before the study begins, there are likely to be some items that almost no student misses and others that virtually no students answer correctly. Such items are useless in indicating treatment effects, and decrease test reliability. Content-specific tests give no benchmark (such as a grade equivalent) or any indication of the magnitude of a given gain. What does it mean if the experimental group exceeded the control group by three points? Is that a lot or a little?

When you have adequate testing time and resources, the best strategy in achievement testing in many cases is to give content-specific *and* standardized achievement tests. Each form of testing has strengths and weaknesses offset by those of the other. When we wish to use a test as a covariate, reliability is critical, and a standardized test is almost always best. Standardized tests correlate better with other measures, so they should be used in most correlational studies, unless the correlation computed also involves variables relating to what was taught in school. For example, if we wanted to know the effect of student time on-task in mathematics class on mathematics achievement, we would want to use a standardized test (and a content-specific test if possible) as covariates, but we would definitely want a content-specific test as measure of the dependent variable (although a standardized test could be given in addition). While the standardized test would do a better job of controlling for overall student mathematics achievement, whatever the students were learning when they were on-task would be much more likley to be reflected in the content-specific test.

Constructing Content-Specific Tests.   In constructing a content-specific achievement test for research, there are several principles to keep in mind. The most important is content validity; the test should match what is taught in school. In experimental comparison studies, in which two or more groups learn similar content with different methods, it is critical that the test cover material to which all groups have been exposed. Otherwise, the test will be biased in favor of one or another treatment. The longer the test, the better it will cover the content and the higher the test reliability will usually be, but under no circumstances should an achievement test be a "speed" test, which students must rush to complete. Speeded tests tend to be relatively low in reliability and give high scores to students who can write quickly, are low in test anxiety, or are good guessers rather than to students who know the material. In other words, the test should be short enough to be completed easily within the allotted time by all but the slowest students.

In making an achievement test, it is important to avoid items that are giveaways, "trick" items, items that can have more than one right answer, or confusing items. Tricky items give high scores to students who are clever about tests in general rather than students who have learned what was taught in class. When there is only one possible answer, fill-in-the-blank is better (and more difficult) than multiple choice. For example, the question, "What is the capital of Canada?" is a better assessment of that knowledge than the question, "Which of the following is the capital of Canada: (a) Paris; (b) Mexico City; (c) Ottowa; (d) Dublin." Matching questions (for example, "match the explorer with the country that sent him") should also be avoided, as they too may reward partial knowledge and "testwiseness." The goal of an achievement test item is not to separate "smart" students from others, but rather to reliably separate students who have learned something from those who have not. Ideally, every item should be passed by some students and failed by others. As noted above, an item that everyone passes or everyone fails is of little value.

If possible, it is good practice to pilot test an achievement test on a class that has just learned the material. For example, if you were about to do a ten-week experiment on a new science program for seventh graders, you might pilot your test on eighth graders who had covered the same science content in the previous year (if you piloted the test on seventh graders who had not had the relevant science unit, the scores might be too low to be of any use). The results of the pilot testing would tell you if the test is too long or too short, and would pinpoint any items that are too easy, too difficult, or too confusing. You might wish to compute a correlation (see Chapter 9) between each item score and the student's total score, and reject items with low item-to-total correlations. You should compute a reliability coefficient (see Chapter 9) on the entire test to see that the reliability is adequate.

Questionnaire Scales

In most studies that take place in schools, we wish to know about student affect (emotions), personality, attitudes, and other noncognitive variables. These variables are usually more difficult to measure and interpret than are achievement and aptitude measures. For example, how can we measure student self-esteem? There are several well-known scales, but even if they are substantially correlated with one another, which is "true" self-esteem? Is a very high score on a self-esteem scale an indication of very high self-esteem or of wishful thinking? While we can usually take an achievement test at face value (a spelling test measures spelling), a questionnaire scale must be shown to reliably and validly measure what it is supposed to measure. This was discussed earlier under *Reliability* and *Validity*.

For most types of noncognitive variables (such as self-esteem, attitudes toward school and toward various subjects, attitudes toward other students, locus of control, test anxiety, and many personality dimensions), there exist well-validated, widely used scales. Published scales are cat-alogued in the *Mental Measurements Yearbook* (Buros 1978), and Shaw and Wright (1967) list published as well as unpublished attitude scales. Sources of measures are usually referenced in articles in which they are used. In general, it is better to use such a well-established scale than to attempt to create a new one. If it is done properly, scale construction is a difficult and time-consuming process. There is no sense in reinventing the wheel if it is unnecessary to do so. Using a well-established scale has the following advantages: (1) It often has norms which help you describe your sample; (2) it usually has reliability and validity information avail-able; and (3) it helps tie your study in with previous literature.

Constructing Questionnaire Scales.   While you should use a well-established scale whenever possible, there are several circumstances un-der which you might wish to create your own scales, or modify existing scales. In some cases, existing scales may not get at the particular attitudes or personality characteristics you want to measure. Established scales are often very long, because scale length is strongly related to reliability. If you are measuring several variables, you may not have time to have your subjects complete long scales, so you might shorten an existing scale or create your own. Shortening scales is often a good idea for another reason: Well-established scales may contain items that have no relevance to a particular research question. For example, many self-esteem scales include items on family relations that have little relevance in some school projects, but may get the researcher in trouble with research screening committees as well as teachers and parents. If these items are of no use, they may be deleted, although deleting items may make it impossible to use the norming, reliability, and validity estimates published by the au-thors of the scale. In this case, the researcher might have to compute reliability coefficients on the shortened scale.

If you make a new scale, it is a good idea to pattern it on an existing scale, using a response format and instructions to students that have already been tried out. It is also imperative to pilot the scale on a sample like the one with which you will do your research. This will allow you to compute a reliability coefficient and to identify weak items, such as items that everyone answered the same way, confusing items, or items that do not correlate well with the total scale score.

Open versus Closed Form.   When you construct a questionnaire scale, you may use either "closed-form" questions or "open-form" ques-tions. Closed-form questions have a restricted set of possible responses, as in the following examples:

1. I like this class (circle one).
    Strongly Agree   Agree   Disagree   Strongly Disagree

2. In a five-day school week, how often do you usually assign homework?
   a. every day
   b. four days
   c. 1 to 3 days
   d. I do not assign homework.

In an open-form question, the respondent may give any response, as in the following:

How do you feel about using microcomputers in your class?

Open-form questions are difficult to code and are disliked by many respondents because they take too much work. However, in some cases they are desirable (if used sparingly) if you want respondents to give complex opinions that do not lend themselves to closed-form questions.

Principles of Questionnaire Construction.   In making your own questionnaire, keep the following in mind:

- Be as simple and clear as possible. Use short questions and short responses if you can.
- Avoid questions with double negatives, such as "My job is not the worst I have had."
- If you use multiple-choice questions, be sure that all possibilities are covered. For example, you might ask primary teachers the following question:
   1. What grade(s) do you teach?
      a. first grade
      b. second grade
      c. third grade
      d. combination of first and second grades
      e. combination of second and third grades
      f. ungraded
      g. other (specify) _____
      In the above question, if you stopped at "c" you might miss important information about what grades are taught, and you might frustrate a teacher who teaches a combined or ungraded primary class and wouldn't know how to respond. Providing "other (specify) _____" is always a good idea if it is possible that you have left out a legitimate response.
- Be explicit in your questions. Instead of "How often does your principal visit your class?" with responses of "never," "occasionally," and "frequently," you might ask:
      In the past four weeks, how many times has your principal visited your class?
      a. never
      b. once
      c. 2 to 3 times
      d. 4 or more times
- Avoid questions with two parts, such as "Do you agree that teacher accountability is a bad idea because it takes too much time for testing?" A respondent might agree that teacher accountability is a bad idea but not for

the stated reason, and might therefore have difficulty answering. This could be broken into two or more questions.

- Avoid vague questions. Instead of "Do you like teaching?" you might ask:

  If you could do it all over again, would you choose teaching as a career?
  a. yes
  b. not sure
  c. no

- Give points of reference or comparison whenever possible. Instead of asking students "Do you like your English class?" you might ask:

  Please rank your major academic classes from most favorite (1) to least favorite (4).
  Mathematics_____
  Social Studies_____
  English_____
  Science_____

- Underline words that are critical to the meaning of the questions, especially the word "not." For example:

  "Do you believe that teachers should <u>not</u> be required to attend workshops outside of school hours?"

- Ask only important questions. Respondents dislike long questionnaires or questionnaires that ask too many unimportant questions.

See Bradburn and Sudman (1979) and Payne (1951) for more on questionnaire construction.

Sociometric Questionnaires

A widely used and powerful measure of peer relations is the sociometric questionnaire (Moreno 1934). In it, respondents are asked to name others who have certain relationships with them. For example:

"If you were going to play a fun game at recess, who in your class would you want on your team?"
"Who are your best friends in this class?"

After each question would appear several spaces on which students could indicate their choices. Sociometric data are usually coded as the number of choices received by each individual from all others, an indication of popularity (or other characteristics, depending on the sociometric questions). Sociometry is especially useful in studying intergroup relations, such as relationships between blacks and whites, Anglos and Hispanics, nonmainstreamed students and mainstreamed students, boys and girls, and so on. The advantage of sociometry for studying these relationships is that it provides a means of assessing intergroup relations without saying anything about race, sex, mainstreaming, etc., making the questionnaire less susceptible to "social desirability bias" (that is, saying what you think you are supposed to say rather than what you really think) than a question such as, "Do you have any friends of a different race than your own?" If a sociometric question is used to measure intergroup relations, the responses for each student might be coded as, "choices from white students" and "choices from black students." The number of white-white, white-black, black-white, and black-black choices made by the group as a whole would be the focus of the analysis. See Moreno (1934) for more on sociometry.

Interviews

Questionnaires are a convenient means of collecting attitudinal and perceptual data, but they require that the researcher reduce his or her research questions to a set of items that may be too limited or limiting. An alternative to questionnaires is the interview, in which individuals are asked specific questions but allowed to answer in their own way. In an interview, respondents can be asked to clarify or expand on responses, making the data from an interview potentially richer and more complete than that which can be obtained from a questionnaire. Interview data, however, is certainly much more difficult and expensive to collect and analyze.

Constructing an Interview Protocol. In an interview study, the researcher creates an "interview protocol," which consists of a set of questions that the interviewers will ask of each respondent. The protocol might also contain notes to the interviewer, indicating courses of action to take in response to certain answers. For example, we might use interviews to study teachers' behaviors and attitudes relating to the presence of mainstreamed children in their classes. One question on the interview protocol might be, "Do you have any mainstreamed students in your class?" If the teacher says no, all subsequent questions about the teacher's behavior toward mainstreamed students would be irrelevant, and the protocol might direct the interviewer to skip several questions. The interviewer might be directed to ask for clarification if the teacher says no, to see if the teacher is unclear about the definition of "mainstreamed." The researcher should also write an interviewer's manual that describes exactly how the respondents should be approached, how the interview should be conducted, and how the data should be recorded.

Questions in an interview protocol can be either "open-form" or "closed-form," as described above. Also, a mixed strategy can be used; respondents may be given closed-form questions and then asked to elaborate if they make certain responses, as in the example below:

> Do you feel that it is part of your job to learn about students' home lives?
> a. Yes, definitely
> b. Only if there is a problem with a student in school that may be related to a problem at home

    c. No

    d. Not sure—(interviewer: ask for elaboration)

The sequencing of interview questions may be very important, as earlier questions may set the tone or context for later ones, and may allow unintended bias to enter into the responses. Let's say that an interviewer asks, "Do you know any students who have been seriously beaten up by other students in this school?" and later asks, "Do you feel safe in this school?" The first question might evoke unpleasant memories that could influence the responses to the second question. If the questions were asked in the opposite order, the response to the more general question might be quite different. For this reason, it is often a good idea to use a "funnel" strategy, beginning with general questions and working toward specific ones. Respondents may be allowed to answer more open-ended questions in their own words (for example, "What kinds of things does your teacher do when you do something he or she thinks is good?") before you zero in on particular issues (for example, "Does your teacher ever give you points, stars, stickers, or other rewards when you do something he or she thinks is good?"). Again, asking specific questions before letting respondents respond in their own words risks putting words in their mouths. After respondents have given an answer in their own words, the interviewer can continue to probe to get more and more specific answers.

If at all possible, it is a good idea to get a copy of interview protocols and interviewer's and coder's manuals from researchers who have done work related to the study you are planning. Usually, if you write to the author(s) of an interview study and offer to pay any costs of reproduction, they will send you these materials.

For more on interview construction, see Yarrow (1960).

Piloting the Interview Protocol.   In interview studies, it is critical to pilot test the instrument on respondents similar to the intended subjects of the main study. No one can make a perfect interview protocol in advance, but after it has been used with several respondents, the weaknesses in the protocol can be identified and corrected. Pilot testing also provides important training for interviewers, and almost always brings up many issues that need to be solved in advance, such as pacing, how long to wait for a response, what to do when respondents say "I don't know" or give other noncommittal answers, how to determine that an answer is complete, and so on. Resolving these issues in advance does much to reduce unwanted differences between different interviewers, and is likely to increase the ultimate reliability of the interviews.

Recording Interviews.   The responses to the interview may be tape-recorded or videotaped for coding later, or they may be summarized by the interviewer during the interview. Taping is preferable, because it gives a permanent record of what was actually said instead of what the interviewer thought was said. This helps prevent the possibility that the interviewer's own bias might enter into what is recorded. However, tapes are sometimes difficult to understand, especially if several individuals are speaking at once. For this reason, it is often a good idea to have the interviewer take notes and to tape the interview, as a double check on the interview responses.

Preventing Bias in Interviews.   The issue of potential bias is very serious in interviews, even if responses are taped, because interviewers can easily lead respondents to give the "right" responses. Even if the interviewers stick to a prepared text and otherwise follow preestablished guidelines for dealing with various responses, their body language and tone of voice can indicate which answer the respondent is "supposed" to give. For this reason, it is important to train observers very carefully, to monitor them closely, to try not to make them aware of the study hypotheses, and above all to emphasize that what you want is accurate data, not data that confirm one or another hypothesis. In an experimental study, it is important to arrange the interviews so that the interviewer cannot tell whether a respondent is from the experimental group or the control group. If there is more than one interviewer, the interviewers should each spend the same proportion of their time in each experimental group, so that differences between interviewers are not interpreted as differences between treatments or classes.

Coding Interview Responses.   Once the interviews are completed, the responses to all open-form questions ordinarily have to be coded for analysis. For example, the responses to the question, "Has inclusion of mainstreamed students in your class made your attitude toward teaching better or worse?" might be coded as "much better," "somewhat better," "no difference," "somewhat worse," or "much worse." Categories such as these can be chosen in advance, or they can be created after the interview to summarize the data that have been collected. The researcher should write a coder's manual, consisting of specific definitions for each category, with examples for each (for example, what kind of response qualifies as "much better" and what kind "somewhat better").

When interview responses are coded, it is essential to compute a reliability coefficient that indicates how closely two independent coders agreed on how to score responses. The two coders should listen to the same tapes separately or read the same protocols and make their ratings independently. There are two methods of computing reliability for coding interview questions. We can compute a correlation between ratings made by one coder and ratings made by another (see Chapter 9 for computing correlations). Alternately, we can divide the number of times the coders agree on a coding category for a particular item by the number of agreements plus the number of disagreements. If the coders cannot agree at least 80% of the time, the categories should be redefined or changed, perhaps by reducing fine distinctions or gradations, until the coders can agree on them. For example, if the coders in the mainstreaming example described above could not differentiate reliably between "much better" and "somewhat better" or "much worse" and "somewhat worse," we might collapse the coding categories from five to three: "better," "no difference," or "worse."

If the items in your interview protocol are summed to form scales, you should compute scale reliabilities as described above (and in Chapter 9). See Bradburn and Sudman (1979), Payne (1951), and Yarrow (1960) for more on planning and conducting interviews.

Behavioral Observation

While we can often learn a great deal by asking teachers or students what they do, we can often learn even more by actually observing them in the classroom. Behaviors typically observed in classroom research fall into two categories: *high-inference* and *low-inference*. High-inference behaviors require the observer to use a great deal of judgment. For example, teachers might be rated on their warmth, activeness, or enthusiasm. Because so much judgment is required on the part of the observers, it may be difficult to observe high-inference behaviors reliably. Most classroom observations involve low-inference behaviors, which require less observer judgment. These include student time on-task (attending to materials or activities at hand), student-student or student-teacher interaction, or the number of questions asked by the teacher per minute. Low-inference behaviors may be difficult to observe reliably if they require much judgment on the part of the observer. For example, "student smiling" is a low-inference behavior, but it might be difficult to observe reliably, because it requires that the observer be able to see the student's face clearly. In addition, it may often be hard to determine whether a student is smiling or not.

Low-inference observations of behaviors that can be counted per unit time (for example, per minute, per hour, per day) are required for single-subject and time series studies (see Chapter 3), and they are frequently used in experimental and correlational studies as well.

Unlike paper-and-pencil measures, behavioral observation systems are rarely standardized, and most researchers who develop observation schemes do not publish their systems in full. Some observation methods can be located in such sources as *Mirrors for Behavior* (Simon and Boyer 1967) and *Evaluating Classroom Instruction* (Borich and Madden 1977), but the best way to obtain an unpublished observation system used in a particular article is to write to the authors for their observation manual. Making your own observation scheme is a difficult and time-consuming task, so your efforts should be directed at locating one that will meet your needs rather than making your own. If existing observation systems do not meet your needs, you should at least pattern your observation system on a well-validated existing scheme and change the definitions of behaviors to fit the requirements of your study. General guidelines for constructing your own behavioral observation system are presented below.

Constructing a Behavioral Observation System. If you make your own observation system, your first task will be to write a detailed description of each behavior you wish to code and a procedure for observation. You will need to make the following decisions:

1. How will you define each observation category? This is not as easy as it sounds. For example, you might define "on-task" as attending to assigned work. But there will be many ambiguous situations. What if a student stops paying attention for an instant? What if he drops his pencil and stops work to pick it up? What if he is raising his hand? What if he has finished all assigned work and is waiting for the next instruction? What if the student is facing forward in the direction of the teacher but doesn't appear to be listening? What if a student is not facing the teacher but does appear to be listening? What if the observer just can't decide? All of these problems will probably arise on the first day of observation. It is imperative that you try out an observation system (yours or someone else's) before the study begins to decide what to do in ambiguous situations.

2. How will you schedule your observation sessions? For example, you might observe each class for one period every day for two weeks or every other day for four weeks. You might observe each class all period or all day, or alternate between four different classes for 15-minute observations in each class every hour, and so on. The best schedule to use depends on the goals of your observation and your resources; behavioral observation takes a lot of time and observers are ususaly expensive, so using them wisely is critical. In general, if you are using a single-case design, you will want to observe very frequently for as long as it takes to fulfill the design. For example, if you are using an ABA design, you will need to observe long enough to establish a stable baseline, a stable treatment effect, and a stable reversal. If you are trying to characterize what teachers do all year, you might observe each class for a week at a time for several weeks spaced out over the school year (this is usually better than spacing out one-day observations over the year, because it is sometimes hard to get a sense of what is going on in a class in a single day's observation).

3. *Within an observation session, whom will you observe?* Depending on the purposes of your research, you may decide to observe a single individual, such as the teacher or a single student. You could observe all students, or a small group of students randomly chosen to represent what the class is doing, or you might observe the teacher and the class.

4. *What schedule of observation will you use?* You will need to decide how frequently and how long to observe each individual you are observing.

If you are observing a single individual on a simple, low-inference behavior such as on/off-task, you could observe whether or not a student is on- or off-task every five seconds, perhaps observing for five seconds and then recording for five seconds, alternating this way all period. You might simply record that a student is on-task until he or she goes off-task, record the time, and then record the time when the student is on-task again. You might observe a student or teacher for 60 seconds, and code whatever he or she was doing during most of that time. If you choose six students to represent the class or if you observe all students in the class, you might observe each student in turn, spending a set amount of time observing each student. There are many possibilities, but the within-session scheduling is critical—you should try out your observation system before you begin your study to be sure that the within-session scheduling is feasible and makes sense.

Reliability and Bias in Behavioral Observation.   Reliability is especially critical for behavioral observation measure. When a questionnaire scale is unreliable, it will not correlate well with other measures, increasing the possibility of a false negative error. However, the low reliability is unlikely to *bias* the results in any particular direction. On the other hand, in behavioral observation, unreliability (even small unreliability) can introduce *systematic* bias. For example, let's say we are studying the effect of the explicitness of teacher directions on student time on-task (attention to academic tasks). We would write very specific definitions of explicitness of directions and of on-task behavior, and design a procedure for noting explicitness of directions and subsequent student time on-task. We might decide to observe classrooms for 50 minutes per day every day for two weeks, and record the behavior of six selected students once per minute.

The potential for bias in this study lies in the fact that an intelligent observer is likely to guess the study hypothesis—that explicitness of directions is positively related to time on-task. Observers should *never* be told study hypotheses because of the possibility that this will lead to systematic bias. In many cases, however, the hypothesis is obvious. In this study, observers might tend to rate students about whom they are unsure as "on-task" when they have just observed the teacher giving explicit directions, but "off-task" when the teacher has been more vague. They might rate directions as "explicit" if they seem likely to be followed, but "not explicit" if not.

To avoid bias, it is important to avoid giving observers a stake in the study outcome. For example, it is bad science to have a coinvestigator (who will become a coauthor) do the observations, or to give observers the impression that you will not be satisfied with their work unless they come back with the "right" data. If it is impossible to keep your hypotheses secret from your observers, you must be especially clear that what you expect is honest data, not data that confirm your hypotheses.

The other way to reduce bias in behavioral observation is to increase reliability. Reliability is enhanced by having two observers (the second may be the researcher himself or herself) observe the same behaviors at the same time, either in the field or on a videotape. The goal is to have both observers record exactly the same observations. This is rarely possible, so reliability coefficients are computed to determine how close to 100% agreement the observers are. There are essentially two formulas used for this: *occurrence reliability* and *overall reliability*. Overall reliability indicates the percentage of all observations on which both observers saw the same thing. Let's say we have two observers who observe a student working for ten intervals of one minute each. The results of their observations are presented in Figure 5–1.

In Figure 5–1, Observer 1 records the student as on-task in all intervals except intervals 2 and 8. Observer 2 also records eight on-task and two off-task intervals, but he saw the student off-task in intervals 2 and 5. The formula for overall reliability is as follows:

$$\text{Overall Reliability} = \frac{\text{Number of Times Observers Agreed}}{\text{No. of Agreements} + \text{No. of Disagreements}}$$

Thus, the overall reliability is $8/(8+2) = 8/10 = .80$; the observers agreed on eight intervals, but disagreed on interval 5 and interval 8.

FIGURE 5–1   Example of Computing Reliability Between Observers

Interval	Observer 1	Observer 2	Match
1	on	on	agree
2	off	off	agree
3	on	on	agree
4	on	on	agree
5	on	off	disagree
6	on	on	agree
7	on	on	agree
8	off	on	disagree
9	on	on	agree
10	on	on	agree

Overall reliability is always computed in studies using behavioral observation. However, overall reliability can be falsely inflated if most observations fall into one or two categories. It is entirely possible that overall reliability could be high even if there is little or no agreement on behaviors that are less frequently seen. In the above example, the student was on-task most of the time (this is usually the case). Every time both observers agreed that the student was on-task, reliability was increased. But what if we were especially interested in off-task behavior? Is off-task behavior being reliably observed? To determine this, we compute occurrence reliability. The formula for occurrence reliability is presented below.

$$\text{Occurence Reliability} = \frac{\text{No. of Times Both Observers Saw Behavior}}{\text{No. of Times Either Observer Saw Behavior}}$$

For Figure 5–1, occurrence reliability for on-task behavior is 7/9, or .78, because one or the other observer recorded on-task in nine intervals, but they both agreed the behavior was on-task in only seven intervals (they disagreed in intervals 5 and 8). However, occurrence reliability for off-task behavior is only 1/3, or .33. Of the three intervals in which one or the other observer saw off-task behavior, they only agreed in one. This level of reliability is unacceptably low. The low occurrence reliability for off-task would indicate that more observer training is needed, even though the overall reliability (.80) might have been considered sufficient.

When is Reliability Adequate?   As with paper-and-pencil scales, there is no established minimum for reliability; higher is better, but there are some behaviors that are difficult to observe as reliably as other behaviors. In the example described above concerning explicitness of directions and time on-task, it would be surprising if reliability for explicitness of directions, which takes considerable judgment, were as high as for time on-task. However, as a rule of thumb, many investigators train their observers until they have an overall reliability of at least .90, and occurrence reliabilities on critical variables of at least .80. They then repeat reliability observations in the field (by having two observers observing at the same time) several times spaced over the course of the study. An average overall reliability of .80 and occurrence reliabilities of .70 would usually be considered reasonable minimums. If lower reliabilities are found, retraining should be done.

Increasing Reliability of Behavioral Observations.   Reliability can usually be increased by giving observers more practice, but it can be enhanced from the start by providing each observer with an observer's manual containing very clear definitions for each behavior, decision rules to use in ambiguous situations, and examples of problematic situations and how to code them. As noted earlier in discussing the observation of time on-task, there must be some rule explaining what to do if a student is momentarily off-task, is facing the teacher but appears not to be listening, is raising his or her hand to be called on, is apparently finished with the task at hand, and so on. Similar decision rules are needed for observations of all behaviors. These decision rules are virtually impossible to anticipate; they typically come up during pilot observations. It is less important what decision rule is followed for these ambiguous situations than that some rule be established before beginning the observations that will count.

Writing the Observation Manual.   To develop the observation manual, you should write the best behavior definitions possible, and then try them out in a setting similar (or identical) to the setting in which the research will take place. In a few hours of observation, most of the definitional or procedural problems that will eventually come up will arise. You should then train an observer or observers, and return to the pilot setting to see if you and your observers can observe reliably using your observation categories. Compute overall and occurrence reliabilities after each session to see whether or not you and your observer(s) agree adequately on each observation category. If you find that some of your categories cannot be reliably observed, you might then change the definitions to resolve ambiguities, or collapse two or more categories into one to avoid having to make difficult distinctions. For example, let's say that in your original system you had as categories "friendly conversation between students" and "arguing between students." In practice, it might be impossible to reliably distinguish between these categories. If the distinction is critical to your research, you might try setting rules for distinguishing between these categories (i.e., students are considered to be arguing if and only if their voices are raised and they are not smiling), or making a fallback decision rule (students are considered to be having a friendly conversation if they are talking unless it is very obvious that they are arguing). However, if the distinction is not critical to the research, these categories can be collapsed into a single "student talk" category that does not require as much judgment on the part of the observer. See Good and Brophy (1978) and Hersen and Barlow (1976) for more on behavioral observation.

SAMPLING

One very important aspect of research design, especially in survey research, is determination of the appropriate sample. As the word implies, a sample is a part of a larger whole. In educational research, we are usually interested in groups that are much too large to include in a single study. For example, we might be interested in the opinions of members of the National Education Association toward teacher accountability. It would be impractical (and unnecessary) to send a questionnaire to every NEA member. Instead, we can select a *sample* of all NEA members that will be representative of the entire group.

The most important principle in sampling is that each member of the population from which the sample is drawn should have an equal and known probability of being selected. The larger the sample drawn, the smaller the sampling error will be.

Let's say a researcher wants to conduct a survey of the 1,000 secondary math teachers in a large school district to determine their knowledge of and attitudes toward microcomputers. He plans to interview each teacher by telephone, so it is impractical (and unnecessary) for him to interview all of them. He might therefore choose a random sample of 100 teachers who will represent the entire population. That is, each secondary mathematics teacher in the school district will have a known and equal probability (one chance in ten) of actually being selected to be interviewed.

The random assignment would proceed in a fashion similar to that described for random assignment to treatment conditions in Chapter 2. The researcher might obtain a list of all secondary mathematics teachers in the district, and assign them numbers from 000 to 999. Then he would consult a table of random numbers (available in most statistics texts) and, starting on a randomly chosen line, begin taking three-digit numbers. If the first line he chose in the random numbers table were

$$9868871247980621...,$$

he would select teachers numbered 986, 887, 124, 798, 062, etc., skipping over any numbers that repeat themselves, until he had 100 names (plus a few more to serve as replacements for any teachers he could not reach).

Cluster Samples

Often, it is more convenient to randomly sample clusters of individuals rather than individuals. For example, if we wanted to find out how much fifth graders in a particular school district know about nutrition, it would be much easier to test whole classes or all fifth graders in a few schools than to separately test randomly selected individuals. To do this, a researcher might obtain a list of all 500 fifth-grade classes in a district and sample 100 of them, just as math teachers were sampled in the earlier example. Then, all students in these classes could be tested.

Stratified Random Samples

One way to be sure that a sample is like the population from which it was drawn is to stratify on important characteristics. For example, if we wanted to interview a subset of students about their racial attitudes in a student body that is 70% white and 30% black and equally balanced by sex, we might make sure that our sample reflects these proportions by stratifying on race and sex. Let's say there are 1,000 students, and we plan to interview 200. We would list the 350 white boys and randomly select 10% of them, and we would repeat this with the 350 white girls, the 150 black boys, and the 150 black girls, to get a final 10% sample that reflects the overall race and sex composition of the school. When a particular category is rare, we may wish to oversample it. For example, if the student body had been 90% white and 10% black, we might have randomly selected half of the black students (50) but only 5/90 of the white students (50), because we are especially interested in getting the views of students of both races. However, if a school mean is computed, we would have to weight the black and white samples' scores to recreate their actual proportion in the school. To find the weight for each score, multiply the true proportion of each group in the population by the reciprocal of the proportion sampled. In the above example, the true proportion of black students in the school was 1/10, while the proportion sampled was 1/2. We would therefore multiply $1/10 \times 2/1 = 1/5$. Thus, we would multiply each black student's score by 1/5. For whites, the multiplier would be $9/10 \times 90/5 = 81/5$. The mean computed on the weighted scores would approximate the overall mean for the school that would have been obtained had we interviewed all students.

Samples of Convenience

It should be noted that it is rarely feasible to randomly select a sample from among all individuals to which we want our findings to apply. That is, if we want to know the opinions of American seventh-grade teachers, it would be very difficult to obtain a list of all seventh-grade teachers in the United States and then randomly select a sample of them. Thus, in practice, researchers usually select from among a smaller group (for example, seventh-grade teachers in the Townville Public Schools) and then make an argument that their findings are likely to apply to seventh-grade teachers in similar school districts (see Cornfield and Tukey 1956). When such a sample is drawn, it is important to describe the teachers and the district in some detail, so that others may reasonably assess the relevance of the findings to other settings. For example, if we know that Townville is a rural town in the Midwest, and the teachers are all white with an average age of 43 and 18 years of experience, we would have an idea that the findings would apply better to similar settings than to urban or suburban school districts with less experienced or younger teachers. Samples of convenience are usually less problematic in experimental, single-case, or correlational research, where we are interested in relationships between variables. However, in survey research or other descriptive research, in which our interest is more in *levels* of variables rather than relationships between them, we must be very careful about applying findings to other settings or samples. We could certainly not make valid conclusions about all U.S. teachers on the basis of a survey of Townville teachers.

Missing Data

Missing data is a serious problem in sampling, especially if there might be important differences between missing and nonmissing individuals. Let's say a researcher wants to find out about eighth graders' experiences with the police. She administers a questionnaire to a sample of eighth graders during their English classes one day, and gets 90% of all eighth graders in her sample to return questionnaires. Is this adequate? Perhaps not, because many of the absent students are likely to be truant, and truant students undoubtedly have different experiences with the police than nontruant students. This researcher should thus try to locate every eighth grader in her sample, even if she has to go to the students' homes, if she wants an accurate picture of eighth graders' experiences with the police. In a study in which no obvious factors differentiate respondents from nonrespondents, a lower response rate might be acceptable. However, when response rates are low (as in a mail survey), it is important to doggedly follow up a sample of nonrespondents to see if they are different from respondents. For example, a researcher might mail a questionnaire to 500 principals. Even after mailing two reminder letters, only 300 (60%) return their questionnaires. The researcher might list the remaining 200 principals, randomly select 50 of them, and repeatedly call them or even visit them to be sure they handed in their questionnaires. If the questionnaires obtained in this way are similar to the original 300, the researcher could feel confident that the sample is unbiased. If this is not the case, he probably needs to obtain most of the remaining questionnaires at whatever cost and trouble it takes. If the 300 questionnaires received are not representative of the 500 in the full sample, they will certainly not be representative of the larger population from which the 500 principals were drawn.

Missing data are less of a concern when we are studying a relationship between variables than when we want to know about a level of a certain variable. In the above example concerning students' contacts with the police, locating the last 10% of the students (many of whom are likely to be truants) is absolutely critical if the purpose of the study is to describe the frequency and type of student-police contacts in a typical American junior high school. However, if the purpose of the study were to find the relationship between students' contacts with the police, grades in school, attitudes toward school, and antisocial beliefs, getting every last student might not be as much of an absolute requirement, although it would still be important.

When repeated followups are impossible, the characteristics of non-respondents can often be inferred from other sources and compared to the characteristics of respondents. For example, in the study of principals described above, we might know the location and sex of each principal. If we determined that respondents and nonrespondents were equally likely to be from urban, rural, or suburban schools and were equally likely to be female, this would help us assume that differences between respondents and nonrespondents are not overwhelming. Another tactic is to compare respondents to successive reminders. If principals who responded right away resemble those who responded a month later (after one reminder) and those who responded two months later (after two or three reminders), we might assume that nonrespondents are not too different either. If early and late responders are not the same, we might infer that nonrespondents resemble late responders.

See Bradburn and Sudman (1979), Dillman (1978), and Payne (1951) for more on survey methods.

Sample Size

Sample size is a critical element of research design. The best way to reduce the possibility of false negative error without increasing the chance of false positive error in experimental or correlational research is to increase the number of subjects involved in the study. If the sample is too small, the chances are good that no statistically significant results will be obtained. A conclusion that there are no significant effects or correlations is an honorable and legitimate finding if we have some confidence that our design makes false negative errors unlikely. However if we have no idea whether the failure to find effects occurred because they do not exist *in fact* or because there was insufficient sample size, the researchers might as well have stayed home. They know no more at the end of the study than they did when they began. Journals do publish articles in which hypotheses were not supported, but they rarely do so if there is a good chance that the reason the hypotheses were not supported is that the sample was not large enough or the study was not strong enough to detect true effects.

When is Sample Size Adequate?   When is a sample large enough? Some statistics books suggest a sample size of at least 30 in each group as a rule of thumb. This is the point at which data from a sample with an underlying normal distribution begin to conform to the normal distribution (see Chapter 9). However, every additional subject in a study adds to the ability to find a true effect if it is there, or to be confident that if no significant relationships are found, it is due to the fact that none exists. Each additional subject does add less to statistical power, so as the sample gets bigger, it takes even bigger increases to get further increases in statistical power. For example, it is much more important to increase a sample from 20 to 30 than from 100 to 110.

To illustrate the effect of sample size on statistical power, consider an experiment in which high school seniors are given coaching for the quantitative portion of the SAT. Some number of students are randomly assigned to the coaching group, while an equal number are randomly assigned to a noncoaching control group. SAT scores have a theoretical mean of 500 and a standard deviation of about 100. We will use a t-test to see if the two groups are the same or different following coaching. How large a difference in SAT quantitative scores would we need to get a significant difference, assuming $p < .05$?

Figure 5–2 illustrates how much of a difference in SAT quantitative scores would be needed to show statistical significance with no more than a 5% chance of making a false positive error ($p < .05$) for different levels of sample size in each of two groups.

As Figure 5–2 shows, increasing the sample size dramatically reduces the group differences required to produce a significant t statistic. If 30 students received coaching and 30 were in the control group, we would have to see group differences of more than half a standard deviation, or 52 SAT points—a huge difference, because many factors other than coaching (for example, prior knowledge, motivation, IQ, etc.), enter into the SAT score. If we considered a quarter standard deviation (25 points) a sufficient difference for practical importance, but only used 30 subjects in each group, we would be running a risk that a true, important difference could exist, and we would fail to detect it—a common false negative error. If we had used a larger sample and found no statistically significant differences, we would have had some confidence that it was because such differences do not exist (that is, coaching makes no difference), but with a small sample we would be unsure.

FIGURE 5–2   Differences Required to Produce a Significant t, $p < .05$

Number in Each Group	d.f.	Critical Value of t for $p < .05$	Difference Required in SAT Points	Difference Required in Standard Deviations
5	8	2.31	146	1.46
10	18	2.10	94	.94
20	38	2.02	64	.64
30	58	2.00	52	.52
50	98	1.99	40	.40
100	198	1.98	28	.28
500	998	1.96	12	.12
1000	1998	1.96	9	.09

The relationship between sample size and the differences needed for statistical significance are essentially the same for statistics other than t (see Chapter 9), and they apply equally to experimental and correlational research. In survey research, there is similar relationship between sample size and standard error of the mean, a measure of the accuracy of a given estimated mean (see Chapter 9).

Of course, there are drawbacks to large studies. A large study will cost more, be harder to manage, and take more trouble to set up and analyze than will a small one. In a large study in which the researcher must rely on teachers or others to implement a treatment or administer a test or questionnaire, it may be difficult to monitor the study closely enough to be sure that everyone is doing what they should do. A small, carefully done study is generally better than a large, sloppy one, and if there is a true difference or relationship between variables, a researcher may be more likely to detect it by being sure that his or her procedures are carefully followed than by increasing sample size.

In addition to the factors discussed above, one consideration in deciding on an appropriate sample size is the size of the effect (or correlation) you anticipate. For example, effects of different instructional methods on student achievement tend to be small, because so many other factors determine student achievement. For an experimental study of instructional methods, 100 students in each treatment group would not be unrealistic. If random assignment of classes or teachers rather than individuals is used, you would want five or more classes in each treatment group (if possible) to minimize the possibility that an unusual class or teacher would heavily influence the outcome (see Chapter 2). In contrast, in a carefully controlled laboratory study, in which treatments are given to students one at a time, 20 or 30 students per treatment group might be sufficient.

Statistical Significance versus Practical and Theoretical Importance.   It should be noted that use of large sample sizes may allow an effect of little practical or theoretical importance to be statistically significant. For example, suppose we compared a computer drill-and-practice program in mathematics to traditional instructional methods. Let's say that after a year, the computer group gained significantly more than the control group on the California Achievement Test. However, the actual difference is only 10% of a grade equivalent, or 5% of a standard deviation in mathematics achievement. Such a result would tell us two things. First, the fact that there is a statistically significant difference in mathematics achievement between the computer group and the control group does imply that the computer drill-and-practice program is effective. However, this result would also tell us that the differences are so small that they are of little practical importance, and probably would not justify major expenditures on computers or computer drill-and-practice software. Furthermore, differences of this size would be a shaky foundation on which to build a theory based on the superiority of computer-assisted instruction.

Some methodologists propose a rule of thumb that a difference between experimental and control groups should not be considered important unless it is at least a quarter of a standard deviation. Others suggest a third or even a half of a standard deviation. That is, if the standard deviation of an achievement measure is 16, an experimental-control difference would have to be at least 4 to be considered of any practical or theoretical significance. However, such rules of thumb must be interpreted loosely, depending on the variable in question. If a treatment could reliably increase individuals' IQ scores by 2 points (only 13% of a standard deviation), or could reliably increase SAT quantitative scores by 15 points (about 15% of a standard deviation), these might be considered important effects, probably more important for most practical purposes than an increase of a half standard deviation in a variable such as liking of school.

It is sometimes argued that large sample sizes should not be used, because with large samples, "anything will be statistically significant." However, in a study without major sources of bias, this is not true. If there are no differences between two or more treatments or no relationship between two or more variables in fact, no statistically significant effects will be found. A large study that finds small effects adds to knowledge, because such a finding is probably reliable; the chances of making a false negative error are slim. In a small study that finds no differences, there is always the possibility that true effects (even large ones) do exist, but were undetected because of a combination of small sample size and unreliable measures, inadequate program implementation, and so on. In other words, when a small study fails to find statistically significant effects, we know little more than we did before the study was begun.

In general, if you have the resources to do a large study, if you can handle large amounts of data, and if you can be sure that procedures will be followed conscientiously, there is no such thing as too large a study. A good study design is one that will add to knowledge no matter what the result is. The larger the study, the more likely this is to be true.

See Kish (1965), Lazerwitz (1968), Shavelson (1981), and Sudman (1976) for more on sampling and sample size.

EXERCISES

1) Describe the flaw in this statement: The reliability of a self-esteem scale was found to be .95 in three studies. It is therefore clear that it is a valid measure of self-esteem.

2) Describe four procedures you might use to validate a test designed to measure teaching skills.

3) Describe two methods of assessing the reliability of a scale that is designed to measure math aptitude.

4) A questionnaire measure of aggressiveness was administered to a group of sixth graders. A short form of the same questionnaire was administered to a group of third graders. What might you expect about the reliability of the measure in these two situations?

5) Discuss the relative benefits and drawbacks of the use of standardized versus content-specific achievement tests in experimental comparison studies: a) as pretests or covariates; b) as posttests or dependent variables.

6) Design an observation system to assess the amount of time teachers use open-ended versus closed-ended questioning techniques. You are assessing a total of 20 classes, 4 in each of 5 schools. You have 2 full-time observers. Specify behavioral definitions, recording format, reliability procedures, and schedule of observations.

7) You are conducting a survey to determine how principals' time is allocated. You want to use a national sample. Design a short questionnaire and define a sampling procedure for your survey. Include a procedure for following up subjects who do not respond.

chapter 6

Internal and External Validity: Is This a Good Research Design?

There are two principal criteria that a research design must satisfy if it is to add to knowledge. These are internal validity and external validity. Internal validity refers to the degree to which a research design rules out explanations for a study's findings other than that the variables involved appear to be related because they are in fact related. If a study high in internal validity finds a certain result, it is likely that the result is a true finding rather than a result of some flaw in the design. Any possibility that the findings might be due to defects in the research design reduces internal validity. External validity, or generalizability, refers to the degree to which the findings of a particular study using a particular sample have meaning for other settings or samples, particularly settings or samples in which we have some practical interest.

Several threats to internal and external validity common in educational research are presented below (see also Campbell and Stanley 1963; Cook and Campbell 1979).

THREATS TO INTERNAL VALIDITY

Passage of Time

One common error in educational research is the use of a pre-post design with no comparison group. For example, a researcher might give students an attitude test in January, and then begin a program of giving attractive certificates to students who get the best scores on each of several quizzes. He might give the attitude test again in May, and since he observes improved attitudes, he concludes that the certificate program improved students' attitudes. However, this design does not control for passage of time. Any number of other events unrelated to the certificate program might have improved student attitudes. It may be that attitudes naturally improve toward the end of the year, or that they are unusually low in January, and so on. Our inability to rule out these alternative explanations makes a pre-post comparison low in internal validity.

Testing Problems

Several recurrent threats to internal validity are posed by problems of testing. Some of the most common of these problems are discussed in the following sections.

Pretest Effects.   One problem relating to testing is that the fact of being pretested can have an influence on the posttest. In a study that simply pretests individuals, gives them some treatment, and then posttests them, the fact of being pretested would probably increase posttest scores, either by giving the subjects practice on the items or by making subjects sensitive to the issues addressed on the posttest. When we compare an experimental group to a control group (or compare two or more treatments), all groups experience the same pretest, so any effects of pretesting are usually not problematic. However, pretests may affect different treatments in different ways. This problem is discussed in Chapter 2.

Comparability of Tests.   Another issue relating to testing involves making sure that whenever test scores are being compared, the tests are the same. If gain scores are computed by subtracting pretest scores from posttest scores, the pre- and posttests must be identical or the results are meaningless.

It should go without saying that when tests are compared to one another, they should be the same, and should be given under the same conditions. However, serious design errors do sometimes occur due to unequal testing conditions. For example, in one published study, students were randomly assigned to two conditions. In one, the students worked in small groups, while in the other they worked alone. The students who worked in small groups were then allowed to take their final tests together, while those who worked alone took their tests individually. Obviously, the results of the tests taken under such different conditions should not have been compared to one another, because the students who took the tests in small groups had an advantage (their groupmates' help) not shared by the other students.

Ceiling and Floor Effects.   Another problem relating to testing is ceiling and floor effects. A ceiling effect is displayed by a distribution of scores when a measure has a maximum possible score and many scores are at or near the maximum (this is discussed in Chapter 9). For example, if we gave a 50-item test and half of the scores fell between 45 and 50 items correct, we would have a ceiling effect. Similarly, if many scores fell between 0 and 5, we would have a floor effect on the test.

Studies involving student grades often have problems with ceiling and floor effects, because most grading systems only go from F to A (that is, F is the "floor" and A is the "ceiling"). An example of a grading study in which false conclusions were drawn because of ceiling and floor effects was recently published. In the study, first graders were asked just after they received their first reading grades to predict their next grades. Most students predicted that they would receive the same grade, and most actually received the same grade on the next report card. However, in cases where students predicted a higher grade, they tended to get either as high a grade or a higher grade than they got before, and when they predicted a lower grade, they got an equal or lower grade on their next report card. The statistics used showed a strong relationship between predicted changes and actual changes, leading the researchers to state that the predictions were in some sense self-fulfilling, as students worked harder (or less hard) to make them come true.

However, this is instead a case of ceiling and floor effects. Because almost all students made A's or B's, and almost all students predicted A's and B's for themselves, there were both ceiling *and* floor effects. A student who made an A could only predict an equal or lower score, and he or she could only get an equal or lower score (a ceiling effect, because there is no grade higher than A). A student who made a B was most likely to predict a B or an A, and was most likely to move up, if he or she changed at all, because few grades lower than B were given (a floor effect). Since both the predictions and the changes could only go in one direction for all practical purposes, the relationship between predicted change and actual change virtually had to be positive.

Ceiling effects typically cause problems in studies investigating different growth rates of students of varying degrees of ability or past performance. Let's say we were evaluating an instructional program designed to increase student science achievement. We pretest the students, administer the program, and then posttest them using the same test. Looking at students with different pretest levels, we would probably find that students who got 95% correct on the pretest would increase from pre- to posttest less than students who got 60% on the pretest, because the test only goes up to a "ceiling" of 100%, restricting the potential growth of students who started at 95% to only 5%. If we concluded on the basis of these results that the program was more effective for students who initially started low than for students who started high on the test, we would be making a serious error. The students who began with high scores might have learned as much or more than those who started with lower scores, but the test could not register their learning (because of its "ceiling" at 100%).

Floor effects are most typically problems that make pretests or covariates useless. For example, if we tested students who had never studied Swahili on their knowledge of Swahili, we would get a floor effect—most scores would be at or near zero. This would make the Swahili pretest useless as an indication of how much students were likely to gain from a class in Swahili. Ceiling effects also make pretests useless. They are relatively unusual in research on academic achievement, but they are common in attitude research, when it happens that almost all subjects have positive attitudes before an attitude-improvement program begins.

Finally, ceiling and floor effects make score distributions deviate from the normal distribution, making it inappropriate to use parametric statistics (see Chapter 9). A variable exhibiting a ceiling or floor effect is unlikely to correlate well with other variables, making false negative errors likely.

Inadequate Reliability and Validity.   Other problems relating to testing have to do with the reliability and validity of the measures. These issues are discussed in Chapter 5.

Selection Bias

Perhaps the most common cause for low internal validity in experiments and correlational studies is that samples being compared to each other are not equal. In one published article, the author of a logic game conducted a study to evaluate the game. He pretested the IQ of an "experimental" class of students in a summer school elective course on logic and a "control" class that was taking a required summer school class in remedial mathematics.

The students in the logic class played the logic game, while those in the remedial math class received their regular instruction. The students in the logic class gained several points on the IQ test, almost certainly because they had had practice on the same questions two weeks earlier. The remedial math class students also gained on the IQ test, but not nearly as much. It is hardly surprising that very low performing students would learn less from having taken an IQ test than would students who were so interested in mental activity that they would take a voluntary summer school course in logic!

The only ways to be sure that selection bias is ruled out are to compare the same subjects under two or more different conditions or to compare two or more groups of subjects who were randomly assigned to groups (see Chapter 2). However, many important questions could never be asked if we absolutely required that subjects be randomly assigned to different treatments or that the same subjects be tested under two or more different conditions. For example, we could never study such issues as whether blacks and whites have equal opportunities to go to college since we cannot randomly assign students to be black or white. We could never study a question such as, "Do freshmen at Yale learn more than freshmen at East Overshoe Community College?" because Yale's more stringent entrance requirements and higher tuition insures them a better qualified and wealthier student body. However, these questions are still important. Sophisticated correlational procedures (described in Chapter 4) have been developed to attempt to overcome selection bias by statistically "controlling" for relevant differences between groups, but when group differences are substantial, selection bias can never be ruled out as an alternative explanation for any findings.

Statistical Regression

Very bright parents have children who are, on the average, less bright than themselves (although still brighter than average). However, it is just as true that very bright children have parents who are (on the average) less bright than themselves. The reason for this is that whenever we choose an extreme group on any measure, that group will tend to be less extreme on any other measure, even if the two measures are highly correlated. Parents' and children's IQs are highly correlated, but the intelligence of children of bright parents or of parents of bright children "regresses" toward the population mean because for an individual to be outstandingly bright, many somewhat random events must all be going in the same direction. The individual's genes, home environment, schooling, temperament, and life experiences must all be conducive (or at least not detrimental) to high intelligence, and the chances that all these factors will be outstanding in a parent and his or her son or daughter are small.

By the same token, if we select a group of students who score outstandingly on a test, for example all students who score above 780 on the PSAT (Preliminary Scholastic Aptitude Test), this group will score well *but not as well* on the average on a very similar test, such as the SAT. This is true because everything (luck, skill, preparation, being in a good mood) must be going right for students to get such a high score. Furthermore, any measure of human aptitudes or attitudes has some random variability, or error, such that the same individual would get somewhat different scores each time he or she was tested. When an individual gets an outstanding score, it is likely that random error operated in his or her favor. Again, it is unlikely that all the variable factors that go into getting a score as high as 780 on the PSAT will be so positive on a second test, or even on a second administration of the same test. Similarly, students who score below 220 are likely to show an increase on a similar test, because it is unlikely that all the factors that produced such a low score will be so negative on a second test.

Statistical regression problems come up from time to time in educational research. A school district research director once did what he called an "IQ band study," to see how well the district was doing with students of varying IQ levels. He was delighted to report that the district was doing famously with its low-IQ students, whose achievement test percentile ranks were substantially ahead of their IQ percentiles, but he was at a loss to explain why the district was doing so poorly with its high-IQ students. The district was contemplating major expenditures on programs for more able students, based on the research director's misinterpretation of data that were clearly exhibiting regression effects (that is, students who were chosen for extreme scores on one test (IQ) were closer to the mean on a second test (achievement)). If he had chosen students with outstanding achievement test scores, he would have found that these students were achieving above their IQ percentile scores, and he might have made exactly the opposite conclusion about which type of student the district was serving best!

Statistical regression problems often come up when two groups that have been selected on the basis of one test are compared to one another. For example, if we compared students selected on the basis of a test for special education to similar students who were not put in special education, or if we compared students assigned to Algebra I to students assigned to Math 9, statistical regression effects would have to be considered (see Chapter 2 for more on statistical regression).

Attrition

Even when two groups are initially equivalent, they may lose their equivalence because of dropouts or other changes in the samples. When these occur at random and equally in the different groups, attrition is not a serious problem, but sometimes attrition is *caused* by a particular treatment, and this may invalidate the study. A classic example of this is a grade-to-grade promotion policy introduced in a small southern school district, where students had to pass a test to be promoted to the next semester. The school district reported massive increases in test scores in the upper grades. This experiment was reported in newspapers, journals, and magazines across the country, and many school districts have implemented promotion testing based in part on this experiment. However, after a moment's reflection, it should be clear that the school district was systematically removing low achievers from its upper grades, so that the average scores in those grades were bound to increase. In other words, even if the promotion policy had no effect on any individual's academic performance, the built-in attrition in the upper grades would make it appear that there was a substantial improvement.

Attrition might also be a problem in a study of an especially difficult new science course, as students who could not keep up would drop out, leaving only the most able students in the class. A successful high school dropout prevention program might lead to a lowering of average achievement test scores in the high school because low achievers (who are most likely to drop out) might be staying in school to take the tests!

Teacher, School, and Class Effects, and Other Confounding Variables

In experiments in which one treatment is compared to another, the critical task is to eliminate by proper research design all sources of differences between the treatment groups other than the effects of the treatments themselves. In field research, this can be difficult. Experimental research in schools often suffers from three characteristic confounding variables: teacher effects, school effects, and class effects.

Teacher effects.   Teacher effects refer to the effects on students of the particular abilities or other characteristics of their teachers. If we compare Ms. Reynolds's class using Method A to Mr. Yager's class using Method B, we cannot separate the differences between treatments from the differences between the teachers.

School effects.   School effects are similar to teacher effects in their ability to confound treatment differences if treatments are located in different schools. However, when schools are similar to one another in student and teacher characteristics, school effects tend to be much smaller than teacher effects (see, for example, Coleman et al. 1966).

Class effects.   Class effects refer to the effects students in the same class have on one another. Let's say that a researcher has Mr. Pappas teach one class using Method A and one using Method B. The classes are equal in past academic achievement, but it just so happens that there is a small group of troublemakers in the Method B class. These students disrupt the Method B class enough to make it inferior to the Method A class on a final test, even though there are in fact no differences between Methods A and B.

Teacher, school, and class effects, and ways to minimize them, are discussed in Chapter 2 (also see Glass and Stanley 1970; Hopkins 1982; Page 1975; Slavin 1983).

Other confounding variables.   There are other confounding variables that are threats to internal validity. In many experiments in schools, experimental groups are given extra resources, aides, or outside attention not given to untreated control groups. Unless these resources are considered part of the treatment, they confound interpretation of study results, as it is unclear whether the effects are due to the treatments or to the additional resources. Poor monitoring of treatment implementation or unclear specification of procedures to be used can lead to wide variations in treatment implementation, making interpretation of what happened impossible. Researchers must clearly specify what the treatments are and how they are to be implemented, and then observe the implementations to be sure that they remain true to the model the researcher specified. See Chapter 8 for more on maintaining the integrity of an intervention.

THREATS TO EXTERNAL VALIDITY

External validity refers to the degree to which the results of a study can be applied to subjects or settings other than the one in which the research took place. It is possible that a study can be high in internal validity but low in external validity; a true finding may have little or no applicability to situations outside of the exact conditions under which the study was done. Several common threats to external validity are discussed below.

Lack of Internal Validity

For a study to have external validity, it must first have internal validity. There is no point in trying to generalize from findings that are themselves in doubt.

Nonrepresentativeness

It is almost never possible to study the entire population to which we want our findings to apply. In research in schools, we usually hope to be able to generalize from the particular population we work with to a much larger population, such as all inner-city seventh-grade math students, all seventh-grade math students, all math students, or all students.

In survey research, representativeness is particularly important. We should certainly not want to say that the opinions of the teachers or students in a particular school are representative of the opinions of all teachers and students. In order to insure representativeness, survey researchers use sophisticated probability sampling methods, which allow them to know the chances that a particular individual will have to be selected into a sample. For example, if a researcher wanted to study the opinions of members of the National Education Association, she could obtain a mailing list for the NEA and decide in advance to survey one NEA member in a thousand. She could then randomly select 1/1,000th of the names (probably using a computer to do so), and survey those teachers. If the response rate was high, this procedure would insure that the sample chosen was representative of the entire NEA membership. Sampling of blocks of individuals can also be done. For example, if we wanted to study teachers' interactions with their colleagues, it might make sense to randomly select some number of schools, and then survey all teachers in those schools.

National surveys, however, are very expensive and difficult to do. More often, educational researchers study a few classes or schools, note the characteristics of their samples, and then allow the reader to decide to what other populations the results might apply. Findings from a study involving fifth graders will be more likely to apply to similar fourth grades than to ninth grades, a study in algebra classes will have more relevance to geometry than to history, and a study in the inner city will have more relevance to other inner-city settings than to the city's own suburbs. Typically, a finding becomes established as real and important when it is replicated in as many places, conditions, student characteristics, and subject areas as possible. In general, it is important at the beginning of a program of research to select samples that are not atypical. For example, in an investigation involving foreign language instruction, it would be better to study Spanish or French than Russian because relatively few students study Russian. A study of a new form of social studies instruction would have more generalizability if it took place in an average suburban high school than if it took place in a special magnet school for the performing arts, and so on.

For more on sampling, see Chapter 5.

Artificiality

Perhaps the most common problem of external validity in educational research is artificiality, where a study (usually an experiment) is conducted under such special or unusual conditions that it is difficult to generalize to settings in which we have any interest (such as classrooms). Many published experimental studies are conducted in actual laboratory settings, or more typically in classrooms for very short periods under unusual conditions. The degree to which laboratory or laboratory-like settings are appropriate depends, of course, on the purpose of the study and the degree to which the results are expected to influence practice. For example, consider a study on memorization strategies. A researcher has some students memorize nonsense words in blocks of three, some in blocks of six, and some in blocks of nine. The study takes place in a fifth-grade classroom, and lasts a total of two hours. Whatever the results, this study might add to basic knowledge about memory. If the researcher wanted to suggest that the research has importance for classroom practice, it would not be too farfetched to guess that math facts or irregular spelling words might best be memorized in specific blocks, although research on learning of those particular bits of information under more normal conditions for a much longer time would be needed to establish this. On the other hand, it would be farfetched to suggest that the study findings might apply to teaching of social studies or algebra.

In another example, a researcher takes two groups of kindergarten students and gives them felt-tip markers and coloring books. One group of students receives candy rewards based on how many pictures they complete, while another receives no rewards. After they work for an hour, the candy rewards are removed, and the number of pictures colored after the removal of the rewards is noted in each group. Suppose that the students who were previously rewarded colored fewer pictures than those who were never rewarded. This research might add to basic understanding of the relationship of rewards to performance of tasks that are already enjoyable to students, but its generalizability to other classroom tasks and typical classroom situations must be independently established, since coloring with felt-tip pens does not resemble many classroom tasks, candy rewards do not resemble the kinds of rewards usually given in class (for example, grades, praise, stars), and kindergarteners are not typical of elementary school students.

When research is specifically formulated to inform practitioners, generalizability to the practical situation is especially critical. Promotion of instructional methods based on highly artificial studies is all too common. For example, most of the studies conducted to evaluate one widely used instructional strategy involved interventions of from three days to two weeks and provided the experimental groups with additional instructional time and/or aides not available to the traditionally taught control groups. The generalizability of these studies to real classroom settings is questionable.

Reactivity

There is a principle of physics that states that there is a limit on what we can learn from nature because there are many phenomena that we change in the act of studying them. Human behavior is a set of phenomena that is particularly sensitive to being studied, which means that we can rarely know if what we are observing would be the same if we were not observing it. This is true because people tend to act differently if they know they are being observed or studied. We call this problem *reactivity*, because subjects' reactions to being studied confound interpretation of what is being studied.

In research in schools, reactivity is a particular problem, because teachers, principals, and other staff often have a substantial interest in looking good to outsiders and may have a strong stake in one or another outcome of a research project. For example, if teachers know that a research project is studying time on-task, they might try to increase their students' time on-task artificially in order to look good to the outside researchers. If a school wants a new program for gifted students, they would want an evaluation of an experimental gifted program evaluated in their school to come out positive, and so on.

Hawthorne effects.   One form of reactivity is called a *Hawthorne effect*, which is the tendency for subjects to do better just because they know they are in an experiment. A Hawthorne effect could come about because the novelty of a new treatment provides short-term motivation that makes a treatment look more effective than it would over a longer period, or because of the participants' awareness of being in an experiment. The study that gave the Hawthorne effect its name (Roethlisberger and Dickson 1939) involved workers in the Hawthorne (Illinois) Western Electric factory. The effects of various levels of lighting on worker productivity were studied. It was found that regardless of the lighting level chosen, productivity increased whenever the lighting level was changed, even when the lighting was reduced to the brightness of moonlight! The increase in productivity was ascribed to the attention given the workers, their knowledge that they were in an experiment, and their desire to look good to the experimenters rather than to anything about the lighting per se. In educational research, Hawthorne effects are problematic in experimental studies comparing attractive new methods to untreated control groups. Methods of reducing Hawthorne effects are discussed in Chapter 2 and Chapter 8.

John Henry effects.   The other side of a Hawthorne effect is called a *John Henry effect* (named after the fabled man who died demonstrating that he could drive railroad spikes faster than a machine). This refers to situations in which individuals in an untreated control group are determined to "beat" the new technique being evaluated in the experimental group. For example, if some teachers in a school have been randomly assigned to use a new method while others continue with their usual methods, the teachers in the untreated control group may feel that they will look bad if the new method is found to be better than whatever they are doing, and they might redouble their efforts to make their classes look better. Means of avoiding John Henry effects are discussed in Chapter 2 and Chapter 8.

Mistaken Causal Models

It is theoretically possible for a study to be high in internal and external validity, and still be wrong or useless. This might occur when the theory on which the research is based is inadequate to encompass the data collected. Every study is (or should be) guided by some theory, or at least by some notion about what the variables under study and the connections between them might mean. We might observe a relationship between the Dow Jones average and student time on-task, but unless we have a theory that might explain this relationship, the observation has little value. More common in social science research is misinterpretation of findings. For example, one published study found that teachers who made accurate assessments of their own popularity among their students were more popular with their students than those who made inaccurate self-assessments. This was interpreted as meaning that sensitivity to students' opinions was an important component of a teacher's popularity. However, since most teachers (and others) tend to believe that they are reasonably popular, it is more likely that the teachers who were *in fact* more popular seemed to make more accurate self-assessments than those who were less popular (but believed themselves to be popular).

Mistaken models of causality are most common in correlational research. The issue of direction of causality in correlational research is discussed in detail in Chapter 4.

EXERCISES

List threats to internal and external validity in the following studies:

1) Two teachers decided to compare two methods of teaching in their own classes. They selected two methods, and randomly assigned themselves to use one or the other.

2) A study compared the use of a fast-paced teaching strategy (a new lesson was introduced daily) with a mastery model (a new lesson was introduced only when 90% of the students scored at least 90% on a test). At posttest, students were tested using content-specific tests for their own program. Percent correct was used as the dependent variable.

3) A new individualized chemistry curriculum was compared to the standard curriculum. Students were pre- and post-tested with a content-specific chemistry test. Mean scores of 220 students in 8 classes randomly assigned by class to experimental (individualized) or control groups were:

	Pre	Post
Individualized	2%	78%
Control	6%	69%

No significant differences were found in an analysis of covariance with pretest as the covariate.

4) A study assessed the effects of a 12-hour teacher workshop (given over a 4-week period) in group process on class management skills. One hundred teachers were randomly assigned to workshop or no treatment, but only 37 teachers attended all sessions of the workshop. These 37 and the 50 control teachers were then systematically observed over 3 weeks and the groups were compared in terms of their class management skills and their students' behaviors.

5) Twenty students enrolled in a special program for students with learning problems were compared with a matched sample of 20 students in the regular program. The students in the two groups were matched for IQ. Math achievement was measured over an academic year to assess the effectiveness of the special program.

6) Two hundred math students were selected and then randomly assigned to one of two groups to assess the effectiveness of two new curriculum programs in increasing math achievement. After two weeks, an achievement measure was administered and the scores of each of the two groups were compared with their own pretest scores on the same test. Results showed significant gain for both groups. The researchers concluded that both programs were effective.

7) A researcher wanted to study the effects of an experimental procedure for studying math facts on student learning of their multiplication facts. He used the experimental procedure with a randomly selected half of a third-grade class, working with each student one at a time in a separate room, and then compared these students' performances on a multiplication facts test with those of the untreated students.

8) Two fifth-grade teachers disagreed about the best way to teach U.S. history. Mr. Norman felt that lively, stimulating lectures were best, while Ms. Cooper emphasized class discussion and debate. They decided to do an experiment. Each teacher taught one unit to his or her class using his or her favorite method, and then they switched classes and taught a second unit to the other teacher's class. The students taught by Ms. Cooper's method scored higher on both unit tests, so Ms. Cooper concluded that discussion is better than lecture for teaching U.S. history.

9) A researcher compared two methods of teaching algebra by randomly assigning 6 gifted fourth-grade math classes to one or the other method.

chapter 7

Planning the Study

CHOOSING A PROBLEM

The first, and perhaps the most important step in carrying out successful educational research is to choose a good research topic. This chapter discusses some of the first decisions involved in coming up with a research plan that is both important and feasible.

Criteria for a Good Research Topic

In considering a topic to study, you should keep in mind the following criteria.

Does the Topic Interest You? A research project, even a small one, takes an enormous amount of work. If you don't care about the end results, it will be hard to keep on when the going gets tough.

Is the Topic Important? Education is an applied field, more like engineering than like physics, in that it uses basic principles to solve practical problems. One critical test of the importance of an educational research project is whether or not the results of the research could ultimately improve the practice of instruction. This does not mean that basic or theoretical research should not be done; improvements in instruction often come about as direct or indirect products of attempts to understand such issues as basic learning processes or teacher characteristics. However, an important research topic in education can almost always be traced in relatively few steps from the research findings to actual practice (see Slavin 1978).

Does the Topic Build on Previous Research?   It would be absurd to say that nothing should ever be done for the first time. However, science generally progresses by building on previous research. A well-designed study that answers an important question posed by recent findings usually makes a more lasting contribution to knowledge than a creative approach to some problem that comes from out of the blue.

Is the Topic Timely?   A good topic should build on previous research, but there are some fields that have been so overworked that one more study will not make much of a difference unless it takes a completely new tack. For example, there are scores of studies of student evaluations of professors (probably because such data are so easy to collect). Another study along this line would probably not make much of a contribution. Also, it is important to do research on currently "live" issues. For example, the efficacy of open schools was a "live" issue in the early 1970s. Now, such studies would have less impact, regardless of their findings.

Other Considerations in Choosing a Topic

Few people have unlimited ability to study whatever interests them. If you are a graduate student, your resources are likely to be quite limited, and if you have not done research before, you may feel uneasy about taking on a major project without at least a good role model. For these reasons, you will probably want to attach yourself to a research project going on in your university if you can. Ask around to see what is happening; you may find the best opportunities outside of your own department, or even in another university in your area or in a local school district. Researchers are usually quite receptive to having graduate students work with them, because the graduate students' thesis or dissertation advances the goals of the larger project at a relatively small cost (especially if the graduate student does not require a salary). If you work on such an ongoing project, your range of topics will of course be limited to the general focus of the project, but this disadvantage may be outweighed by significant advantages in terms of help with research design, research costs, availability of subjects, and apprenticeship with experienced researchers.

Besides the availability of ongoing research projects, your choice of topics may be constrained somewhat by requirements of your department. You may be expected to work directly under a professor in your department or to choose a topic that relates to research going on in the department. Be sure you understand the formal requirements as well as the informal expectations of your department with regard to choice of research topics.

GATHERING PRELIMINARY INFORMATION

Once you have a general idea of the topic you would like to study, you are ready to start a more systematic review of the literature. If you are a graduate student, you will need a literature review as part of your thesis or dissertation proposal. Even if this were not the case, you would want to have a fairly thorough knowledge of the literature before defining the specific questions you will ask in your own research. The literature review will inform you as to the degree to which your topic is a currently "live" issue and will help you avoid proposing a study that has already been done (perhaps several times). A clear knowledge of how your study will build on the existing literature is critical before beginning to collect data.

Widely Focused Literature Search

Your first step in searching the literature should be to look through the *Current Index to Journals in Education* (CIJE), which contains abstracts of articles published in educational journals and indexes of these articles organized by subject and by author. Look for articles relating to your topic under as many different subject headings as you can think of, because articles on the same topic may be listed under different headings. Start with the most recent edition of CIJE and then work backwards in time. When you find recent articles on your topic, read them and use *their* reference lists to locate additional references. This will focus your search on the most important references, those that are cited by researchers currently working in this area. You can save yourself a great deal of work if you can locate a review in your area in such journals as the *Review of Educational Research* or the annual *Review of Research in Education*. It is a good idea to scan the tables of contents of these publications for the last five years to see if a review in your area exists. The reference lists in these reviews will be an excellent place to start in your own literature search.

In your initial search, begin with published articles in high-quality research journals in which all articles must pass a rigorous review to be published. You can waste a great deal of time trying to locate unpublished articles, dissertations, or articles in obscure publications. While useful information often does appear in unpublished or obscure sources, the proportion of useful to useless information in articles that have not been subjected to rigorous review is low. Only when you have firmly established the topic you will study and have a good understanding of the *published* literature on it should you begin to investigate unpublished literature.

List of Primary Resources
for Information Gathering
in Education

Below are listed the most widely used resources for gathering information on educational research. Ask your reference librarian for additional suggestions. Also, see Woodbury (1976) for additional sources of information.

> *Current Index to Journals in Education (CIJE)*. Phoenix, Ariz.: Oryx Press, 1969-Date. Lists articles from more than 700 education-related journals.
>
> *Resources in Education (RIE)*. Washington, DC: Superintendent of Documents, Government Printing Office, 1966-Date. Lists unpublished documents in education, such as government reports, conference papers, and technical reports.
>
> *Educational Research Information Centers (ERIC)*. Maintains a combined list of the articles from CIJE and RIE that can be accessed by computer. See your reference librarian for details on this service.
>
> *Education Index*. Indexes a variety of educational publications and other sources.
>
> *Psychological Abstracts*. Washington, D.C.: American Psychological Association, 1927-Date. Contains lists and abstracts of psychological publications, including most high-quality educational journals and books, and some unpublished technical reports. Can be accessed by computer.

MAKING THE PROPOSAL

As soon as you have a general idea of the topic you wish to study and a good understanding of the literature relating to it, you will need to begin work on a proposal. If you are a graduate student, you will need a formal proposal for your committee or advisor; if not, you will still need a proposal as a plan of action.

The primary parts of a research proposal are discussed below. (Note: if you are a graduate student, your university may have specific requirements concerning the contents of a research proposal.)

Statement of the problem.   This section briefly introduces the questions you want to answer in your research, and discusses the importance of the problem for the practice or theory of education. For example, for a study of grades based on improvement over past performance, you might briefly discuss the importance and history of grading, discuss previous attempts to make grading more effective, and then specifically propose and justify a method of grading based on improvement and state the problem as, "Does grading based on improvement over past performance increase achievement more than traditional grading practices?"

Hypotheses. In this section, you should specifically state your hypotheses concerning the outcomes of the study. You may have major and minor hypotheses that you wish to identify as such. A hypothesis should be stated in simple terms that strongly suggest the methods you plan to use. Below are listed several hypotheses.

> Fourth-grade students who receive grades based on improvement over their own past performance will have significantly higher achievement, controlling for pretests, than will students who are traditionally graded. (Implies an experimental study.)
>
> Ninth grade students will have significantly more positive attitudes toward learning-disabled classmates than they will toward behaviorally disturbed classmates. (Implies a correlational study.)
>
> A program of giving rewards to disruptive students for conforming to class rules will improve the behavior of these students. (Implies a single-case experiment with replications.)
>
> Teachers who give essay tests will be significantly higher in ratings by their students than teachers who give only objective tests. (Implies a correlational study.)

Some graduate schools prefer that you state your hypotheses in null form (for example, the experimental and control treatments will have *equal* effects on the mathematics achievement of seventh graders). See recent dissertations from your university for conventions in stating hypotheses.

Literature Review. A summary of the research relevant to the topic should appear in the proposal. This need not be an exhaustive review, but should clearly show how the literature supports or leads to the hypotheses. A well-written literature review should critically explore the ideas and data presented by earlier researchers. It should not simply catalogue articles: "So-and-so (19XX) found this. Such-and-such (19XX) found that." Instead, the review should critically assess the previous literature, pointing out faults and limitations of the existing research as well as strengths and consensus. At the end of the review, future areas for research should be suggested, with the research you are proposing prominent among these suggestions. The review should inexorably lead to your own project. For examples of literature reviews, read several in the *Review of Educational Research* or the *Review of Research in Education*.

Procedures. This section should lay out your research plan in detail, including the following:

Subjects and Sampling Plan
Procedures, including Experimental Treatments
Measures
Anticipated Analyses

Schedule.   At the end of the proposal, you should anticipate the time schedule for completion of each activity, from contacting schools or other sources of subjects as potential research sites to completing the data analysis and writing up the project. This is especially important, because planning backward from the beginning of the proposed data-gathering or implementation period will give you an idea of dates by which each task must be accomplished.

Roughing out and Discussing the Proposal

A research proposal is rarely written all at once. In general, you will want to rough out the main features of the proposed research (especially the statement of the problem, hypotheses, procedures, and variables to be measured) and then discuss them with anyone who will listen—professors, graduate students, colleagues, teachers, administrators, and so on. In these discussions, you will be seeking judgments concerning the importance, reasonableness, and feasibility of the plan, as well as the adequacy of the research design. These topics are discussed in the following section. You may have to revise your ideas many times before settling on a research plan.

Evaluating the Proposal

As you are developing your proposal, keep the following criteria for a good study in mind:

The problem is important.   An important problem builds on previous research, and advances a theory that has importance in improving the practice of education. It is either new (the same study has not already been done), or it is a replication or extension of a previous study that is both important and has not been overreplicated already. In either case, an important study has clear links to previous research and informs some important theory.

The project is feasible.   A feasible problem is one on which good data can be brought to bear with the resources available to the researcher. A researcher might believe that SAT scores are declining because of a gradual deterioration in social responsibility, but this problem does not lend itself to brief investigation. A project is feasible if the researcher has adequate resources to accomplish it. Some critical resources to consider are:

A researcher with adequate ability, experience, and motivation to complete the project

Adequate access to appropriate sites and subjects (for example, good relationships with school districts that might serve as research sites)

Adequate funds for data collection and project implementation

Adequate labor for project monitoring, and data collection and analysis (either the researcher has adequate time to devote to the project or other assistance is available)

Adequate time to set up and complete the project

The research design is appropriate.   As noted in Chapter 1, a good research design is one in which the results will add to knowledge regardless of what they are. In evaluating a research design, consider all possible outcomes. For each, consider how confident you might be that the outcome was genuine (that is, that you were not making false positive or false negative errors), and how much that outcome would add to knowledge. Take the standpoint of a critic of your own study and try to think of flaws in your design that might invalidate the findings. Study Chapter 6 carefully to be sure that your study is adequate in both internal and external validity.

PLANNING PROCEDURES

Once a study begins, it is usually rather difficult to make substantial changes in the procedures being used. For this reason, a detailed plan of procedures to be followed must be prepared well in advance of the beginning of the study. If you are doing an experimental study over a significant time period, where teachers will actually be implementing the various treatments, you will need to write a teacher's manual. If you are using behavioral observation or interviews, you will need an observer's manual or an interviewer's manual. Regardless of the kind of study you are doing, it is a good idea to write out in advance exactly what you plan to do and when you plan to do it, and to try to anticipate courses of action for various possible situations or problems.

Teacher's Manuals

No matter how well you train teachers to implement a particular experimental treatment, it is always important to provide teachers with a detailed description of what they are supposed to do. Most teachers who participate in research are very conscientious and want to be sure that they are doing what the researcher expects of them. A detailed manual makes it possible for teachers to review the treatments as they implement them. Manuals should definitely be provided to teachers in all experimental conditions that involve any methods different from whatever the teachers were doing before the experiment. It is also a good idea to provide "control" teachers with a manual explaining any information about recordkeeping or measurement relevant to them or even describing a formalized technique that is essentially what they were already doing. Providing control teachers with as much attention as possible, including their own manual, may help prevent the problems of Hawthorne effects (the novelty of the experimental treatment rather than the treatment effect itself causing a positive result) or John Henry effects (the control teachers working especially hard to "beat" the experimental treatment). See Chapters 2 and 6 for more on Hawthorne and John Henry effects.

Writing teacher's manuals for experimental treatments is a fine art. Teacher's manuals need to be detailed and explicit without being overly long. They need to provide a rationale for the treatment the teacher is to implement, even if the "treatment" is really the control group, but they must be light on theory and heavy on practical information. A good teacher's manual anticipates and provides solutions to problems that are likely to come up in the course of the intervention.

Contents of the teacher's manual.   A teacher's manual might consist of an overview which summarizes the major features of the intervention, a step-by-step description of what to do, and a section on "troubleshooting" that discusses problems that may arise.

The bulk of the teacher's manual should be directed toward clarifying what teachers are expected to do. Teachers should be given a means of introducing their methods to students, possibly even including speeches to give to the students, or at least very explicit methods to use to be sure that students understand what they are going to do. Teachers should be given clear directions about how they should organize their class periods and what activities should take place over the course of a week. There should be instructions on any record-keeping requirements (such requirements should be kept to a minimum). Any details of measurement, such as the frequency and nature of behavioral observations or interviews, should be explained.

There are many practical issues that should be addressed. What should teachers do about grading? Discipline problems? Absences? Parent questions or concerns? What kind of changes will teachers need to make in special programs they already have, such as pull-out programs for reading, special education, volunteer tutoring, or Title I? Will teachers have to keep students out of band practice? How will mainstreamed students and very low achievers be handled? What about gifted students?

How much leeway will you allow teachers in their implementation of the program? For example, will you allow teachers to supplement project procedures with their own methods and materials, and if so, to what extent? It is important to give teachers some leeway to make pedagogical decisions, but it is also critical that the integrity of the program be maintained so that the study does not degenerate into a comparison of teachers rather than methods. It should be made clear in the teacher's manual what the essential elements of the program are, so that teachers can know what they can and cannot modify.

A "troubleshooting" section should be included in the teacher's manual to attempt to anticipate problems that will arise and to suggest solutions. What if some students refuse to participate? What if students try to cheat? What if the experimental method causes too much noise or activity? If these problems are frankly discussed in advance, teachers will feel more confident that they can handle the treatments.

Finally, a teacher's manual should tell teachers where they can go for help, including telephone numbers of project staff (home as well as office numbers) to call if they run into problems.

In a nonexperimental study that involves teachers, you may still wish to prepare a teacher's manual to explain what teachers are expected to do with regard to testing, observations, interviews, etc. (see below).

Pilot Testing

Under ideal conditions, it is very helpful to pilot test experimental treatments or other procedures before assessing them formally in a large study. A pilot test gives the researcher an idea of what the method will actually look like in operation and what effects (intended or not) it is likely to have. By generating many of the practical problems that will ultimately arise, a pilot test enables you to avert these problems by changing procedures or at least to discuss them in the final form of the teacher's manual. For a completely new method, a pilot test is especially important. It is practically impossible to invent a method that will work without a hitch the first time. If a pilot test is not possible, you should at least have several teachers read and react to the manual. It is also a good idea to pilot test questionnaires, interview procedures, behavioral observation schemes, and tests before using them in your study (see Chapter 5).

Observer's Manuals
and Interviewer's Manuals

These manuals are discussed in Chapter 5, under *Behavioral Observation* and *Interviews*. As in the case of teacher's manuals, the key to effective observer's and interviewer's manuals is clarity, completeness, and anticipating problems or exceptions.

Testing Instructions

Regardless of the length or complexity of your study, if you are depending on teachers to administer tests or questionnaires, you will need to prepare a brief instruction sheet explaining how these instruments are to be given. These testing instructions should include indications of how the tests should be introduced to students (possibly including a speech for teachers to read to students), how much time to allow, what to do if students ask questions, and so on. You might pattern your instructions on those used for standardized tests or questionnaires.

Overall Study Plan

Regardless of the kind of study you are planning, it is a good idea to write out a detailed study plan well before the study is to begin. The plan should include every task that will need to be done before the study begins, with dates by which they should be done. For example, a study plan might include dates by which a brief description of the project should be written and sent to school districts (see Chapter 8), school district approval obtained, teachers selected, measures and other materials sent to printers, manuals written, observers trained, teachers trained, pretests administered, implementation begun, and so on. Obviously, these dates should be "backward planned" from a date on which the implementation will begin. For example, if we want to do a 12-week study in the spring semester, we might decide to begin around February 1. All other dates would be established with reference to this date, with generous amounts of time allowed for each activity because a 12-week study cannot start much after February 1 without forcing posttesting after Memorial Day (spring activities, preparations for the end of the year, and increased absenteeism make testing in June something to be avoided if possible).

Consent, Confidentiality, and Human Subjects Review

In the past decade, increased public concern over real and potential abuses of persons or data by researchers has led to action on the federal and local levels to protect the rights of subjects in research. Almost all research that is done under federal grants or under the auspices of a university must be reviewed by a human subjects review committee. This committee, which exists in every university, considers any risks involved in the research and weighs them against any benefits to the individuals directly involved in the research as subjects and to society as a whole.

Human subjects review and informed consent. The human subjects review process was primarily developed to protect subjects from risk involved in medical experiments or psychological experiments involving deception or potential psychological disturbance. One major provision of human subjects regulations requires that subjects be informed of any risks involved in the study and that they be instructed that they are free to withdraw from the project at any time. Since minors do not have the right to give or withhold consent to participate in research, this means that when consent is needed in research involving students, it must be obtained from parents. Getting parents to return informed consent forms adds considerably to the difficulty of doing research in schools both for the researcher and for the teachers and building administrators.

As of this writing, both legislation and practice are changing with regard to informed consent for nonrisky research in schools. School districts have always had the right to modify and evaluate instruction without obtaining parent permission, and instructional research can often be approved by human subjects review boards on this basis without requiring parent permission. That is, if a school district is willing to take responsibility for a project evaluating a new instructional method or new instructional materials, the requirement for parent permission may be waived. More recently, the U.S. Department of Health and Human Services has considered dropping human subjects review requirements for all nonrisky research in schools. Current regulations can be obtained from human subjects review committees or from federal funding agencies.

Regardless of what the federal government decides, school districts vary widely in their own procedures with regard to informed consent; some districts are more stringent than the federal government, while others avoid asking parental permission as much as they can.

Confidentiality.   Another major issue in research in schools is confidentiality. Human subjects review boards may require that specific procedures be followed to insure the confidentiality of any data that could be traced to an individual. Beyond any legal issues, it is an ethical requirement that sensitive data, such as delinquency records, special education evaluations, and any information about parents be kept strictly confidential. Many school districts have policies that make it difficult or impossible to have personally identifiable information leave the district. Research can be done under these circumstances by having a school district employee with a list of students cut off or black out students' names on all tests and questionnaires and replace them with numerical codes before sending them on to the researcher. Maintaining such strict confidentiality may convince human subjects review boards and school districts to relax their consent requirements, because one of the few risks of research in schools is that damaging or embarassing data about individual students will leak out. When it is clear that the researcher will never see personally identifiable data, this concern is alleviated.

Confidentiality of educational data is also a major concern of the Privacy Act, a federal statute specifically dealing with who may have access to educational records. The Privacy Act specifically forbids making personally identifiable data available to persons outside of the school district. The Privacy Act is interpreted variously in different school districts, and there is also discussion about it at the federal level. If it is applicable to your project (ask an experienced researcher, a school district administrator, or your university lawyer), you will need to follow a procedure such as the one outlined above to avoid taking personally identifiable data away from the school district.

EXERCISES

Develop a timetable of preparations and implementation for a six-week study of a new instructional method that you intend to begin November 1 in a junior high school. The study will involve one behavioral observer, pretesting and posttesting, and one day of teacher in-service.

chapter 8

Gaining Access to Schools and Implementing the Project

As soon as you have decided on a problem, a design, procedures, and measures, you are ready to start looking for sites in which to do your research. If your research involves college students as subjects in laboratory settings, obtaining subjects may not present a serious problem, as many university departments require that undergraduates serve as subjects in studies or give them extra credit for doing so. Similarly, if the subjects are to be your own students or students in your own department, gaining access to subjects may not present a substantial problem. However, if you plan to do your research in schools other than any in which you are employed, your ability to get your research accepted and properly implemented will depend on many factors. For example, your ease of access to the school will depend on the nature of your study and what it requires from the school district, the extent and level of your contacts in the district, and your own resources, including your own reputation or that of your institution as well as your money, personnel, and other tangible resources. This chapter discusses issues related to the problem of getting access to schools and implementing your project in the school setting.

Designing An Acceptable Study

The most important determinant of your ability to get access to schools is the project itself. Anyone in the school district who has the power to approve or disapprove your study will be concerned with the following questions.

What will the study cost the district?   If the study will cost the district any money, its chances of being approved are minimal. If your study requires anything consumable (such as paper, ditto masters, or workbooks), be prepared to provide these materials to the schools. However, even if no money or materials are required, there are many other costs that will concern school officials. For example, how much teacher time will you require? If you require minimal teacher time, or if you can compensate teachers for time they must spend outside of school hours or pay for substitutes to cover teachers' classes so that you can meet with them during school hours, your chances of having the study approved are much greater than if you are asking for additional uncompensated teacher time. You may also run into problems with teachers' unions if you require much additional teacher time outside of class. How much noninstructional student time do you need? In the current concern about the amount of time spent on instruction, many schools are hesitant to take even a couple of periods of student time for noninstructional activities, especially if they are already overburdened with tests mandated by the school district or the state. If your study is a test of an innovative instructional method that sounds promising, school officials are likely to see time needed for assessment as a necessary cost that may be made up for in more effective instruction, but if it is a questionnaire or interview study or a laboratory study that takes place in a school building, they may see every minute of time spent on the study as a minute of instruction lost.

How dangerous is the study?   A school district is a bureaucracy, and bureaucracies tend to avoid taking risks. If there is a chance that your study will cause serious physical, emotional, or educational harm to even a single child, you should not be doing it. However, there are many innocuous kinds of measures or procedures that some school districts will not let you use for fear of arousing parent (or student) complaints. Sensitive measures top this list. These include any questions about students' families, especially potentially embarrassing information. Some school districts are sensitive about allowing measures of student self-esteem, sociometric measures (such as "Who are your friends in this class?"), and even many personality measures. Many districts are reluctant to allow questions about sex, drug use, delinquent activity, and the like, and some are hesitant about attitude-toward-teacher scales. The only nonachievement measures you can be confident will be approved are questionnaire scales such as "liking of school," "liking of math/science/English," and so on.

Certain procedures may also be seen as dangerous by the district officials. For example, anything that might affect student grades or the grading system may be seen as dangerous, especially in secondary schools

(because grades are important to students going to college). Any curriculum that could be seen as calling into question traditional values or roles
might be considered dangerous in many districts. Sex education, death
education, and family life education fall into this category. Even if the
school district might include these subjects in its curriculum, it may be
reluctant to let an outsider do so. In fact, any project at all has some
danger to a school district, because unless you work in the district in
which you plan to do your study, the district has limited control over you.
You must be sensitive to school officials' natural anxiety about letting
you do your study. This anxiety seems to be greatest in districts in which
the school administration is especially sensitive to parents' concerns,
where a tiny but vocal group of parents can cause a program to be dropped.
This is most often the case in well-to-do suburban districts and often in
urban districts, but is less likely to be true of rural districts. School districts
will obviously also be cautious if they have recently had a bad experience
with outside research. If you are a graduate student and do not work in
the school district in which you would like to do your research, you will
be seen as particularly dangerous. Try to involve a regular faculty member
(hopefully known to the district officials) in your project, especially in the
initial stages of gaining access.

What are the benefits of the study to the district?   As much as school
district officials may occasionally seem overcautious, overly bureaucratic,
or picky, most educators do value research, and will often go out of their
way to help you do your study if it seems important, even if it is unlikely
to have much of a direct benefit to the school district itself. Many school
officials have had to do a master's thesis or a doctoral dissertation, so
they may be sympathetic to someone who needs their help to do research.
However, the chances that a school district will approve a project rise
dramatically if the project has a direct benefit to students, teachers, or
district staff. Studies that are likely to benefit the school system are usually
either evaluations of promising instructional methods, or research that
will provide information on a topic about which the school district is
concerned. Indirect benefits may also be important in making a project
valuable to a school district. For example, if you are testing learning-
disabled students and make your test results available to the school
administration, this may be enough of a benefit to increase your chances
of being accepted. If your study does not have an inherent benefit to the
participants, you might want to offer the schools something to show your
appreciation. For example, you might organize a field trip for students to
see your university or to see your computer, or you might simply agree
to come in after the study is over to explain to students what the study
was about, what researchers do, and why their work is important. Any-

thing too lavish is out of line, but something you can offer by virtue of your special knowledge or position can leave everyone feeling good about your project.

Of course, it is possible to get schools to allow you to do research that does not benefit them or has many features that they see as negative or even somewhat dangerous, but the fewer benefits and more costs or dangers your research entails, the harder it will be to gain access to schools and to get their active participation during the project.

Brief Project Description

Before approaching a school district, write a brief (four to five pages double-spaced) description of the project, including the following: (1) a brief, nontechnical (jargon-free) rationale; (2) a clear description of the procedures to be used, including the number of schools, teachers, and students you will need to involve, the duration of the project, the method of random assignment (if any), and the treatments to be used; (3) a description of the measures; (4) a description of the assistance you will need from the district; (5) a paragraph on how you will make sure that the study will not cost the district anything; (6) a description of how you will insure confidentiality of any individually identifiable data; and (7) a paragraph on how the project will benefit the district and/or improve general understanding of an important issue in educational research. You should attach copies of any questionnaires or observation instruments you will use. If you are a graduate student, you should include a paragraph indicating who your adviser is and how involved he or she will be in the project (the more involvement the better).

Choosing a School District

Your first step in approaching a school district is deciding which district to approach. Obviously, you will need a district that has the number and kind of classes you need. For example, if you need a large number of handicapped students, you will need to go to a large school district or to an intermediate education district serving several small districts. You may need integrated classes or mainstreamed classes or gifted classes. There may only be one district in your area that has the kinds of schools or students you need.

Virtually all school districts have some standard procedure for reviewing research projects. A large or medium-sized district will have a director of research who will be involved in screening research proposals from outside the district. There may be a research screening committee in the district, and research projects may or may not have to go before the school board. In a small district, an assistant superintendent or superintendent may be able to make decisions independently, perhaps subject to review by the school board. Large and medium-sized districts are likely to have formal, written guidelines for outside research; small ones may or may not.

Contacts

The best way to get access to schools in most school districts is to have a contact in the school district. The contact need not be your best friend; a friend of a friend or a friend of a colleague will do. The reason a contact is important is that, as noted above, outside research is always at least a little dangerous to the school districts. They want some assurance that you are trustworthy and know what you are doing. If someone in the district is willing to vouch for you, or even better, take responsibility for your project, the district officials' fears will be allayed. The best contacts are individuals who have enough line authority to take responsibility for your project. If you need to involve only one school in your study, the principal's support will do. If you will need many schools, the assistant superintendent for instruction, regional superintendents, or anyone to whom principals must answer are the best contacts. If your study will involve special education, the director of special education will be the best contact, but only if your study will take place in special education classes (not in mainstreamed classes, where the director of special education has little authority). Similarly, if you need reading teachers, the director of reading will be a good contact. Subject matter supervisors (for example, mathematics, English, social studies, science) are good contacts for research in their respective areas, especially in secondary school research. The supervisor of elementary education is usually the best contact for elementary school research.

Having a contact in a school district who does not have line authority over the teachers or schools you will need for your research is still a great help, but your best use of these contacts is to ask them to introduce you to someone who does have such authority. Examples of contacts who are unlikely to have enough line authority to take responsibility for you are individual teachers; directors of psychological services, pupil personnel, social work, or other special services; directors of staff development and others in this department; supervisors or specialists who are not the district-level directors in their areas; vice principals; and so on. The director of research is likely to be a good contact for getting district-level approval for a project, and will usually be helpful in soliciting schools or teachers. Department heads in secondary schools can be good contacts if your research can be done in one department, but you will usually need support from the building principal as well.

Some sort of contact, especially for any project that will involve several classrooms for a significant time period, is so important that in making your decision where to do your research, you should consider first the district in which you have the best contacts. If you are a graduate student, your adviser's contacts or those of other faculty members in your department may be especially useful.

One reason that contacts are so important is that large and moderate-sized school districts and any districts near universities may receive dozens of requests to do research each year. They must screen them to be sure that the schools do not become laboratories for the local universities. Anything too sensitive, dangerous, costly, time-consuming, or ill-conceived will probably be rejected regardless of who proposes it. However, this still may leave the district with more worthwhile and practical projects than it can possibly approve. If someone who has authority over the classrooms in which the project will take place says he or she will take responsibility for the project, the research becomes part of that person's discretionary power to introduce innovations and to oversee activities in the schools. Put another way, research directors rarely like to tell principals that they cannot do something they want to do (within reason) in their own buildings, and research directors are even less likely to tell superintendents, assistant superintendents, or regional superintendents that they cannot do something in their areas of control. Active support from a powerful person in a school district, especially a small to medium one, may allow you to bypass much or all of the screening process. On the other hand, if you present a proposal to a school district in which you have no contacts, there is no guarantee that it will be accepted (regardless of its merits). And worse, the district may take from a month to a year to give its decision. This time period is, of course, much shorter if you have a contact who calls the research director to ask for a quick decision. If your project must be passed upon by the school board, the same principles apply; school boards generally accept the recommendations of research directors on noncontroversial projects, and they are also unlikely to contradict decisions of principals and other school officials in their areas of authority.

Other Factors in Choosing a District to Approach

There are many other issues to consider in deciding which school districts to approach with your research plan. Some districts have absolute, unbendable policies against certain kinds of research. No matter how good your contacts, you will not be able to get the district to approve such a project. Districts that are undergoing crises, such as recent or impending strikes, school closings, reductions in force, new busing, or any kind of problem directly related to a research project, should be avoided if possible. School districts are most receptive to research when they are feeling secure, not threatened.

Many researchers find that it is much easier both to get access to schools and to actually conduct research in small to medium-sized rural districts at some distance from a university than in urban or suburban districts or districts near universities. Most urban and suburban districts and districts close to universities have a good deal of research and all kinds of new programs going on in them each year. Another researcher may be tolerated, but few people in such districts will be overjoyed to have more research in their schools.

Rural districts, on the other hand, are less frequently approached by researchers. Because they may not have the resources to bring in many new programs, they are more likely to look on research, especially research on promising instructional methods, as an exciting opportunity. Parents in rural districts seem to have greater trust in the schools to do their job than parents in urban or suburban districts, and the rural school district is less likely to be highly politicized. For these reasons, the school district may be more likely to approve your research plan as being sound and beneficial to students (or at least not detrimental), with less concern about slighting the sensibilities of one or another group of parents. Project approval in a rural district is likely to be more informal and quicker than in a highly bureaucratized, large district, and teachers are more likely to give some time (within reason) to making the project work.

Approaching a School District

In general, it is best to begin to approach school districts to discuss your project as soon as you can, so that you can give the district time to respond to your proposal and to work through the many channels that may be necessary. Also, the earlier you start, the greater the chance that if your negotiations with one district fall through, you will be able to find another district and still keep to your schedule. For a fall semester study, the previous spring is usually a good time to start; for a spring study, October is usually adequate. If you are approaching districts that are known to take a long time to approve research projects, you will want to start earlier.

First Contacts

Your first step in approaching the school district should *not* be to mail your brief project description to the director of research. The reason for this is that as soon as your proposal lands on the research director's desk, it will probably be considered a final proposal and will be approved or disapproved as it is. At the point when the director of research receives your proposal, you want to be as sure as you can be that it will be acceptable to the district and, if possible, that you have the backing of at least one person with line authority over the area in which you want to do your research.

If you have a contact with someone who has such authority, your first step should be to arrange a meeting with him or her to discuss your project. If you have a contact who does not have adequate authority, have that person suggest someone who has the line authority you need, and then arrange a meeting with this person, with or without your original contact in attendance. If you have no contacts in the district, you should still try to set up a meeting with the person in charge of the day-to-day operation of the area of the school district in which you plan to do your research (for example, the district supervisor of mathematics, supervisor of elementary education, director of special education, etc.). In general, if you are contacting someone you don't know, it is best to write a letter in which you describe your project in one or two paragraphs, and say that you will be calling in about a week to set up a meeting time to discuss the project. About ten days after you send the letter, call the person to set up a meeting time. He or she may wish to have other district officials attend, including the director of research or selected principals. If you are a graduate student, you should have your adviser attend the meeting if possible.

Meeting with School Officials

Before the meeting, you need to look at your proposal and decide what parts of it are absolutely critical to your research, and what parts are negotiable. Are you willing to do the research with a somewhat smaller sample? Can you change the grade level or subject matter if necessary? Are some of your measures more necessary than others? Can you reduce the number of hours of testing or training? Your proposal will spell out what you would like to do, but you should be prepared to negotiate on certain details. You may wish to present your plan to colleagues or friends, both for practice and to get an idea of the kinds of questions your proposal might elicit.

In the meeting, you should explain your project completely, being very clear about what the project will add to the science and/or practice of education, what will be provided to the district, what will be required of the district, and how the project will benefit the students and teachers directly involved. You will need to discuss the measures you plan to use, and you may wish to distribute copies of the measures and of anything else that will give the person with whom you are meeting a better idea of what you are proposing. The plan should sound complete, but also flexible. Your basic tone should be one of confidence that the project can and should be done, but that you are willing to modify certain details to respond to problems that the school district might foresee. When you have given your description and answered any questions, ask whether or not the study sounds acceptable, or if not, whether there are changes you could make that might make it acceptable. If there are particular features of your procedures or measures that the people with whom you are talking find objectionable or problematic, you might either suggest alternative procedures, or state that these features are nonnegotiable.

By the end of the meeting, you should have a good idea how acceptable and feasible your project will be. The people with whom you are meeting may have the power to accept or reject your proposal on the spot. If not, they will tell you what next steps you need to follow to get acceptance. Of course, even if they accept the project, you will need to talk with individual principals or teachers in the schools in which you plan to do your research. You should get suggestions from the people with whom you are meeting regarding schools that might be receptive to your project.

If your meeting goes well, and the project you have agreed to by the end of the meeting is the same as the project you described in your brief project description, you may distribute copies of the project description to those present. If you have made significant changes, you will want to modify the project description and send it to the people who attended the meeting as soon as possible. They will need a written project description to remind them of what your are planning and to share with others if they are to help you get through additional red tape and into individual schools.

Following your meeting, you may need to send a copy of your brief project description to the director of research or whoever screens research for the district. It is best if someone you met with is willing to take responsibility for the project and agrees to send your proposal to the research director with his or her own cover letter. This virtually assures acceptance in many districts. If this is not possible, you should send in your proposal with your own cover letter summarizing the project in one or two paragraphs, stating with whom you met, and saying that they indicated support for your idea. You should send copies to the people with whom you met and indicate that you are doing so in the letter to the research director. If the research director did not attend your initial meeting, he or she will probably call one of the people with whom you met, so this is important.

As soon as district staff have approved your project, it may have to go before the board of education. This is not usually a significant barrier, as the research director (or whoever approves your project) is unlikely to allow your project to go before the board if there is much of a chance that it will be rejected. However, having to go before a board of education does add significantly to the time it takes to get a project approved.

Approaching Individual Schools

When you have approval from the central administration, you will be able to approach individual schools. From the time you get project approval, you will need to identify the people from whom you will need passive approval (usually principals and other administrators) and those from whom you need active assistance (usually teachers). The people from whom you need active assistance should be approached as directly as possible.

There are many ways that you can approach individual schools. You might arrange to attend a regularly scheduled principals' meeting to explain your project and ask for volunteers. You might have central office administrators suggest schools that are likely to meet your needs. They might call the principals of these schools to tell them that you will be calling (and thereby assuring them that your project has district-level support), or you can contact the principals directly to set up meetings with them in their buildings. In these meetings, you should explain your project with an emphasis on the practical details: how many classes you'll need, what will be asked of teachers, how much testing time is involved, and so on. Principals generally ask more practical questions than central office administrators, so you should be ready to handle such questions.

It is not generally a good idea to depend on an administrator to actually choose principals for you, or to depend on a principal to choose teachers. The problem is that you want schools and teachers to volunteer to participate in your study. It can be very bad for a study if teachers or other participants feel that they were forced to take part. It is good to have administrators indicate that they support your project and would be pleased if teachers decide to participate. In most districts, this support is critical. But there is a big difference between encouragement and compulsion. In your conversations with district administrators and principals, you should emphasize that you do not want them to exercise their authority to compel teachers to participate. When you meet with principals, you might emphasize that you are asking for their support and a chance to present your proposal to the teachers themselves, but you are not asking the principal to "deliver" some number of teachers.

Some principals will want you to speak to their teachers at the same time as you speak to them, but in general you will need to come back later for a meeting with teachers. This is the most critical meeting in your efforts to do your study; it sometimes happens that central office administrators and principals are enthusiastic about a project, but no group of teachers will agree to participate. Teachers as a group tend to be very practical, and they are (as they should be) usually much more concerned about the well-being of their students than about research. If they perceive a project as impractical, disruptive to their instructional efforts, or too difficult to do, they will reject it (or accept it halfheartedly, which can be worse), regardless of how important the study or the researchers are. Teachers survive on great reserves of common sense. If your project doesn't make sense to them, they are unlikely to participate.

If you are using any kind of random assignment, you will need to emphasize the importance of random assignment in meetings with principals and teachers. This is ordinarily a small problem if you are randomly assigning classes taught by the same teachers in a departmentalized school to experimental and control classes. In this case, each teacher will receive training and/or materials for the experimental treatment and will not mind very much having half of their classes randomly excluded from the experimental group; in fact, they may prefer to try something new with only a few classes rather than all their classes.

If you are randomly assigning teachers or classes to treatments, you have a bigger problem. In this case you will need to clearly explain to teachers that volunteering to participate in the study means that they will have a 50% chance to receive the experimental treatment (if you have one experimental and one control treatment). This is less of a problem when you are comparing two relatively attractive treatments, or when the "control" treatment receives materials but not procedures received by the experimental group, because in this case all teachers who participate are receiving something. However, if the control group in your study is completely untreated, it is particularly important to promise that control teachers will receive all of the materials and training received by experimental teachers, but at the end of the study.

The most difficult experimental comparison design to convince teachers to use is one with random assignment of individual students to classes. This is easiest to accomplish if students were about to be assigned to new classes anyway, as at the beginning of the year or at the start of a special class. It is also not as difficult when, for example, all of the math classes in an elementary school at a particular grade level meet at the same time, so that the students taught by two or more teachers can be pooled and then randomly assigned to treatments without forcing changes in teachers' entire schedules. However, individual random assignment is always disruptive, especially when it breaks up classes that have been together for some time. You may find that teachers will accept everything about your study except the random assignment. Teachers and principals take grouping decisions seriously, and if you are asking them to randomly assign groups that stay together for several weeks or more, you may be asking for trouble. If your random assignment would have the effect of untracking a tracked school, you will have especially strong resistance, as teachers often do not believe that they can handle wide ability ranges in one class (although research generally shows no difference in achievement between tracked and nontracked classes; see Esposito 1973).

In addition to soliciting their participation, when you meet with teachers you are setting a tone for your further relationship with them. Obviously, you want to appear competent and trustworthy, and you want to be clear that you are not trying to force anyone to participate. It is very important that you come across as a scientist and not an advocate.

If it is obvious that you are trying to "prove" that the experimental group is better than the control group, you are asking for a Hawthorne effect (the experimental teachers will try to prove you right) or a John Henry effect (the control teachers will try to prove you wrong) or both. These effects take the science out of experimental research. Even when the structure of the design makes it obvious that you are testing a treatment in which you have some emotional investment, you can clearly communicate to teachers that your commitment is to an honest evaluation, not a whitewash, and that you expect them to give each treatment their best, for the sake of their students as well as the study.

It should go without saying that teachers (like everyone else) resent a condescending or superior attitude. They should be treated as partners in a scientific enterprise. You have expertise in research methods and statistics, and they have expertise in practical classroom management and instruction. Even if you are or were an outstanding teacher yourself, you must respect teachers' diverse styles and skills and refrain from trying to tell teachers how they should teach (except in regard to the experimental procedures).

Overplanning

One characteristic of field research is that things go wrong. If things are going to go completely wrong, it is best that they do so at an early stage in your project, so that you can pick up the pieces and start again. However, this assumes that you have plenty of time.

If you absolutely must have a study done by a certain time, you should probably overplan. That is, you should approach more than one school district, and ask for more schools and classes than you will need as a minimum. In the case of multiple school districts, you must, of course, tell each district that you are also negotiating with another, unless you have the resources to do the research in both places. You certainly do not want to have a district go through all of the work to approve your project only to have you unexpectedly pull out at the last minute, but school district officials will understand that until they can give you final approval, you may have to approach more than one district. Similarly, you may approach more schools and teachers than you wish to involve to make sure that you have enough.

IMPLEMENTING THE PROJECT

Once you have gained access to schools, your task becomes one of maintaining good relationships with the people with whom you will be working (especially teachers) and at the same time maintaining the integrity of the research by making sure that testing and treatment implementation are done according to your criteria. You will need to be sensitive to the fact that teachers and administrators have a great many things to do, among which your research may not be a top priority. Teachers and administrators usually have a large but finite reservoir of good will toward research in general and (hopefully) toward your project in particular. You need to get reliable implementation and good data from the school without overdrawing on that reservoir.

Getting Along with Schools

If your study will involve only a small number of teachers and a very short time period, you will probably be in and out of the school before too much can go wrong. On the other hand, if you will be involving many teachers for a longer time, it is vital to establish the right sort of relationship with the school staff. Below are listed a few general principles to follow in getting along with schools.

Follow through on promises. School people are often promised things that are never delivered. You want to establish a reputation right away as someone who always follows through on a promise. If you don't think you can provide something that teachers want, say so. If you promise teachers a ream of paper each, you might give them two. Teachers should feel that you are sympathetic to their problems and doing everything you can to get things to go smoothly for them.

Emphasize confidentiality. As implied above, you must make it clear that your interest is in variables or programs, not in individual teachers, and that you will not release to the school district the kind of data that could influence personnel decisions. Teachers sometimes feel that a researcher is an arm of the administration, and occasionally, administrators will attempt to use research to get information on individual teachers with whom they are having difficulties. Never let yourself be put in such a position.

Be a scientist, not an advocate. Make it clear to everyone involved in your research that your interest is in accurate data, not in proving that program A is better than program B.

Make friends with secretaries. Presumably, you will have made friends with the principal and the staff involved in your project in the course of getting access to classrooms. However, it is also a good idea to make friends with other important individuals in the school such as the school secretaries, who can be invaluable in making sure that materials get to teachers, helping you locate teachers who are not in their classrooms, and so on. By the same token, making friends with custodians and other nonteaching staff can help a great deal in making things go smoothly in a long study.

Try to arrange free access to classrooms. If teachers are implementing experimental treatments for several weeks or more, you will want to visit classrooms frequently, both to be sure that the teachers are sticking with the program and to be there to answer questions. Sometimes schools (especially secondary schools) expect you to specifically arrange each visit, as though you were a supervisor. Having to arrange visits may limit your ability to be in the classrooms when you are needed or to see how the treatments are being implemented. If you can convince the teachers and school administration of your need to have relatively free access to observe classes, this is very helpful. If you do schedule visits and announce them in advance, stick scrupulously to your schedule and notify the school if you can't make it on a given day.

Try not to inhibit teachers' abilities to make pedagogical decisions. While you must be clear with teachers about what you expect them to do, you should also try to allow them enough latitude to make important pedagogical decisions within the confines of the experimental treatments. For example, in a study of a new instructional method, try to leave to the teacher's judgment such matters as grading, disciplinary procedures, and special modifications for students with special needs.

Avoid use of administrative muscle. The fact that you are in the school building means that someone in the school or district administration allowed or even pushed for your project to take place. Their authority can be helpful in the unusual case in which teachers or principals refuse to do something critical to the research when they have previously committed themselves to do so. However, bringing pressure from higher authority should be the last resort in a severe case. Teachers and principals usually resent such pressure. It is far better to attempt to work out problems with the people involved. A teacher or principal who feels coerced, usurped, or hostile toward the research can usually find some way to damage the project; it is your task to call on their professionalism and good nature to get the project done, not to depend on the line of authority (unless absolutely necessary).

Remember that you are a guest. When you are doing research in a school, it is wise to remember that you are there as a guest of the school or school district. *You may make requests but not demands.*

Respect teachers.   No one who sees what teachers do every day should have anything but the greatest respect for them. Because they are dedicated and professional, most teachers are always looking for ways to improve their teaching. However, nothing alienates teachers faster than arrogance. Teachers are more willing to participate enthusiastically in research when it is clear to them that the researcher values their perspective and their input, and takes their practical needs and problems seriously. A researcher who fails to incorporate teacher suggestions, or who takes the attitude that the practicalities of classroom life are beneath him or her, will be unlikely to get maximum cooperation from teachers.

Maintaining the Integrity of the Research

It is possible that a researcher could follow the principles listed above and get along fine with school staff, but nonetheless fail to have his or her research implemented properly. Below are three more principles to help insure that your project is implemented in classrooms as you intended.

Observe during testing.   If at all possible, it is a good idea to observe classes when their teachers give them tests or questionnaires. It is not usually a good idea to have project staff actually *administer* the tests, because the novelty of an outsider giving tests can create excitement or even poor behavior among the students. However, if you or someone on the research staff is present, you can answer questions as they arise, make sure that testing procedures are carefully followed, and note any irregularities or reactions to testing that may become important later on in understanding the results.

Get every makeup test possible.   You should make a considerable effort to get every legitimate test you can from every student in your study. It is rarely a problem getting valid tests from students present on the initial testing day, but makeup tests are much more difficult to obtain, because after the testing period teachers want to get on with their teaching instead of giving tests to a few students.

One way to maximize makeups is to station yourself or a staff member in the school for a couple of days after the initial testing to give makeup tests. If you cannot do this, you should provide teachers with a list of missing tests as soon as possible after the initial testing to remind them of who needs makeup testing. It is important to get as close as possible to a 100% return because missing data may upset the equality of your classes; a student who does not take a test does not count in the study, even though he or she received the treatments.

Monitor the project. During project implementation, visit classes as often as possible (especially in the early weeks). You should not try to take over teachers' classes, but it is a good idea to be present often, to answer questions as they arise. You should give teachers your office and home telephone numbers, but for some reason, teachers rarely call researchers when they run into problems. If you're not at least checking in with teachers frequently, you might never hear about what is going wrong until it is too late. When you are visiting a classroom and see a teacher doing something incorrect, you should bring it to his or her attention as diplomatically as possible, and out of the hearing of students and others. Although most teachers want to do a conscientious job and welcome suggestions, they are naturally somewhat sensitive about criticism.

As part of your monitoring, you may wish to make a list of the activities you consider absolutely essential in your treatments, and check them off as you observe. You may wish to use observers specifically trained to observe these activities to confirm that teachers are doing what they are suppose to be doing.

Reporting Back Your Findings

As soon as possible after the end of your study, you should report your findings to the people who were involved in your research. It is simple courtesy to provide this information, and it will help maintain your own reputation and that of research in general in the district where you worked. You should send copies of your research reports to the participants, and you may wish to hold a workshop or make formal presentation of the results as soon as you have them.

EXERCISES

Discuss what aspects of the following studies may lead to acceptance or rejection of a project proposal by a school:

1) A study of factors related to altruism in children that involves testing 50 pairs of students for 10 minutes each.

2) A study of an instructional program using peer tutoring and group process training to improve math problem-solving skills and social interaction. The study involves 10 hours of teacher training, with substitutes for teachers during training time to be paid for by the researchers.

3) A study of a new teaching method involving frequent tests. Materials to be supplied by the school district.

4) A correlational study of teacher methods (as reported by teachers)

and student achievement and attitudes. Requires two 40-minute test periods for teachers and students.

5) A correlational study of parental discipline methods as reported by students and school structure (authoritarian, permissive) as reported by teachers.

chapter 9

A Practical Guide
to Statistics

WHAT ARE STATISTICS?

Statistics are simply convenient ways of summarizing characteristics of data in a form we can understand and use. For example, we could note that the scores on a health test in Mrs. Garcia's class were 37, 45, 21, 50, etc., but it is more useful to say that the mean (average) score was 40.6, or that 68% of the scores fell between 30.4 and 50.8. If we wanted to compare Mrs. Garcia's first-period class and fifth-period class on the same test, the list of scores would be impossible to interpret, but if we know the mean score and the dispersion (scatter) of the scores, we can easily make this comparison.

This chapter describes the principal concepts behind the use of statistics and presents computational procedures for the most widely used statistics. This is meant to be an introduction to the principal statistics needed for research in education, not a complete treatment of the subject. A section at the end of this chapter lists several statistics books that go into far more detail.

Scales of Measurement

Nominal scale. A nominal scale simply uses numbers as "names" for certain categories or individuals. Numbers in a nominal scale have no relationship to one another; school number 48 is neither "three times" school number 16 nor 32 units more than school number 16.

Ordinal scale. Numbers in an ordinal scale are in a definite order, but there is nothing known about the distance between each number. A student's rank in class is an example of an ordinal scale; student number 4 is definitely higher in rank than student number 8, but the ranks do not indicate how different the two students are in academic achievement.

Interval scale. In an interval scale, scores differ from one another by the same amount, but there is no meaningful zero point. An example of an interval scale is the thermometer; 67 degrees is the same amount hotter than 66 degrees as 34 is hotter than 33, but 66 degrees is not "twice as hot" as 33 degrees. Many aptitude and attitude scales use interval scales. One person cannot be "twice as smart" or "twice as happy" as another, but scales can be constructed to have equal intervals between each score.

Ratio scale. A ratio scale is an interval scale with a true zero point. An amount of money is a ratio scale, because it *is* meaningful for a person to have twice as much money (or have twice as many books, or be twice as old) as someone else.

Statistics by Calculator

Although there once was a time when researchers computed statistics by hand or used cumbersome and limited calculators, the computer is now the tool of choice for statistical analysis. Chapter 10 presents an introduction to the use of the computer for statistical analysis. However, just as the advent of the calculator did not free children from the need to understand long division, easy access to computers does not free researchers from having to understand how to calculate statistics by hand. Experience with calculating statistics by hand is critical for understanding the results of statistical analyses performed by the computer.

However, this does not mean that we must start from scratch. There are now inexpensive calculators that perform many of the routine calculations that form the basis of the statistics described in this chapter. No one should ever again try to figure statistics with nothing but a sharp pencil and a table of square roots. It is strongly suggested that you use a hand calculator to compute not only the basic arithmetic functions but also as many of the following statistics as possible.

Critical Calculator Functions for Social Science Statistics*

STATISTIC	SYMBOL
Mean	$\overline{x}$, μ
Variance	s^2, s^2_{n-1}, σ^2

*Note: The meaning of these symbols are explained later in this chapter.

Standard Deviation	s, s_{n-1}, σ
Square	x^2
Sum of Squares	Σx^2
Square Root	$\sqrt{x}$

Many of the major manufacturers of hand calculators (for example, Texas Instruments, Casio, Sharp, Radio Shack) have calculators that perform all of the above functions (and many more) for under $30.

Using your calculator, you should refigure for yourself all of the examples presented in this chapter. This will help you get a feel for how statistics work and will prepare you for the exercises presented at the end of the chapter.

Measures of Central Tendency

Mean.   The mean of a set of numbers is simply their average, the sum of the scores (Σx) divided by the number of scores (see Examples 9–1 and 9–2).

Median.   The median of a set of numbers is the middle score, above and below which half of all the scores fall. If there is an odd number of scores, the middle number is the median. If there is an even number of

Examples of Mean, Median, and Mode.

EXAMPLE 9–1	EXAMPLE 9–2

EXAMPLE 9–1

```
              18 ⎫
              16 ⎬  4 scores
      Mode  12 ⎨  above median
              12 ⎭
              10 ⟵── Median
               9 ⎫
               8 ⎬  4 scores
               6 ⎨  below median
               2 ⎭
         Σx  =  93
          N  =   9
```

$$\text{Mean} = \bar{x} = \frac{\Sigma x}{N} = \frac{93}{9} = 10.33$$

Median = 10   (middle score)

Mode = 12   (most frequent score)

EXAMPLE 9–2

```
              16 ⎫  3 scores above median
              13 ⎬
               8 ⎭
               7    ⟵── Median  = 7.5
               5 ⎫  3 scores below median
               5 ⎭
              ──
         Σx  =  54
          N  =   6
```

$$\text{Mean} = \bar{x} = \frac{\Sigma x}{N} = \frac{54}{6} = 9.0$$

Median = 7.5   (halfway between 7 and 8)

Mode = 5   (most frequent score)

scores, the median is the number halfway between the two middle scores (see Examples 9–1 and 9–2).

Mode.   The mode is simply the most frequent score (see Examples 9–1 and 9–2).

When to Use the Mean, Median, or Mode

The *mean* of a set of scores is usually the most useful piece of information about those scores, and it serves as the basis of most other statistics comparing sets of scores. The *median* is most often used to characterize a set of scores that are not distributed evenly, because it is not influenced by extreme scores. For example, let's say a teacher gave a test on subtraction with renaming. Ten students scored from 75% to 100% correct, but two students completely forgot how to subtract and got zeros. This situation is illustrated in Example 9.3.

EXAMPLE 9–3

100	
100	
95	
90	
85	
85	← Median = 85
85	
80	
75	
75	
0	
0	

$$\Sigma x = 870$$
$$N = 12$$

$$\text{Mean} = \frac{\Sigma x}{N} = \frac{870}{12} = 72.5$$

$$\text{Median} = 85$$

In example 9–3, the mean would not be a good measure of central tendency, because the two zeros influence the mean too much; the mean of 72.5 is less than the scores eight of the ten students got. However, the median is minimally influenced by extreme scores, and does tend to fall among the scores that most individuals received.

The *mode* is sometimes used to help describe an unusual distribution of scores, since scores usually cluster around the most frequent score (the mode), no matter how the scores are distributed. (See *Skewed Distributions*, below).

Measures of Dispersion

After the mean, the most important piece of information about a set of scores is the degree of dispersion (scatter) around the mean. Consider the following sets of scores here:

EXAMPLE 9–4	EXAMPLE 9–5
85	70
70	68
65	65
60	62
45	60
Σx = 325	Σx = 325
N = 5	N = 5
Mean = $\dfrac{\Sigma x}{N}$ = $\dfrac{325}{5}$ = 65	Mean = $\dfrac{\Sigma x}{N}$ = $\dfrac{325}{5}$ = 65
Median = 65	Median = 65

The scores in Examples 9–4 and 9–5 have the same means and medians, but they are obviously quite different. In Example 9–4, the scores vary widely from 85 to 45, while in Example 9–5, they vary only from 70 to 60.

One easily computed measure of dispersion is the *range*. To find it, simply subtract the lowest score from the highest score as follows:

Range = highest score − lowest score

Using the data from Examples 9–4 and 9–5:

Example 9–4: Range = 85 − 45 = 40
Example 9–5: Range = 70 − 60 = 10

Standard Deviation and Variance

The range has limited usefulness because it is dependent on the values of only two scores. Much better measures of dispersion that form the basis (with the mean) of most statistics are called the variance (s^2) and the standard deviation (s) (which is just the square root of the variance).

To compute the variance and standard deviation, follow these steps:

1. List the scores (x) in any order.
2. Add up the scores (Σx).
3. Square each score (x^2).
4. Add up the squared scores (Σx^2).
5. Count the number of scores (N).

6. Compute the variance:

$$s^2 = \frac{\Sigma x^2 - \dfrac{(\Sigma x)^2}{N}}{N - 1}$$

7. Compute the standard deviation:

$$s = \sqrt{s^2}$$

Example 9–6 illustrates the computation of variance and standard deviation.

EXAMPLE 9–6

x	x^2
8	64
7	49
5	25
3	9
2	4

$\Sigma x = 25 \quad \Sigma x^2 = 151$
$N = 5$

$$s^2 = \frac{\Sigma x^2 - \dfrac{(\Sigma x)^2}{N}}{N - 1}$$

$$= \frac{151 - \dfrac{(25)^2}{5}}{5 - 1}$$

$$= \frac{151 - \dfrac{625}{5}}{4}$$

$$= \frac{151 - 125}{4} = \frac{26}{4} = 6.5$$

$$\text{Mean } (\bar{x}) = \frac{\Sigma x}{N} = \frac{25}{5} = 5$$

$$\text{Variance } (s^2) = 6.5$$

$$\text{Standard Deviation } (s) = \sqrt{6.5} = 2.55$$

The formulas for sample variance and standard deviation are extremely important to understand, as most of the statistics presented in this chapter are based on these statistics. As noted earlier, if you have a hand calculator that computes means, variances, and standard deviations, you will save yourself a great deal of time working problems in the following sections.

The formulas given above are for the variance and standard deviation of a *sample*, which is almost always our interest in educational research. However, there is a slightly different formula for the variance and standard deviation of a *population*, which we compute only if we have the scores of every individual to whom we want our measures to generalize. These formulas are as follows:

$$\text{population variance } (\sigma^2) = \frac{\Sigma x^2 - \frac{(\Sigma x)^2}{N}}{N}$$

$$\text{population standard deviation } (\sigma) = \sqrt{\sigma^2}$$

The formula for the population *mean* is the same as that for the sample mean but it has a different symbol (μ):

$$\text{population mean } (\mu) = \frac{\Sigma x}{N}$$

The Normal Curve

Let's say we assembled 100 children of the same age and measured their height, and found the mean to be 50 inches. We would expect most scores to fall close to 50 inches. This is illustrated in Example 9–7, where each "X" indicates the height of one child.

EXAMPLE 9–7 – The Normal Curve

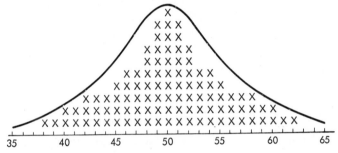

The bell-shaped curve illustrated in Example 9–7 is called the *normal curve*. It is based on laws of probability concerning random deviations from a population mean. For example, the mean height of all the children in this instance is 50 inches. However, many factors add to or subtract from the mean for each individual. These might include heredity, sex, nutrition, and so on. It is known that people with tall parents and people with good nutrition are taller than people with short parents or poor nutrition, and that at certain ages, boys tend to be taller than girls. Further, there is a large component of random chance in getting a particular combination of genes. Most people are "average" on these factors and random chance may add to or subtract from height independently of the other factors. Since these factors may cancel one another out to some degree, most people fall around the average height. To be especially tall requires that all the random factors line up in the same direction: A very tall child will usually have a tall father, a tall mother, good nutrition, be a boy, and have luck going in the tall direction. A very short child would be likely to have all the factors going in the opposite direction. Since it is statistically unlikely that all these factors will work in the same direction, individuals far from the mean (in either direction) are rare in relation to the number that fall near the mean.

Anyone who has played craps or other games with dice has some idea of the normal curve.* The mean score on the roll of two dice is seven. There are six different ways to get a total of seven (1–6, 2–5, 3–4, 4–3, 5–2, 6–1), so most scores fall at or near seven. Two thirds of all rolls will be 5, 6, 7, 8, or 9. In contrast, there is only one way to roll a two (1–1) or a twelve (6–6), so these are much less common. As in the case of height, very high or very low scores are relatively uncommon. Both dice must be extreme in the same direction (high or low) to produce an extreme score, and this is relatively unlikely.

Many distributions in nature conform to the normal curve, and are thus called "normally distributed." This includes such important human characteristics as height, weight, intelligence, strength, speed, longevity, and so on. Standardized test scores are usually normally distributed, as are grades and other measures of human performance (but see below for examples of skewed (non-normal) distributions).

The normal curve has several important properties:

1. It is symmetrical around the mean, meaning that about as many scores will fall above the mean as below it. This also means that the mean, the median, and the mode of a normal curve are the same.
2. It is bell-shaped, because most scores cluster around the mean.
3. It has no upper or lower limits. In a normally distributed population, scores extremely far from the mean are rare or unlikely, but they are not impossible.

One of the most important properties of the normal curve for statistics is that if we are given the mean and standard deviation of a normally distributed population, we can predict how many individual scores will fall in a given range. For example, we know that 68% of all scores will fall between one standard deviation below the mean and one standard deviation above the mean. Figure 9–1 shows the proportions of a normally distributed population that will fall within given portions of the normal curve. (Appendix 1 at the end of this volume gives the proportions of a normally distributed population that will fall between the mean and any number of standard deviations from the mean.)

As an illustration of the meaning of Figure 9–1, consider IQ scores, which have a mean of about 100 and a standard deviation of about 15. The distribution of IQ is approximately normal. This implies that approximately 68.3% of IQ scores fall between 85 and 115 (that is −1s to +1s) and 95.4% fall between 70 and 130 (−2s to +2s). About 84.1% of all scores fall below 115 (+1s). This can be determined by adding the pro-

---

*Distributions of scores from rolls of two dice actually form a binomial curve, which is similar but not identical to a normal curve.

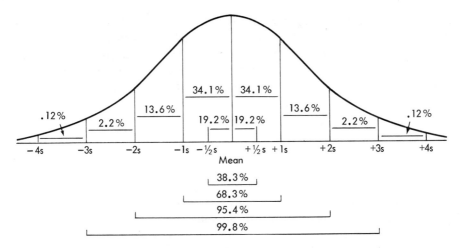

FIGURE 9-1   The Normal Curve

portion below the mean (50%) to that falling between the mean and +1s (34.1%).

By subtracting this from one, we can see that only 15.9% of all scores fall above 115 (1 − .841 = .159). If students in a school district have normally distributed IQ scores with a mean of 100 and a standard deviation of 15, and admission to a gifted program requires that students have an IQ of at least 130 (+2s), we can predict that only 2.3% of the students will qualify (1 − (.50 + .341 + .136) = 1 − .977 = .023).

Several familiar scales are based on the normal curve. For example, Scholastic Aptitude Test (SAT) scores are set up with a theoretical mean of 500 and a standard deviation of 100. Thus a score of 600 is one standard deviation above the theoretical mean; if the mean were in fact 500, 68.3% of all SAT scores would fall between 400 and 600. The limits of the scale are set at 200 and 800, or −3s and +3s, respectively. Little is lost by setting these limits, as 99.8% of all scores should fall in this range (see Figure 9–1).

z-Scores

It is often important to be able to compare scores on different tests. For this purpose, we can change the raw scores to standard scores with a mean of zero and a standard deviation of one. The formula for this transformation is as follows:

$$z = \frac{x - \bar{x}}{s}$$

Where x = an individual score
    $\bar{x}$ = the group mean
    s = the group standard deviation
    z = the standard score

For example, we might want to know whether a student with an IQ of 85 ($\bar{x} = 100$, $s = 15$) is performing up to her ability level on a math test on which she got a 35 ($\bar{x} = 50$, $s = 5$). She is 15 points below the mean on both tests, so it looks as though she is performing at her ability level. However, let's compute the z-scores for each test.

$$\text{IQ: } z = \frac{85 - 100}{15} = \frac{-15}{15} = -1.0$$

$$\text{Math: } z = \frac{35 - 50}{5} = \frac{-15}{5} = -3.0$$

As a comparison of the z-scores shows, the student scored much worse relative to other students on the math test ($z = -3.0$) than on the IQ test ($z = -1.0$).

Another frequently used standard score that avoids the problem of negative numbers and fractions is the Z-score, which has a mean of 50 and a standard deviation of 10. The formula for Z is:

$$Z = 10_z + 50 = 10\left(\frac{x - \bar{x}}{s}\right) + 50$$

Thus, a z-score of $+1.0$ would equal a Z-score of 60, and a z-score of -1.5 would equal a Z-score of 35.

Percentile scores.   A percentile score indicates where a score falls in a distribution in terms of how many scores fall below that score. A score in the 10th percentile exceeds only 10% of all scores. The 50th percentile is the median of the distribution. Thus, the mean of a normal distribution is in the 50th percentile, a score one standard deviation above the mean is in the 84th percentile, and so on.

Skewed Distributions

Not all distributions of scores are normal. Most non-normal distributions are *skewed*. A skewed distribution typically has scores bunched up around the low or high end of a scale, with small numbers of scores several standard deviations in the other direction. A typically skewed distribution is income. The median family income in the U.S. in 1975 was $13,772. That is, half of all households earned more than that figure, and half earned less. However, the *mean* income was $22,105. The mean is so much higher because of the impact of millionaires and others with very high incomes, who are small in number but have a strong impact on the mean. A graph of income might look like that in Figure 9–2.

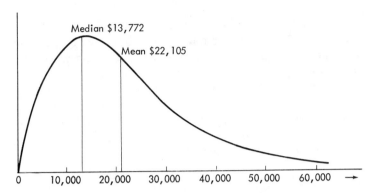

FIGURE 9–2   Hypothetical Graph of Income (Positively Skewed Distribution)

The income distribution predicted in Figure 10.2 is an example of a *positively skewed distribution*, so called because very high values skew the mean. An example of a *negatively skewed distribution* is a ceiling effect on a test. Let's say a teacher gave a test, and half of the students got scores between 90% and 100%. This is a case of a ceiling effect, because no matter how much students knew, they could not get a score higher than 100% (that is, there is a ceiling of 100%) and many students approached that ceiling. A ceiling effect is diagrammed in Figure 9–3.

Note that in Figure 9–3, the mean is strongly influenced by the few very low scores, just as income (Figure 9–2) was strongly influenced by the few individuals with very high incomes. In both of these cases, the median is a better measure of central tendency than the mean. The assumptions underlying the normal distribution will not hold in these cases, so parametric statistics (such as t, F, and r) should not be computed on variables with strongly skewed distributions (see parametric versus nonparametric statistics, later in this chapter).

FIGURE 9–3   Ceiling Effect (Negatively Skewed Distribution)

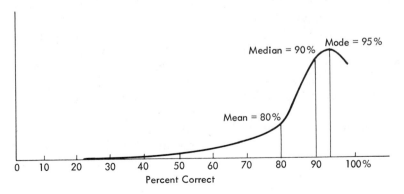

Kurtosis

Some non-normal distributions are not skewed, but deviate from the bell shape diagrammed in Figure 9–1. These are distributions with non-normal *kurtosis*. An example of such a distribution is the age (in years) of fifth graders on January 1. The vast majority of fifth graders would be 10 years old on January 1, but a few would be older or younger, producing a distribution that is more bunched up in the middle than a normal distribution. Parametric statistics can usually be used on distributions with non-normal kurtosis if the degree of kurtosis is not extreme.

Standard Error of the Mean

How good an estimate of the population mean is a sample mean? The statistic that indicates this is called the *standard error of the mean*, (s_m), whose formula is

$$s_m = \frac{s}{\sqrt{N}}$$

Where s = sample standard deviation
       N = number of scores in the sample
      s_m = standard error of the mean

Let's say we chose a random sample of 100 third-grade students in a school district with 5,000 third graders. Their mean reading vocabulary score is 17.5, with a standard deviation of 5.0. The standard error of the mean (s_m) would be:

$$\frac{s}{\sqrt{N}} = \frac{5.0}{\sqrt{100}} = \frac{5.0}{10.0} = 0.5$$

What this statistic implies is that there is a 68.3% chance that the true mean (the mean we would have obtained by testing all 5000 students) is within ±.5 of 17.5. The means of all possible samples of 100 students would be normally distributed around the true mean, with a standard deviation of about .5. In survey research, two standard errors of the mean is often called *sampling error*, as in "37% of the registered voters interviewed thought that President Nixon should be impeached, with a *sampling error* of ±3%." This would mean that there is a 95.4% chance that the true mean (that is, the mean that would have been obtained if all registered voters in the U.S. were interviewed) would be within 3% of 37%.

STATISTICAL
COMPARISONS

Up to this point, we have discussed only statistics that describe distributions of scores. However, we are often interested in comparing distributions to other distributions or to preestablished parameters. (A *parameter* is a statistic describing some aspect of a distribution, such as the mean or standard deviation.) The following sections discuss statistics used for such comparisons.

The Concept
of Statistical Significance

As is illustrated in the discussion of the standard error of the mean (above), each time we choose a random sample from a larger population, the mean of that sample on some variable will be somewhat different from means of other samples from the same population on that variable. Consider an experiment in which we flipped a fair coin in several sets of 100 trials. We would expect to get 50 heads *on the average*, but in each set of trials the number of heads would vary somewhat. Let's say a psychic claims that he can influence the outcome of coin flips. He flips the coin 100 times and there are 55 heads. Is his claim of psychic powers justified?

The answer to this depends on how frequently we would see this many heads in 100 flips *at random*. If 55 heads is not unusual in 100 flips, we would conclude that we cannot rule out the possibility that the psychic has no power over coins. If 55 heads is unheard of, we would have reason to believe that this result is not likely to be due to random sample-to-sample variation, but is due to true psychic powers.

The null hypothesis (H_0).   This discussion brings us back to the concept of the null hypothesis, briefly introduced in Chapter 1. In the case of comparisons of the means of two different samples, the null hypothesis might be that the means do not differ.

$$H_0: \mu_1 = \mu_2$$

Note that the null hypothesis is written using the symbol for the *population* mean (μ) rather than the *sample* mean ($\bar{x}$). The reason for this is that even though we collect data on a sample (such as sophomores at State University) our hypotheses are meant to apply to a much larger population (such as all sophomores or all college students).

Our task is to provide overwhelming evidence that the null hypothesis is untenable. To do this, it is not enough to show that two sample means are not identical ($\bar{x}_1 \neq \bar{x}_2$). Even if the two samples were randomly selected from the same population, we would expect some differences in the sample means due to random variation (chance). The task is to determine whether or not the differences are beyond those that would be expected by chance.

Consider the experiment initially presented in Chapter 1, concerning the effects of viewing different movies on preschoolers' aggressive behavior. Thirty preschool children were randomly assigned to see either the violent movie or "Mary Poppins". Afterwards, they were allowed to play with a set of toys, and the number of aggressive acts committed were observed by observers who did not know which movie the children had seen. Two possible sets of outcomes are depicted in Example 9–8. Each "X" represents the number of aggressive acts for a single child.

EXAMPLE 9–8

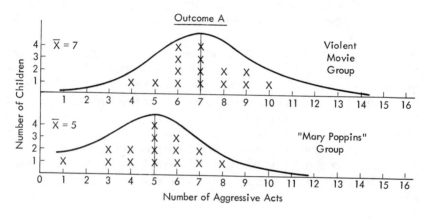

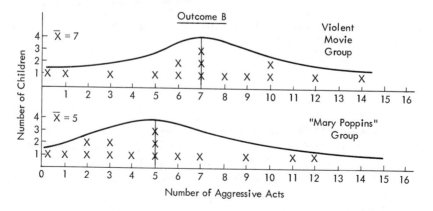

As was noted in Chapter 1, even though the means for the groups are the same in Outcomes A and B, Outcome A clearly shows that students who saw the violent movie exhibited more aggressive behavior than those who saw "Mary Poppins." The null hypothesis (which states that the means of the two groups are the same) does not appear to be tenable; sample-to-sample variation in means would probably not produce such a sharp difference in distributions by chance.

In Outcome B, the distributions of scores overlap too much for us to be able to say that the means are not different due to mere chance variation.

Criteria for Rejecting the Null Hypothesis

Obviously, inspection of graphs is not a sufficient means of determining whether or not two groups differ. To do this, we must use statistics that tell us how likely it is that the difference between two means might be due to chance variation. If the likelihood of this difference is small, we can reject the null hypothesis; if it is not small, we must continue to believe the null hypothesis.

In education, psychology, and other social sciences, the most commonly accepted criterion for rejecting the null hypothesis is that the observed results would be seen only 5% of the time due to random sample-to-sample differences. This is expressed as an *alpha* level of .05. When the level of statistical significance (alpha) is set at .05, it is still possible that the null hypothesis is true (which is to say that the differences we observe might just be due to mere random sampling error), but it is unlikely (there is only a 5% chance). Occasionally, researchers will set alpha at 1% (.01), to give themselves 99 chances in 100 that if they decide to reject the null hypothesis of no significant differences, they will not be incorrect.

Type I and Type II Error

There are two types of errors that can be made in testing a null hypothesis. Type I, or *alpha error*, is related to the concept of false positive error, introduced in Chapter 1. Type I error occurs when we mistakenly reject the null hypothesis. Type II, or *beta error* (discussed earlier as false negative error), occurs when the null hypothesis is false, but we accept it anyway. Type I and Type II error are illustrated in Figure 9–4.

In setting alpha levels, it is important to consider that decreasing alpha decreases the possibility of Type I error, but increases the possibility of Type II error.

FIGURE 9-4   TYPES OF ERROR

	Actual Situation	
	H_o is true (that is, there are no significant differences)	H_o is false (that is, there are significant differences)
We say H_o is true (that is, there are no significant differences)	Correct	Type II, beta, or false negative error
We say H_o is false (that is, there are significant differences)	Type I, alpha, or false positive error	Correct

Rejecting the Null Hypothesis

To understand how we know when to reject the null hypothesis, consider an example in which the standard error of the mean (s_m) is 1.0 for each of two groups, but the means are different. Figure 9-5 shows the hypothetical distribution of means for Group 1, and two possible means for Group 2.

Consider the possibility that the mean for Group 2 takes on a value that is one standard error of the mean (s_m) higher than the mean for Group 1. How often would a score as high as $\bar{x}_1 + 1s_m$ occur by chance (sample-to-sample variation)?

The answer is that a mean as high as $\bar{x}_1 + 1s_m$ or higher would occur 15.9% of the time by chance $[1 - (.50 + .341) = .159]$, much higher than the alpha level (.05) generally accepted as a criterion for rejecting the null hypothesis. Thus, if a mean for Group 2 fell only $1s_m$ higher than the mean for Group 2, we would not have enough evidence to reject the null hypothesis.

FIGURE 9-5

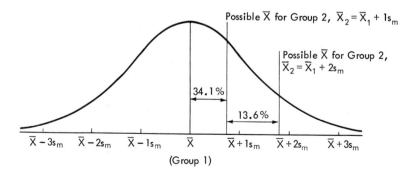

Possible $\bar{X}$ for Group 2, $\bar{X}_2 = \bar{X}_1 + 1s_m$

Possible $\bar{X}$ for Group 2, $\bar{X}_2 = \bar{X}_1 + 2s_m$

34.1%

13.6%

$\bar{X} - 3s_m$ $\bar{X} - 2s_m$ $\bar{X} - 1s_m$ $\bar{X}$ $\bar{X} + 1s_m$ $\bar{X} + 2s_m$ $\bar{X} + 3s_m$

(Group 1)

However, consider the possibility that the mean for Group 2 was *two* standard error of the mean units higher than the Group 1 mean (that is, $\bar{x}_2 = \bar{x}_1 + 2s_m$). Looking again at Figure 9–5, it can be calculated that a mean as high or higher than $\bar{x}_1 + 2s_m$ would be seen by chance only 2.3% of the time $(1 - (.50 + .341 + .136) = .023)$. In this case, the chances that if we rejected the null hypothesis we would be wrong (2.3%) are less than the 5% criterion (alpha level) we established. Thus, we can reject the null hypothesis with some confidence. The observed difference between Group 1 and Group 2 is real, not just an accident of random sample-to-sample variation.

One-Tailed and Two-Tailed Tests of Significance

In most experiments in which we are comparing two groups, we have a strong hypothesis to predict which group will have the higher mean. For example, if a researcher developed a new method of teaching geometry, she would have a hypothesis that the experimental group (which received the new method) would do better on the posttest than the control group (which studied geometry using traditional methods).

However, the researcher would have to allow for the possibility that the experimental students would learn *less* than the control students. If this happened, she would want to know whether or not the difference between the experimental and control groups was statistically significant (that is, more than would have been expected by chance sample-to-sample variation). To allow for that possibility and still maintain an alpha level of 5%, she would have to distribute the 5% equally in the two tails of the distribution, as illustrated in Figure 9–6.

Note that in Figure 9–6, the researcher would reject H_o: $\mu_1 = \mu_2$ only if the difference between the means of Group 1 and Group 2 were $\pm 1.96s_m$, because 47.5% of all scores fall between the mean and $+1.96s_m$ and 47.5% would fall between the mean and $-1.96s_m$ $[1 - (47.5 + 47.5) = .05$; see Appendix 1]. Otherwise, she would have to conclude that the difference

FIGURE 9–6   Two-Tailed Tests, Alpha = .05 (.025 in each tail)

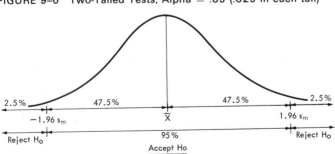

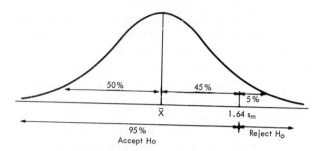

FIGURE 9-7   One-Tailed Test, Alpha = .05 (all in one tail)

between the means for Group 1 and Group 2 could have occurred due to random sample-to-sample variation.

It is possible to restrict attention to one tail of the distribution of sample means by posing a directional hypothesis:

$$H_o: \mu_1 < \mu_2$$

In this case, to disprove the null hypothesis, we only need to show that, in fact, the mean for Group 1 *exceeds* the mean for Group 2. This is somewhat easier to do than to show conclusively that $\bar{x}_1 \neq \bar{x}_2$ because we need only be concerned about one tail of the distribution, not two. If the mean for Group 1 exceeds the mean for Group 2 by $1.64s_m$, we can reject the null hypothesis that the mean for Group 1 is less than that for Group 2 with an alpha level of .05. This is diagrammed in Figure 9-7.

While use of a one-tailed test makes it somewhat "easier" to find significant differences between means, one-tailed tests (and directional hypotheses) are appropriate only when there is no conceivable chance that the results will turn out in a direction opposite to the one hypothesized. For example, it is inconceivable that heating a steel bar will cause it to contract rather than expand, so a directional hypothesis concerning lengths of heated versus unheated steel bars would be appropriate. However, few if any relationships in social science are so well established and reliable that the possibility of a finding in the opposite direction to that hypothesized can be completely ignored. Hence, one-tailed tests should rarely be used in social science research.

The t-Test for Comparisons of Two Independent Group Means

The primary statistic used to determine whether or not means from two different samples are different beyond what would be expected due to sample-to-sample variation is called a t-test. The formula for a t-test is as follows:

Issue Receipt

University of Plymouth (3)

Date: Sunday, January 22, 2012

Time: 12:54 PM

Card number: 0021094296

Item ID: 9000560624

Title: Research methods in education

Due date: 13/02/2012 23:59

Total items: 1

Please keep your receipt until you
have checked your Voyager account

$$t = \frac{\bar{x}_1 - \bar{x}_2}{\sqrt{\dfrac{s_1^2}{N_1} + \dfrac{s_2^2}{N_2}}}$$

Where $\bar{x}_1$ = mean of Group 1
$\quad\ \ \bar{x}_2$ = mean of Group 2
$\quad\ \ s_1^2$ = variance of Group 1
$\quad\ \ s_2^2$ = variance of Group 2
$\quad\ \ N_1$ = number of scores, Group 1
$\quad\ \ N_2$ = number of scores, Group 2

To determine whether or not a t-test indicates that the difference between two means is statistically significant, we must consult a table of critical t's such as appears in Appendix 2. To use this table, we must first compute the degrees of freedom (d.f.) for the analysis, as follows:

Degrees of Freedom (d.f.) $= N_1 + N_2 - 2$

Where N_1 = number of scores, Group 1
$\quad\ \ N_2$ = number of scores, Group 2

We then look down the table for the level of significance (alpha) we have established (.05 or .01) to the appropriate degrees of freedom. The table entry indicates the minimum value of t needed for statistical significance at that level. Note that an alpha level of .05 for a two-tailed test equals an alpha level of .025 for a one-tailed test, and an alpha level of .01 for a two-tailed test equals an alpha level of .005 for a one-tailed test. Also note that as the degrees of freedom increase, the t-distribution approximates the normal distribution and t essentially becomes z (a standard score with a mean of zero and a standard deviation of 1). A t statistic can be either positive or negative, depending on which mean is considered x_1 and which is designated x_2.

Computing t

The steps for computing the t-test using a hand calculator are as follows:

1. List the scores (x) for Group 1 in any order.
2. Square each score (x^2).
3. Add up the scores (Σx).
4. Add up the squared scores (Σx^2).
5. Count the number of scores (N).
6. Compute the mean:

$$\bar{x}_1 = \frac{\Sigma x}{N}$$

7. Compute the variance:

$$s_1^2 = \frac{\Sigma x^2 - \dfrac{(\Sigma x)^2}{N}}{N - 1}$$

8. Repeat steps 1 through 7 for Group 2.

9. Compute t:

$$t = \frac{\bar{x}_1 - \bar{x}_2}{\sqrt{\dfrac{s_1^2}{N_1} + \dfrac{s_2^2}{N_2}}}$$

10. Compare the obtained value of t to the critical value of t listed in Appendix 2. If the absolute value of t (ignoring the sign) is larger than the critical value, reject the null hypothesis; if not, accept the null hypothesis.

To illustrate the use of the t-test, let's return to the comparison of aggressive acts exhibited by children who had seen either the violent movie or "Mary Poppins." Two possible outcomes of this study were diagrammed earlier in Example 9–8, and the data and calculations are shown in Examples 9–9 and 9–10.

As is shown in Example 9–9, the t for Outcome A is 3.21. Looking in Appendix 2, we can see that the criterion for statistical significance at alpha$=.05$ and degrees of freedom of 28 is 2.05 (using a two-tailed test). Because 3.21 > 2.05, we can reject the null hypothesis. In fact, this value of t exceeds the criterion for an alpha of .01 (2.76), so we can say that the chance of the result in Outcome A having occurred due to sample-to-sample variation is less than one in 100. This is abbreviated $p<.01$, since probability (of a Type I error) is less than .01.

In contrast, the t for Outcome B is only 1.49. This does not meet the criterion for statistical significance (2.05), so we must accept the null hypothesis, and conclude that the difference between the means may be due to sample-to-sample variation rather than to different effects of the different movies.

It is interesting to note that if we had had just 20 more subjects in each treatment group and the same means and standard deviations, the t in Outcome B would have been 2.28 with 68 degrees of freedom. This is statistically significant at p < .05. Thus, the value of t depends on three factors: the difference between the means of the two groups, the standard deviations of the groups, and the number of subjects in each group.

Note: If the N's and/or the variance of the two groups being compared in a t-test are equal, the formula given above will be correct. If the N's

EXAMPLE 9-9 (Outcome A)

Violent Movie		Mary Poppins	
x	x^2	x	x^2
10	100	8	64
9	81	7	49
9	81	7	49
8	64	6	36
8	64	6	36
7	49	6	36
7	49	5	25
7	49	5	25
7	49	5	25
6	36	5	25
6	36	4	16
6	36	4	16
6	36	3	9
5	25	3	9
4	16	1	1

$\Sigma x = 105$ $\Sigma x^2 = 771$ $\Sigma x = 75$ $\Sigma x^2 = 421$
$N = 15$ $N = 15$
$\bar{x} = 7.0$ $\bar{x} = 5.0$

$$s^2 = \frac{771 - \frac{(105)^2}{15}}{14} = 2.57 \qquad s^2 = \frac{421 - \frac{(75)^2}{15}}{14} = 3.29$$

$$t = \frac{\bar{x}_1 - \bar{x}_2}{\sqrt{\frac{s_1^2}{N_1} + \frac{s_2^2}{N_2}}}$$

$$= \frac{7.0 - 5.0}{\sqrt{\frac{2.57}{15} + \frac{3.29}{15}}}$$

$$= \frac{2.0}{\sqrt{.171 + .219}}$$

$$= \frac{2.0}{\sqrt{.39}} = \frac{2.0}{.624}$$

$$t = \underline{3.21}$$

Degrees of Freedom (d.f.) = $N_1 + N_2 - 2 = 15 + 15 - 2 = \underline{28}$
Decision (criterion for $p < .05 = 2.05$),
         (criterion for $p < .01 = 2.76$)
Reject Null Hypothesis
       $p < .01$

EXAMPLE 9–10 (Outcome B)

Violent Movie		Mary Poppins	
x	x^2	x	x^2
14	196	12	144
12	144	11	121
10	100	9	81
10	100	7	49
9	81	6	36
8	64	5	25
7	49	5	25
7	49	5	25
7	49	4	16
6	36	3	9
6	36	3	9
5	25	2	4
3	9	2	4
1	1	1	1
0	0	0	0

$\Sigma x = 105 \quad \Sigma x^2 = 939 \qquad \Sigma x = 75 \quad \Sigma x^2 = 549$

$N = 15 \qquad\qquad\qquad N = 15$

$\bar{x} = 7 \qquad\qquad\qquad \bar{x} = 5$

$$s^2 = \frac{939 - \frac{(105)^2}{15}}{14} = 14.57 \qquad s^2 = \frac{549 - \frac{(75)^2}{15}}{14} = 12.43$$

$$t = \frac{\bar{x}_1 - \bar{x}_2}{\sqrt{\frac{s_1^2}{N_1} + \frac{s_2^2}{N_2}}}$$

$$= \frac{7.0 - 5.0}{\sqrt{\frac{14.57}{15} + \frac{12.43}{15}}}$$

$$= \frac{2.0}{\sqrt{.971 + .829}}$$

$$= \frac{2.0}{\sqrt{1.8}} = \frac{2.0}{1.34}$$

$$t = \underline{1.49}$$

Degrees of Freedom (d.f.) $= N_1 + N_2 - 2 = 15 + 15 - 2 = \underline{28}$
Decision (criterion for $p < .05$) $= \underline{2.05}$

Accept Null Hypothesis

of the two groups differ *and* the variances of the groups differ, you should use the following formula:

$$t = \frac{\bar{x}_1 - \bar{x}_2}{\sqrt{\dfrac{(N_1 - 1)\ s_1^2 + (N_2 - 1)\ s_2^2}{N_1 + N_2 - 2}\left(\dfrac{1}{N_1} + \dfrac{1}{N_2}\right)}}$$

Homogeneity of Variances

One important assumption behind the t-test is that the variances of the two samples are similar, or *homogeneous*. This is easily checked. Divide the larger variance by the smaller to compute an F, as follows:

$$F = \frac{s_L^2}{s_S^2}, \text{ d.f.} = (N_L - 1), (N_S - 1)$$

Where s_L^2 = the larger varience

s_S^2 = the smaller variance

d.f. = degrees of freedom

N_L = the number of scores in the group with the larger variance

N_S = the number of scores in the group with the smaller varience

Check the F statistic against the F table in Appendix 3. The degrees of freedom for the numerator is $N_L - 1$; for the denominator, it is $N_s - 1$. Look to the intersection between the degrees of freedom for the numerator and denominator to find the criterion F. If the F value you computed is more than the value in the table, you must conclude that the two variances are not homogeneous and you should use a nonparametric test rather than t (see below).

As an example of this, consider a study comparing the physical strength of learning-disabled boys to that of nondisabled agemates. Each student's strength is tested in several ways and put on a scale from 1 to 10. The results are as follows:

LEARNING DISABLED   NONDISABLED

$\bar{x} = 7.62$ $\bar{x} = 5.92$

$s^2 = 8.40$ $s^2 = 5.12$

$N = 13$ $N = 31$

To test the homogeneity of variances, we proceed as follows:

$$F = \frac{s_L^2}{s_S^2} = \frac{8.40}{5.12} = 1.64$$

d.f. $= (N_L - 1), (N_s - 1) = 12, 30$

The critical value for F at $p < .05$ with 12, 30 degrees of freedom (from Appendix 3) is 2.09, so we cannot reject the null hypothesis that

$s_L^2 = s_S^2$. Thus, the variances can be considered homogeneous, and we can go ahead and compute the t-test to compare the two means.

The t-Test for Comparisons of Two Means from Matched Groups

Occasionally, we wish to test the difference between the means of two *matched* groups for statistical significance. This is most often done when we wish to compare the same subjects under two differenct conditions or at two different times. For example, we might test a group of students on their knowledge of algebra in September and then test them again in December to see if they have learned anything at all. Or consider a situation in which parents have complained that Mr. Durr gives much harder physics tests than Mr. Douce. The principal wants to find out if this is true, so she takes 20 students from a third teacher's physics class and gives them a 30-item test made by Mr. Durr and a 30-item test made by Mr. Douce on the same topic.

The formula for t with matched groups is as follows:

$$t = \frac{\overline{D}}{\sqrt{\frac{s_D^2}{N}}} \qquad \text{d.f.} = N - 1$$

Where $\overline{D}$ = the mean of the difference scores = $\frac{\Sigma D}{N}$

s_D^2 = the variance of the difference scores = $\dfrac{\Sigma D^2 - \dfrac{(\Sigma D)^2}{N}}{N - 1}$

ΣD^2 = the sum of the squared difference scores
N = the number of pairs of scores.

For the comparison of Mr. Durr's test and Mr. Douce's test, the data are as follows:

EXAMPLE 9–11

Student #	Mr. Durr's Test	Mr. Douce's Test	D	D²
1	28	29	−1	1
2	26	30	−4	16
3	25	27	−2	4
4	24	25	−1	1
5	24	22	+2	4
6	23	29	−6	36
7	22	21	+1	1
8	21	22	−1	1
9	21	29	−8	64
10	21	20	+1	1

Student #	Mr. Durr's Test	Mr. Douce's Test	D	D²
11	20	29	−9	81
12	20	25	−5	25
13	20	27	−7	49
14	20	18	+2	4
15	19	24	−5	25
16	18	16	+2	4
17	18	26	−8	64
18	17	21	−4	16
19	16	22	−6	36
20	14	20	−6	36
	$\Sigma x = 417$	$\Sigma y = 482$	$\Sigma D = -65$	$\Sigma D^2 = 469$
	$\overline{x} = 20.85$	$\overline{y} = 24.10$	$\overline{D} = \dfrac{\Sigma D}{N} = \dfrac{-65}{20} = -3.25$	

To compute the t for matched groups, follow these steps;

1. Subtract each individual's score on Test 2 from his or her score on Test 1 to get a difference score (D).
2. Add up the difference scores (ΣD).
3. Compute the mean difference: $\overline{D} = \dfrac{\Sigma D}{N}$
4. Square each difference score and add them up (ΣD^2).
5. Compute the variance of the difference scores as follows:

$$s_D^2 = \frac{\Sigma D^2 - \dfrac{(\Sigma D)^2}{N}}{N-1}$$

$$= \frac{469 - \dfrac{(-65)^2}{20}}{20-1}$$

$$= \frac{469 - 211.25}{19}$$

$$= 13.57$$

6. Compute t:

$$t = \frac{\overline{D}}{\sqrt{\dfrac{s_D^2}{N}}}$$

$$= \frac{-3.25}{\sqrt{\dfrac{13.57}{20}}}$$

$$= \frac{-3.25}{.824}$$

$$= -3.94$$

7. Compare the obtained value of t to the critical value of t listed in Appendix 2 for d.f. $= N - 1 = 19$.

As is clear from Example 9–11, Mr. Durr's test is indeed more difficult than Mr. Douce's test. Ignoring the sign, the t of -3.25 is larger than the criterion value of t for d.f. $= 19$ of 2.09 for p $<$ .05; it is also larger than the criterion value of 2.86 for p $<$ .01.

The t-test for matched groups can also be used in cases where there are different individuals in each group but each individual in one group has a "match" in the other. For example, we might compare two groups of students matched on standardized test scores, in which case difference scores would be computed between each individual in each matched pair. However, remember that matching is inappropriate when the individuals being matched are drawn from two different populations (such as special education and regular classes, Math 9 and Algebra I, etc.; see Chapter 7).

The t-Test for Comparisons of a Sample Mean to a Population Mean

Let's say we wish to know whether or not a given class is different on a standardized test than the population on which the test was standardized. The formula for comparing a sample mean to a population mean is as follows:

$$t = \frac{\bar{x} - \mu}{\sqrt{\dfrac{s^2}{N}}}$$

Where $\bar{x} =$ the sample mean

$\mu =$ the population mean

$s^2 =$ the sample variance

$N =$ the number of scores in the sample

For example, we might wish to know whether the mean mathematics SAT score for seniors at Testville High School ($\bar{x} = 514$) is higher than that for all U.S. seniors ($\mu = 462$).

Chapter 10 describes an SPSS computer program, T-TEST, which computes t-tests for independent and matched groups.

Parametric versus Nonparametric Statistics

Most of the statistics described in this chapter (including t, F, and r) are *parametric* statistics, which means that the parameters (characteristics) of the distributions of scores from which they are derived meet certain assumptions. The most important of these are as follows:

1. The scores are *normally distributed*. Highly skewed distributions (such as distributions with ceiling or floor effects) should not be analyzed using parametric statistics, although modest deviations from normal distributions are allowable.
2. The variances of any two (or more) groups being compared must be nearly equal. This is discussed earlier under homogeneity of variance.
3. The variables must be interval or ratio scales. Ordinal (ranked) or nominal (frequency count) data must be analyzed using nonparametric statistics, described later in this chapter.
4. The samples are randomly assigned to conditions.
5. The observations are independent; the selection of any case is not dependent on the selection of any other case.

Conditions 4 and 5 are frequently violated in educational research. For example, virtually all correlational and descriptive studies (see Chapter 4) violate Condition 4. Condition 5 is violated by experimental studies in which treatments are administered in class groups (regardless of how the samples were assigned to treatments), but the individual student is the unit of analysis. Parametric statistics can be used in such cases if the data conform to Conditions 1 through 3, but the results must be interpreted very cautiously (see Chapters 2 and 4).

ANALYSIS OF VARIANCE (ANOVA)

One major limitation of the t-test is that its use is restricted to comparisons of two samples (or one sample and a population mean). To compare more than two samples, we use analysis of variance, or ANOVA. Instead of a t, ANOVA produces an F statistic. In the case of comparing two samples, $F = t^2$ (that is, a t of ± 2.0 is equal to an F of 4.0).

Comparison of Three Groups: 3 × 1 ANOVA

The simplest extension of the t-test is a comparison of three groups, where the effect of one independent variable (treatment) on one dependent variable is analyzed. This is called a *one-way analysis of variance*, or a K × 1 analysis of variance, where K is the number of treatment groups. A comparison of three groups would thus be a 3 × 1 analysis of variance.

Consider a study in which a researcher wants to compare the effects of individualized instruction, peer tutoring, and traditional instruction on student achievement in spelling. He randomly assigns 30 students to the three groups, 10 per group. The treatments are administered for three months, and then he gives a 20-item test, sampling items from the students' spelling lists. The results are as follows:

EXAMPLE 9-12

Individualized Instruction		Peer Tutoring		Traditional Instruction	
x_1	x_1^2	x_2	x_2^2	x_3	x_3^2
19	361	18	324	16	256
14	196	20	400	12	144
17	289	17	289	15	225
17	289	18	324	11	121
13	169	20	400	15	225
20	400	19	361	18	324
17	289	18	324	14	196
16	256	19	361	14	196
18	324	15	225	13	169
19	361	20	400	10	100

$\Sigma x_1 = 170$ $\Sigma x_1^2 = 2934$ $\Sigma x_2 = 184$ $\Sigma x_2^2 = 3408$ $\Sigma x_3 = 138$ $\Sigma x_3^2 = 1956$

$\bar{x}_1 = 17.0$ $s_1^2 = 4.89$ $\bar{x}_2 = 18.4$ $s_2^2 = 2.49$ $\bar{x}_3 = 13.8$ $s_3^2 = 5.73$

$N_1 = 10$ $N_2 = 10$ $N_3 = 10$

Grand Total $(\Sigma x) = \Sigma x_1 + \Sigma x_2 + \Sigma x_3 =$

170 + 184 + 138 = 492

Total $N = N_1 + N_2 + N_3 =$

10 + 10 + 10 = 30

To calculate the ANOVA, follow these steps.

1. Compute the sum of each set of scores (Σx).
2. Square each score and sum the squares (Σx^2).
3. Count the number of scores in each group (N).
4. Compute the mean for each group $\left(\bar{x} = \dfrac{\Sigma x}{N} \right)$.
5. Compute the variance for each group:

$$s^2 = \frac{\Sigma x^2 - \dfrac{(\Sigma x)^2}{N}}{N - 1}$$

6. Compute the Grand Total $(\Sigma x) = (\Sigma x_1 + \Sigma x_2 + \Sigma x_3)$.
7. Compute the Total $N = (N_1 + N_2 + N_3)$.
8. Compute the sum of squares between groups (SS_B) as follows:

$$SS_B = \frac{(\Sigma x_1)^2}{N_1} + \frac{(\Sigma x_2)^2}{N_2} + \frac{(\Sigma x_3)^2}{N_3} - \frac{(\Sigma x)^2}{N}$$

$$= \frac{(170)^2}{10} + \frac{(184)^2}{10} + \frac{(138)^2}{10} - \frac{(492)^2}{30}$$

$$= 2890.0 + 3385.6 + 1904.4 - 8068.8$$

$$= 111.2$$

9. Compute the sum of squares within groups (SS_W), as follows:

$$SS_W = [(N_1 - 1) s_1^2] + [(N_2 - 1) s_2^2] + [(N_3 - 1) s_3^2]$$
$$= [(9)(4.89)] + [(9)(2.49)] + [(9)(5.73)]$$
$$= 44.01 + 22.41 + 51.57$$
$$= 117.99$$

10. Compute degrees of freedom (d.f.) as follows:

d.f. between groups = $K - 1 = 3 - 1 = 2$
d.f. within groups = $N - K = 30 - 3 = 27$

11. Compute the mean square between groups (MS_B) and mean square within groups (MS_W) as follows:

$$MS_B = \frac{SS_B}{K - 1} = \frac{111.2}{2} = 55.60$$
$$MS_W = \frac{SS_W}{N - K} = \frac{117.99}{27} = 4.37$$

12. Compute F:

$$\frac{MS_B}{MS_W} = \frac{55.60}{4.37} = 12.72$$

13. Look up the criterion F for degrees of freedom (between, within) = (2, 27) in Appendix 3. The criterion for $p < .05$ is 3.35; for $p < .01$, it is 5.49. $F = 12.72$ exceeds either of these criteria, so for $F_{(2, 27)} = 12.72$, $p < .01$.

The ANOVA is summarized in the following form:

Analysis of Variance

Source of Variation	SS	d.f.	MS	F
Between Groups (treatments)	SS_B	K–1	$MS_B = \frac{SS_B}{K-1}$	$\frac{MS_B}{MS_W}$
Within Groups (error)	SS_W	N–K	$MS_W = \frac{SS_W}{N-K}$	
TOTAL	$SS_B + SS_W$	N–1		

FOR EXAMPLE 9-12

Analysis of Variance

Source of Variation	SS	d.f.	MS	F
Between Groups (treatments)	111.20	2	55.60	
Within Groups (error)	117.99	27	4.37	12.72, $p < .01$
Total	229.19	29		

Comparison of K Groups:
K × 1 ANOVA

Computational procedures for any number of groups in a one-way analysis of variance can be easily inferred from those for the three-group comparison (3 × 1) ANOVA. Simply extend the formulas for SS_B and SS_W as follows:

$$SS_B = \frac{(\Sigma x_1)^2}{N_1} + \frac{(\Sigma x_2)^2}{N_2} + \ldots + \frac{(\Sigma x_K)^2}{N_K} - \frac{(\Sigma x)^2}{N}$$

$$SS_W = [(N_1 - 1)\, s_1^2] + [(N_2 - 1)\, s_2^2] + \ldots + [(N_K - 1)\, s_K^2]$$

Chapter 10 describes the use of the SPSS program ANOVA to compute analyses of variance.

Individual Comparisons

It is usually not enough to know that there is a statistically significant difference between three or more groups. We also want to know whether or not differences between particular pairs or groups of treatments are statistically significant. There are many ways of computing individual differences between treatments after an ANOVA has been found to be statistically significant. The easiest is to compute a t-test between each pair of means. This is permissible if you have firm hypothesis about why differences occur between the pairs of treatments, and if the number of such comparisons is small. However, if you are just looking at a set of means at the end of a study and noting which are most different from each other, computing t-tests is not appropriate. With many such comparisons, a few are bound to be statistically significant by chance. Individual comparison procedures (such as Duncan, Tukey, Scheffe, and Newman-Keuls tests) have been devised to take into account the number of comparisons being made. See any of the statistics books listed at the end of this chapter for more on unplanned (*a posteriori*) individual comparisons. Also, the SPSS computer program ONEWAY, described in Chapter 10, computes these statistics.

Two-Factor ANOVA

We often wish to know how two or more factors affect a dependent variable, and how they interact with each other. For example, in the experiment presented in Example 9–12, we might have wanted to know which treatment was associated with the highest spelling scores, whether girls and boys learned equally well, and whether girls and boys profited equally from the different treatments. The questions about which treatments and which sex were associated with the greatest learning are questions of *main effects*; the questions about whether or not boys and girls were affected differently by the different treatments is a question of an *interaction* between treatment and sex. If we analyzed the data presented in Example 9–12 by treatment and sex, we would have a 3 × 2 ANOVA, because there are three levels of treatment and two levels of sex (boy and girl). This design is diagrammed in Example 9–13.

The 3 × 2 design creates six "cells". The data in these cells are presented in Example 9–13, with subscripts indicating the *column* and *row* of the cell. For example, a score in Column 1, Row 2 (girls in individualized instruction) would be designed x_{12}.

To calculate the 3 × 2 ANOVA, follow these steps:

1. Compute the sum for each cell (Σx).
2. Square each score and sum the squares (Σx^2).
3. Count the number of scores in each cell (N).

4. Compute the mean for each cell $\left(\bar{x} = \dfrac{\Sigma x}{N}\right)$.

5. Compute the variance for each cell:

$$s_{cr}^2 = \frac{\Sigma x^2 - \dfrac{(\Sigma x)^2}{N}}{N - 1}$$

6. Compute the total sum for each column (Σc).
7. Compute the total N for each column (N_c).
8. Compute the total sum for each row (Σr).
9. Compute the total N for each row (N_r).
10. Compute the grand total $\Sigma x = (\Sigma r_1 + \Sigma r_2)$.
11. Compute the total $N = (N_{r_1} + N_{r_2})$.
12. Compute the sum of squares between columns (treatments) as follows:

$$SS_{Bc} = \frac{(\Sigma c_1)^2}{N_{c_1}} + \frac{(\Sigma c_2)^2}{N_{c_2}} + \frac{(\Sigma c_3)^2}{N_{c_3}} - \frac{(\Sigma x)^2}{N}$$

$$= \frac{(170)^2}{10} + \frac{(184)^2}{10} + \frac{(138)^2}{10} - \frac{(492)^2}{30}$$

$$= 2890.0 + 3385.6 + 1904.4 - 8068.8$$

$$= 111.2$$

13. Compute the sum of squares between rows (sex) as follows:

$$SS_{Br} = \frac{(\Sigma r_1)^2}{N_{r_1}} + \frac{(\Sigma r_2)^2}{N_{r_2}} - \frac{(\Sigma x)^2}{N}$$

$$= \frac{(242)^2}{15} + \frac{(250)^2}{15} - \frac{(492)^2}{30}$$

$$= 3904.3 + 4166.7 - 8068.8$$

$$= 2.2$$

EXAMPLE 9-13

	Individualized Instruction		Peer Tutoring		Traditional Instruction		Row Total
	x_{11}	x_{11}^2	x_{21}	x_{21}^2	x_{31}	x_{31}^2	
Boys	19	361	18	324	16	256	
	14	196	20	400	12	144	
	17	289	17	289	15	225	
	17	289	18	324	11	121	
	13	169	20	400	15	225	$\Sigma r_1 = 242$
	$\Sigma x_{11} = 80$	$\Sigma x_{11}^2 = 1304$	$\Sigma x_{21} = 93$	$\Sigma x_{21}^2 = 1737$	$\Sigma x_{31} = 69$	$\Sigma x_{31}^2 = 971$	$\Sigma N_{r_1} = 15$
	$\bar{x}_{11} = 16.0$	$s_{11}^2 = 6.0$	$\bar{x}_{21} = 18.6$	$s_{21}^2 = 1.8$	$\bar{x}_{31} = 13.8$	$s_{31}^2 = 4.7$	
	$N_{11} = 5$		$N_{21} = 5$		$N_{31} = 5$		
	x_{12}	x_{12}^2	x_{22}	x_{22}^2	x_{32}	x_{32}^2	
Girls	20	400	19	361	18	324	
	17	289	18	324	14	196	
	16	256	19	361	14	196	
	18	324	15	225	13	169	
	19	361	20	400	10	100	$\Sigma r_2 = 250$
	$\Sigma x_{12} = 90$	$\Sigma x_{12}^2 = 1630$	$\Sigma x_{22} = 91$	$\Sigma x_{22}^2 = 1671$	$\Sigma x_{32} = 69$	$\Sigma x_{32}^2 = 985$	$\Sigma N_{r_2} = 15$
	$\bar{x}_{12} = 18.0$	$s_{12}^2 = 2.5$	$\bar{x}_{22} = 18.20$	$s_{22}^2 = 3.7$	$\bar{x}_{32} = 13.8$	$s_{32}^2 = 8.2$	
	$N_{12} = 5$		$N_{22} = 5$		$N_{32} = 5$		
Column Total	$\Sigma c_1 = 170$		$\Sigma c_2 = 184$		$\Sigma c_3 = 138$		**Grand Total**
	$\Sigma N_{c_1} = 10$		$\Sigma N_{c_2} = 10$		$\Sigma N_{c_3} = 10$		$\Sigma x = 492$
							$N = 30$

Row 1 Total (Boys) $= \Sigma r_1 = \Sigma x_{11} + \Sigma x_{21} + \Sigma x_{31} = 80 + 93 + 69 = 242$

Row 2 Total (Girls) $= \Sigma r_2 = \Sigma x_{12} + \Sigma x_{22} + \Sigma x_{32} = 90 + 91 + 69 = 250$

Column 1 Total (Individualized Instruction) $= \Sigma c_1 = \Sigma x_{11} + \Sigma x_{12} = 80 + 90 = 170$

Column 2 Total (Peer Tutoring) $= \Sigma c_2 = \Sigma x_{21} + \Sigma x_{22} = 93 + 91 = 184$

Column 3 Total (Traditional Instruction) $= \Sigma c_3 = \Sigma x_{31} + \Sigma x_{32} = 69 + 69 = 138$

Grand Total $= \Sigma x = \Sigma r_1 + \Sigma r_2 = 242 + 250 = 492$ Total N $= 30$

14. Compute the total sum of squares between groups as follows:

$$SS_B = \frac{(\Sigma x_{11})^2}{N_{11}} + \frac{(\Sigma x_{21})^2}{N_{21}} + \frac{(\Sigma x_{31})^2}{N_{31}} + \frac{(\Sigma x_{12})^2}{N_{12}} +$$

$$\frac{(\Sigma x_{22})^2}{N_{22}} + \frac{(\Sigma x_{32})^2}{N_{32}} - \frac{(\Sigma x)^2}{N}$$

$$= \frac{(80)^2}{5} + \frac{(93)^2}{5} + \frac{(69)^2}{5} + \frac{(90)^2}{5} + \frac{(91)^2}{5} + \frac{(69)^2}{5} - \frac{(492)^2}{30}$$

$$= 1280.0 + 1729.8 + 952.2 + 1620 + 1656.2 + 952.2 - 8068.8$$

$$= 121.6$$

15. Compute the sum of squares for interaction (treatment $\times$ sex) as follows:

$$SS_{int} = SS_B - (SS_{Bc} + SS_{Br})$$
$$= 121.6 - (111.2 + 2.2)$$
$$= 8.2$$

16. Compute the sum of squares within groups (error) as follows:

$$SS_W = [(N_{11} - 1)\,s_{11}^2] + [(N_{21} - 1)\,s_{21}^2] + [(N_{31} - 1)\,s_{31}^2]$$
$$+ [(N_{12} - 1)\,s_{12}^2] + [(N_{22} - 1)\,s_{22}^2] + [(N_{32} - 1)\,s_{32}^2]$$
$$= [(4)(6.0)] + [(4)(1.8)] + [(4)(4.7)] + [(4)(2.5)] + [(4)(3.7)] + [(4)(8.2)]$$
$$= 24.0 + 7.2 + 18.8 + 10.0 + 14.8 + 32.8$$
$$= 107.6$$

17. Set up an ANOVA table as follows:

Analysis of Variance

Source of Variation	SS	d.f.	MS	F
Between Columns (treatments)	SS_{Bc}	$c - 1$	$MS_{Bc} = \dfrac{SS_{Bc}}{c - 1}$	$\dfrac{MS_{Bc}}{MS_W}$
Between Rows (sex)	SS_{Br}	$r - 1$	$MS_{Br} = \dfrac{SS_{Br}}{r - 1}$	$\dfrac{MS_{Br}}{MS_W}$
Interaction (treatment $\times$ sex)	SS_{int}	$(c - 1)(r - 1)$	$MS_{int} = \dfrac{SS_{int}}{(c - 1)(r - 1)}$	$\dfrac{MS_{int}}{MS_W}$
Within Groups (error)	SS_W	$N - cr$	$MS_W = \dfrac{SS_W}{N - cr}$	
Total	$SS_{Bc} + SS_{Br} + SS_{int} + SS_W$			

18. Compute degrees of freedom (d.f.) and mean squares (MS) as indicated in the above ANOVA table (c = number of columns, r = number of rows). Then compute F's for columns, rows, and interaction by dividing the mean square for each by the mean square within groups (error). The final ANOVA table for Example 9–13 appears on the next page.

Analysis of Variance

Source of Variation	SS	d.f.	MS	F	
Between Columns (treatments)	111.2	2	55.60	12.41, p $<$ .01	
Between Rows (sex)	2.2	1	2.20	0.49	n.s.
Interaction (treatment $\times$ sex)	8.2	2	4.10	0.92	n.s.
Within Groups (error)	107.6	24	4.48		
Total	229.2	29			

19. Look up the criterion F for degrees of freedom (2, 24) in Appendix 3. The criterion for p $<$ .05 is 3.40; for p $<$ .01, it is 5.61. The F for the between columns (treatment) effect is 12.41, which exceeds both of these criteria, so $F_{(2, 24)} = 12.41$, p $<$ .01. Compare the F for the between rows (sex) effect [$F_{(1, 24)} = 0.49$] to the criterion for F with (1, 24) degrees of freedom, which is 4.26. Since .49 is less than 4.26, the sex effect is not statistically significant. Similarly, the F for interaction [$F_{(2, 24)} = 0.92$] does not exceed the criterion for p $<$ .05 with degrees of freedom (2, 24) of 3.40, so it is not statistically significant.

The above ANOVA table indicates that while the treatment effect is statistically significant, neither the sex effect nor the sex $\times$ treatment effect was significant. Note that the treatment effect is similar but not identical to that found in the earlier 3 $\times$ 1 analysis, not including sex as a factor. This difference is due to a change in the within-groups (error) sum of squares and degrees of freedom. Compare the ANOVA table for Example 9–12 to that for Example 9–13. Note that if the sum of squares and degrees of freedom for sex and for the treatment $\times$ sex interaction in Example 9–13 are added to the sum of squares within groups, the total will be the same as for Example 9–12.

c $\times$ r Factorial Designs

Computational procedures for any number of columns and rows are simply extensions of those presented above. The critical formulas are presented below for up to j columns and k rows.

$$SS_{Bc} = \frac{(\Sigma c_1)^2}{N_{c_1}} + \frac{(\Sigma c_2)^2}{N_{c_2}} + \ldots + \frac{(\Sigma c_j)^2}{N_{c_j}} - \frac{(\Sigma x)^2}{N}$$

$$SS_{Br} = \frac{(\Sigma r_1)^2}{N_{r_1}} + \frac{(\Sigma r_2)^2}{N_{r_2}} + \ldots + \frac{(\Sigma r_k)^2}{N_{r_k}} - \frac{(\Sigma x)^2}{N}$$

$$SS_{B} = \frac{(\Sigma x_{11})^2}{N_{11}} + \ldots + \frac{(\Sigma x_{jk})^2}{N_{jk}} - \frac{(\Sigma x)^2}{N}$$

$$SS_{int} = SS_{B} - (SS_{Bc} - SS_{Br})$$

$$SS_{W} = (N_{11} - 1) s_{11}^2 + \ldots + (N_{jk} - 1) s_{jk}^2$$

All other formulas and procedures are the same as those described above.

ANALYSIS OF
COVARIANCE (ANCOVA)

In experimental research in schools, one major problem is that most attributes of students (such as achievement level, self-esteem, attitudes, and so on) are relatively stable before the researcher arrives on the scene. If we randomly assign students to different treatments and give them measures of achievement or attitude, it is likely that, no matter how powerful the treatment, the main determinant of student scores will be their abilities or attitudes before the project began.

For this reason, a posttest-only design is highly susceptible to false negative error, because a true effect may be swamped by student-to-student differences in prior ability or attitudes.

This problem can be at least partially overcome by use of *analysis of covariance* (ANCOVA), in which measures of ability and prior attitudes are "controlled for." Any number of covariates can be used. Covariates are usually pretests, but such measures as standardized test scores, previous grades, and student age may also be used as covariates. When covariates are highly correlated with the dependent variable, analysis of covariance increases statistical power (the ability to avoid false negative errors if there is a true effect). Furthermore, analysis of covariance can make treatment groups that are different on pretests statistically equivalent if the pretest differences are not too large (see below for more on this).

As an example of the use of analysis of covariance, consider a study in which 37 students are randomly assigned to one of two treatments: homework or no homework. Students are pretested on a mathematics test, and then they are given either homework every night or no homework. At the end of four weeks, they are given the same test as a posttest. Example 9–14 summarizes the results:

To calculate the analysis of covariance (ANCOVA), follow these steps:

1. Compute the sums of the pretest and posttest scores (Σx_1, Σx_2, Σy_1, Σy_2).
2. Square each pretest and posttest score and sum the squares (Σx_1^2, Σx_2^2, Σy_1^2, Σy_2^2).
3. Count the number of scores in each group (N).
4. Compute the pretest and posttest means for each group ($\bar{x}_1$, $\bar{x}_2$, $\bar{y}_1$, $\bar{y}_2$).
5. Compute the pretest and posttest variances for each group:

$$s_x^2 = \frac{\Sigma x^2 - \dfrac{(\Sigma x)^2}{N}}{N-1} \qquad s_y^2 = \frac{\Sigma y^2 - \dfrac{(\Sigma y)^2}{N}}{N-1}$$

6. Compute the pretest and posttest grand totals:

$$\Sigma x = \Sigma x_1 + \Sigma x_2$$
$$\Sigma y = \Sigma y_1 + \Sigma y_2$$

EXAMPLE 9–14

	Homework						No Homework				
	Pre		Post				Pre		Post		
x_1	x_1^2	y_1	y_1^2	$x_1 y_1$		x_2	x_2^2	y_2	y_2^2	$x_2 y_2$
12	144	13	169	156		13	169	13	169	169
4	16	5	25	20		11	121	14	196	154
4	16	6	36	24		5	25	4	16	20
0	0	4	16	0		9	81	7	49	63
5	25	7	49	35		0	0	2	4	0
8	64	11	121	88		9	81	10	100	90
9	81	11	121	99		6	36	7	49	42
10	100	10	100	100		12	144	10	100	120
1	1	6	36	6		3	9	2	4	6
4	16	7	49	28		5	25	10	100	50
10	100	12	144	120		13	169	15	225	195
9	81	12	144	108		2	4	0	0	0
8	64	13	169	104		6	36	7	49	42
12	144	14	196	168		12	144	13	169	156
13	169	18	324	234		6	36	10	100	60
2	4	10	100	20		11	121	10	100	110
12	144	17	289	204		4	16	3	9	12
11	121	10	100	110		9	81	8	64	72
						6	36	9	81	54

$\Sigma x_1 = 134 \quad \Sigma x_1^2 = 1290 \quad \Sigma y_1 = 186 \quad \Sigma y_1^2 = 2188 \quad \Sigma x_1 y_1 = 1624$

$\bar{x} = 7.44 \quad s_{x1}^2 = 17.20 \quad \bar{y}_1 = 10.33 \quad s_{y1}^2 = 15.64$

$N_1 = 18$

$\Sigma x_2 = 142 \quad \Sigma x_2^2 = 1334 \quad \Sigma y_2 = 154 \quad \Sigma y_2^2 = 1584 \quad \Sigma x_2 y_2 = 1415$

$\bar{x}_2 = 7.47 \quad s_{x2}^2 = 15.15 \quad \bar{y}_2 = 8.11 \quad s_{y2}^2 = 18.65$

$N_2 = 19$

Grand Total Pre $(\Sigma x) = \Sigma x_1 + \Sigma x_2 = 134 + 142 = 276$

Grand Total Post $(\Sigma y) = \Sigma y_1 + \Sigma y_2 = 186 + 154 = 340$

Grand Total Cross-Products $= (\Sigma xy) = \Sigma x_1 y_1 + \Sigma x_2 y_2 = 1624 + 1415 = 3039$

Total $N = N_1 + N_2 = 18 + 19 = 37$

7. Compute the Total $N = (N_1 + N_2)$.

8. Compute the Grand Total Cross-Products: Multiply each pretest (x) score by its corresponding posttest (y) score and add up the products (Σxy).

9. Compute the Grand Total Cross-Products ($\Sigma xy = \Sigma xy_1 + \Sigma xy_2$).

10. Compute the sum of squares between groups (SS_B) for the posttest as follows:

$$
\begin{aligned}
SS_B &= \frac{(\Sigma y_1)^2}{N_1} + \frac{(\Sigma y_2)^2}{N_2} - \frac{(\Sigma y)^2}{N} \\
&= \frac{(186)^2}{18} + \frac{(154)^2}{19} - \frac{(340)^2}{37} \\
&= 1922.00 + 1248.21 - 3124.32 \\
&= 45.89
\end{aligned}
$$

11. Compute the sum of squares within groups (SS_W) as follows:

$$
\begin{aligned}
SS_W &= [(N_1 - 1)\, s_{y1}^2] + [(N_2 - 1)\, s_{y2}^2] \\
&= [(17)(15.64)] + [(18)(18.65)] \\
&= 265.88 + 335.70 \\
&= 601.58
\end{aligned}
$$

12. Compute the total sum of squares (SS_T) as follows:

$$
\begin{aligned}
SS_T &= SS_B + SS_W \\
&= 45.89 + 601.58 \\
&= 647.47
\end{aligned}
$$

13. Compute the adjusted sum of squares within treatments (SS'_W) as follows:

$$
SS'_W = SS_W - \frac{\left(\Sigma xy - \dfrac{\Sigma x_1 \Sigma y_1}{N_1} - \dfrac{\Sigma x_2 \Sigma y_2}{N_2}\right)^2}{[(N_1 - 1)\, s_{x1}^2] + [(N_2 - 1)\, s_{x2}^2]}
$$

$$
\begin{aligned}
&= 601.58 - \frac{\left[3039 - \dfrac{(134)(186)}{18} - \dfrac{(142)(154)}{19}\right]^2}{[(17)(17.2)] + [(18)(15.15)]} \\
&= 601.58 - \frac{(3039 - 1384.67 - 1150.95)^2}{292.4 + 272.7} \\
&= 601.58 - \frac{(503.38)^2}{565.1} \\
&= 601.58 - 448.40 \\
&= 153.18
\end{aligned}
$$

14. Compute the adjusted total sum of squares (SS'_T) as follows:

$$
SS'_T = SS_T - \frac{\left(\Sigma xy - \dfrac{\Sigma x \Sigma y}{N}\right)^2}{\Sigma x_1^2 + \Sigma x_2^2 - \dfrac{(\Sigma x)^2}{N}}
$$

$$= 647.47 - \frac{\left[(3039) - \frac{(276)(340)}{37} \right]^2}{1290 + 1334 - \frac{(276)^2}{37}}$$

$$= 647.47 - \frac{(3039 - 2536.22)^2}{1290 + 1334 - 2058.81}$$

$$= 647.47 - \frac{(502.78)^2}{565.19}$$

$$= 647.47 - 447.26$$

$$= 200.21$$

15. Compute the adjusted sum of squares between treatments (SS'_B) as follows:

$$SS'_B = SS'_T - SS'_W$$
$$= 200.21 - 153.18$$
$$= 47.03$$

16. Compute degrees of freedom as follows:

   d.f. between groups $= K - 1 = 2 - 1 = 1$
   d.f. within groups $= N - K - 1 = 37 - 2 - 1 = 34$

17. Compute the adjusted mean square between groups (MS'_B) and the adjusted mean square within groups (MS'_W) as follows:

$$MS'_B = \frac{SS'_B}{K - 1} = \frac{47.03}{1} = 47.03$$

$$MS'_W = \frac{SS'_W}{N - K - 1} = \frac{153.18}{34} = 4.51$$

18. Compute F:

$$\frac{MS'_B}{MS'_W} = \frac{47.03}{4.51} = 10.43$$

19. Look up the criterion F for degrees of freedom (1, 34) in Appendix 3. The criterion for $p < .05$ is 4.17; for $p < .01$, it is 7.56. $F = 10.43$ exceeds either of these criteria, so $F (1, 34) = 10.43$, $p < .01$.

The ANCOVA is summarized in the following form:

Analysis of Covariance

Source of Variation	SS	d.f.	MS	F
Between Groups (treatments)	SS'_B	$K - 1$	$\dfrac{SS'_B}{K - 1}$	
Within Groups (error)	SS'_W	$N - K - 1$	$\dfrac{SS'_W}{N - K - 1}$	$\dfrac{MS'_B}{MS'_W}$
Total	$SS'_B + SS'_W$	$N - 2$		

FOR EXAMPLE 9–14:

Analysis of Covariance				
Source of Variation	SS	d.f.	MS	F
Between Groups (treatments)	47.03	1	47.03	
Within Groups (error)	153.18	34	4.51	10.43, p < .01
Total	200.21	35		

Analysis of Variance versus Analysis of Covariance

The capacity of analysis of covariance to increase the sensitivity of analysis is clearly illustrated by comparing the analysis of variance that would have been computed had the analysis used only the posttest data. The analysis of variance is summarized below.

Note that the analysis of variance does not even come close to statistical significance, much in contrast to the analysis of covariance on the same data. The difference in these outcomes derives primarily from removal of most of the student-to-student variation due to achievement differences at the pretest from the within groups (error) term. In general, analysis of covariance increases the sensitivity of an analysis to the degree that the covariate and the dependent variable are correlated. In this case, the covariate (pretest) and the dependent variable (posttest) are highly correlated ($r = .83$), which explains the dramatic difference between the results of the ANCOVA and those of the ANOVA. However, this high a correlation between pretest and posttest would not be unusual for reliable achievement tests.

As noted in Chapter 2, analysis of covariance can be used to make groups that are different on pretests or other covariates statistically equivalent. However, this works well only when the groups are not too far apart on the covariates. When groups are more than approximately one-half standard deviation apart on a pretest or other covariate, analysis of covariance will undercorrect for the difference, making the group that started higher appear to score better than it should. For this reason, results of analyses of covariance should be interpreted very cautiously when group differences on the covariate(s) are large (see Lord 1960).

FOR EXAMPLE 9–14:

Analysis of Variance				
Source of Variation	SS	d.f.	MS	F
Between Groups (treatments)	45.89	1	45.89	
Within Groups (error)	601.58	35	17.19	2.67, n.s.
Total	647.47	36		

Analysis of Covariance for More Complex Designs

Analysis of covariance can be used in any case in which analysis of variance can be used, including factorial designs with multiple treatments. However, complex analyses of covariance are difficult to compute by hand, so these formulas are not presented here. Chapter 10 describes the use of the SPSS computer programs ANOVA and MANOVA for computation of complex (as well as simple) analyses of variance and covariance.

CORRELATION

The concept of the correlation coefficient was presented in Chapter 4. In brief, a correlation coefficient (r_{xy}) expresses the degree to which two variables vary in the same (or opposite) direction. Correlation coefficients can range from -1 to $+1$, as follows:

-1.0	$-.8$	$-.6$	$-.4$	$-.2$	0	$+.2$	$+.4$	$+.6$	$+.8$	$+1.0$

When x is high,   No relationship   When x is high,
y is low, and ◄──────── between x and y ────────► y is high, and
vice versa   vice versa

Example 9–15 illustrates five correlations:

EXAMPLE 9–15

1		2		3		4		5	
x	y	x	y	x	y	x	y	x	y
1	5	1	3	1	5	1	2	1	1
2	4	2	4	2	1	2	1	2	2
3	3	3	5	3	2	3	5	3	3
4	2	4	1	4	3	4	4	4	4
5	1	5	2	5	4	5	3	5	5

Perfect Negative:	Moderate Negative:	No Relationship	Moderate Positive:	Perfect Positive:
$r_{xy} = -1.0$	$r_{xy} = -.5$	$r_{xy} = 0$	$r_{xy} = +.5$	$r_{xy} = +1.0$

Let's say a researcher wants to find out whether there is a relationship between the number of books students read at home on school days and the number of hours they spend watching television. He might ask a sample of 20 students to keep a log for five school days to record the number of books read and hours of television watched. The results of this survey are shown in Example 9–16.

EXAMPLE 9–16

Number of Books Read (x)		Hours of TV Watched (y)		
x	x^2	y	y^2	xy
0	0	8	64	0
0	0	10	100	0
0	0	6	36	0
0	0	7	49	0
1	1	8	64	8
1	1	11	121	11
1	1	9	81	9
1	1	7	49	7
1	1	10	100	10
1	1	6	36	6
2	4	3	9	6
2	4	4	36	8
2	4	8	64	16
2	4	0	0	0
2	4	3	9	6
2	4	6	36	12
3	9	1	1	3
3	9	6	36	18
4	16	2	4	8
4	16	3	9	12

$\Sigma x =$	32	$\Sigma x^2 =$	80	$\Sigma y =$	118	$\Sigma y^2 =$	884	$\Sigma xy =$ 140
$N =$	20	$s^2_x =$	1.52	$N =$	20	$s^2_y =$	9.88	
$\bar{x} =$	1.6	$s_x =$	1.23	$\bar{y} =$	5.9	$s_y =$	3.14	

To compute the correlation coefficients, follow these steps:

1. Compute the sum of each set of scores (Σx, Σy).
2. Square each score and sum the squares (Σx^2, Σy^2).
3. Count the number of scores in each group (N).
4. Compute the standard deviation for each group:

$$s = \sqrt{\frac{\Sigma x^2 - \frac{(\Sigma x)^2}{N}}{N-1}}$$

5. Compute the cross-products by multiplying each x score by its corresponding y score and sum the cross products (Σxy).
6. Calculate the correlation as follows:

$$r_{xy} = \frac{\Sigma xy - \frac{\Sigma x \Sigma y}{N}}{s_x s_y (N-1)}$$

For Example 9–16:

$$r_{xy} = \frac{140 - \dfrac{32 \times 118}{20}}{(1.23)(3.14)(19)}$$

$$= \frac{-48.8}{73.4}$$

$$= -.66$$

Thus, there appears to be a fairly strong negative correlation between books read and hours of television watched $(-.66)$. The more books students report reading, the fewer hours of television viewing they report, and vice versa. But is this correlation significantly different from zero? The next section shows how to test a correlation coefficient for statistical significance.

Testing a Correlation Coefficient for Statistical Significance

To test a correlation coefficient against the null hypothesis,

H_0: $r_{xy} = 0$,

follow these steps:

1. Compute t as follows:

$$t = \frac{r \sqrt{N-2}}{\sqrt{1-r^2}} \qquad \text{d.f.} = N - 2$$

For Example 9–16:

$$t = \frac{-.66 \sqrt{18}}{\sqrt{1 - (-.66)^2}}$$

$$= \frac{(-.66)(4.24)}{\sqrt{1 - (.436)}}$$

$$= \frac{-2.80}{0.75}$$

$$= -3.73 \qquad \text{d.f.} = 20 - 2 = 18$$

2. Compare the computed t to the criterion listed in the t table (Appendix 2) for $N - 2$ degrees of freedom (two-tailed). For $20 - 2 = 18$ degrees of freedom, the criterion for $p < .05$ is 2.10. For $p < .01$, it is 2.88. Since the obtained t (-3.73) exceeds these values (ignoring the sign), we can reject the null hypothesis that $r_{xy} = 0$. The negative correlation between books

read and hours of television watched is statistically significant at p < .01. That is, the more books a student reports reading on school days, the fewer hours of television he or she will report having watched.

Correlations with Categorical Variables

The above example illustrates a correlation between two *continuous* variables, which means that these variables (books read, hours of television watched) can take on any values within a certain range. However, we often wish to compute a correlation between one continuous variable and one categorical (or discrete) variable, which can take on only a limited set of values. For example, we might want to correlate students' SAT scores (a continuous variable) with a variable indicating whether or not their mothers went to college (a categorical variable). To do this, we arbitrarily assign one number to indicate that a student's mother did go to college and a different number to indicate that a student's mother did not attend college. Let's say we assign a 1 to indicate college attendance and a 0 for nonattendance. We might then have two sets of scores as follows:

Mother's College Attendance	Student's SAT Score
1	460
0	512
1	318
1	680
0	295
0	534
1	440
etc.	etc.

To compute the correlation, we would proceed just as in Example 9–16. A correlation between a dichotomous variable (a categorical variable with only two values) and a continuous variable is called a point-biserial correlation (see below).

Other Correlation Coefficients

All correlations can be computed using the formula presented above. However, there are different names used for correlations between different types of variables, and many statistics books give different formulas for these different correlations (although they are arithmetically equivalent to the formula presented above). These names are as follows:

Correlation Coefficient	Symbol	Use
Pearson product-moment	r	x and y are interval or ratio scales
Spearman rank-order	ρ or r_s	x and y are ordinal (ranked scores)
Point-biserial	r	x is interval or ratio score, y is dichotomous (yes-no, male-female, etc.)
Phi	ϕ	x and y are dichotomous

Chapter 10 describes SPSS computer programs for computing correlations. PEARSON CORR is used for Pearson product-moment correlations (and can be used for most other correlations as well). NPAR CORR translates scores into ranks, and then computes either the Spearman rank-order correlation or Kendall's Tau, a related statistic. Phi is an optional statistic in the CROSSTABS program.

Partial Correlation

As noted in Chapter 4, we often wish to explore correlations by *partialling out*, or controlling for, other variables that may cause the original correlation. For example, we might observe a correlation between students' popularity among their peers and their grades. There could be at least two plausible explanations for this: popular students might be attractive to teachers as well as to fellow students, and this may cause them to get better grades, or intelligent students may be more popular than less intelligent students, and their better grades could be a result of higher intelligence. We could explore the original correlation by computing a partial correlation between popularity (number of times a student was named as a friend by his or her classmates) and grade point average, partialling out student IQ.

The correlation matrix for such a study appears in Example 9–17.

EXAMPLE 9–17

	Popularity (x)	Grades (y)	IQ (z)
Popularity (x)	—	.32	.24
Grades (y)		—	.68
IQ (z)			—

To compute the partial correlation, use the following formula:

Correlation between x and y, partialling out z = $r_{xy \cdot z} = \dfrac{r_{xy} - r_{xz}r_{yz}}{\sqrt{1 - r_{xz}^2}\,\sqrt{1 - r_{yz}^2}}$

Using the correlation in Example 9–17:

$$r_{xy \cdot z} = \frac{.32 - (.24)(.68)}{\sqrt{1 - (.24)^2} \sqrt{1 - (.68)^2}}$$

$$= \frac{.32 - .16}{\sqrt{1 - .06} \sqrt{1 - .46}}$$

$$= \frac{.16}{(.97)(.73)} = \frac{.16}{.71}$$

$$= .23$$

Thus, the correlation between popularity and grades is still positive after partialling out the effect of IQ. We can test the partial correlation for statistical significance using a slight variation of the formula described earlier for testing correlation coefficients, with degrees of freedom for the t-test of N − 3. If there were 32 subjects in the study described above, the t-test would be as follows:

$$t = \frac{r \sqrt{N - 3}}{\sqrt{1 - r^2}}$$

$$= \frac{.23 \sqrt{32 - 3}}{\sqrt{1 - (.23)^2}}$$

$$= \frac{(.23)(5.4)}{\sqrt{1 - .05}}$$

$$= \frac{1.24}{.975}$$

$$= 1.27 \qquad \text{d.f.} = N - 3 = 29$$

Looking at the t-table in Appendix 2, it can be seen that the critical value of t (two-tailed) for d.f. = 29, p < .05, is 2.045. We cannot reject the null hypothesis, H_0: $r_{xy \cdot z} = 0$. That is, after partialling out IQ, there is no significant relationship between students' popularity and their grades. This result would suggest that high popularity does not cause high grades and high grades do not cause high popularity, but both grades and popularity are caused (at least in part) by a third variable, intelligence.

Chapter 10 describes an SPSS computer program, PARTIAL CORR, that computes partial correlations.

Linear and Nonlinear Relationships

One important assumption behind the computation of correlation coefficients is that the relationship between x and y is *linear*. If x and y are positively correlated, a higher value of x is associated with a higher value of y (on the average) at any point in the distribution. In a *curvilinear* relationship, higher values of x might be associated with higher values of y at some points in the distribution, but lower values of y at other points. Figure 9–8 illustrates linear and curvilinear relationships.

An example of a possible curvilinear relationship is effort and probability of success. Let's say a researcher told different groups of 30 students that she would reward the student(s) who had (a) the highest single quiz score (probability of success $= P_s = 1/30$); (b) the highest 5 scores ($P_s = 5/30$); (c) the highest 10 scores ($P_s = 10/30$); and so on, to the highest 29 scores ($P_s = 29/30$). We might expect that average effort would be low at $P_s = 1/30$, because less able students would know that they didn't have a chance to win, and also low at $P_s = 29/30$, because able students would know that they had little chance of losing. However, moderate levels of probability of success would be likely to motivate most students. This might produce data like the curvilinear pattern shown in Figure 9–8, where there is a positive relationship between probability of success and effort at low levels of P_s, and a negative relationship between P_s and effort at high levels of P_s. If you suspect a curvilinear relationship in a correlational analysis, graph the data to check out this possibility. The SPSS computer program SCATTERGRAM, described in Chapter 10, produces such graphs, called scatterplots. If there is a nonlinear relationship, the correlation coefficient is meaningless, but other statistics (such as the correlation between x and y^2) may be used to describe the relationship. See one of the statistics books listed at the end of this chapter for means of dealing with nonlinear relationships.

NONPARAMETRIC STATISTICS

As noted earlier in this chapter, one assumption behind the use of parametric statistics (such as t, F, and r) is that the variables involved are normally distributed. This assumption can be violated to some degree, but there are distributions that are so skewed (or non-normal) that parametric statistics should not be used. Also, parametric statistics cannot be computed on nominal or ordinal scales of measurement. There are nonparametric statistics that correspond to most parametric statistics but do not have such restrictive assumptions. Only one nonparametric test,

FIGURE 9–8   Linear, Curvilinear, and Zero Relationships

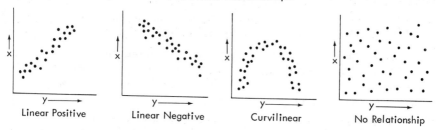

Linear Positive   Linear Negative   Curvilinear   No Relationship

chi square, is presented here; for others, see any of the statistics books listed at the end of this chapter. Also, Chapter 10 describes the SPSS program NPAR, which computes a variety of nonparametric statistics.

Chi Square (χ^2)

The most widely used nonparametric statistic is chi square, which is used whenever data are frequency counts, such as the number of individuals falling into a particular category. The variables in a chi square analysis are always categorical, which means that they can take on a limited set of values. Examples of categorical variables are sex (boy/girl), race (black/white/oriental), treatment (experimental/control), and so on. Continuous variables can be made into categorical variables by combining scores in a limited number of ranges. For example, age (a continuous variable because it can take on any non-negative value) can be made into a categorical variable by categorizing individuals as "9 years old or older" or "younger than 9 years old," or "less than 7," "7 to 9," or "older than 9." The limits for these categories depend on the purposes of the study, but they are often chosen so that an approximately equal number of cases will fall into each category. For example, if a continuous variable is reduced to two categories, the median might be a convenient break point, because half of all scores will be above and below the median. However, it may also be important to make categories that have theoretical or practical meaning, such as "below school age" (0 to 5), "school age" (6 to 12), "teen" (13 to 19), and "adult" (20 and over).

As an example of the use of chi square, consider a study comparing the numbers of times boys and girls who are high school sophomores visit their guidance counselors each year for personal problems. Such a study could not use parametric statistics, such as correlation or analysis of variance, because visits to guidance counselors for personal problems are far from normally distributed; most students never visit their counselors for personal problems, while a small minority do so quite frequently, creating a highly skewed distribution. Thus, we will reduce "counselor visits" to a categorical variable with three levels: no visits, 1 to 2 visits, or 3 or more visits. The data for this study might be as follows:

EXAMPLE 9-18

		Visits to Counselor for Personal Problems			
		0	1-2	3+	
Sex of Student	Boy	$OBS_{11} = 50$	$OBS_{12} = 50$	$OBS_{13} = 10$	$\Sigma r_1 = 110$
	Girl	$OBS_{21} = 30$	$OBS_{22} = 40$	$OBS_{23} = 20$	$\Sigma r_2 = 90$
		$\Sigma c_1 = 80$	$\Sigma c_2 = 90$	$\Sigma c_3 = 30$	$\Sigma x = 200$

The data presented in the six cells in Example 9–18 are frequency counts of all students falling into a particular combination of sex and counselor visits. The cell entries are the number of students "observed" in that category. For example, OBS_{11} is the number of boys (50) who never visited their counselor for a personal problem; OBS_{23} is the number of girls (20) who visited their counselor three or more times. There appears to be a relationship between sex and counselor visits; there are fewer girls than boys who never see a counselor for a personal problem, and more girls than boys who see a counselor at least three times in a year. To compute a chi square to test this, follow these steps.

1. Compute column totals and row totals by adding together the scores in each column or row:

$$\Sigma c_1 = OBS_{11} + OBS_{21}$$
$$\Sigma c_2 = OBS_{12} + OBS_{22}$$
$$\Sigma c_3 = OBS_{13} + OBS_{23}$$
$$\Sigma r_1 = OBS_{11} + OBS_{12} + OBS_{13}$$
$$\Sigma r_2 = OBS_{21} + OBS_{22} + OBS_{23}$$

2. Compute the total number of observations:

$$\Sigma x = \Sigma r_1 + \Sigma r_2 = \Sigma c_1 + \Sigma c_2 + \Sigma c_3$$

3. Make a table of *expected frequencies* by multiplying the column and row totals for each cell and dividing by Σx, as illustrated below:

	Column 1	Column 2	Column 3	
Row 1	$EXP_{11} = \dfrac{\Sigma r_1 \Sigma c_1}{\Sigma x}$	$EXP_{12} = \dfrac{\Sigma r_1 \Sigma c_2}{\Sigma x}$	$EXP_{13} = \dfrac{\Sigma r_1 \Sigma c_3}{\Sigma x}$	Σr_1
Row 2	$EXP_{21} = \dfrac{\Sigma r_2 \Sigma c_1}{\Sigma x}$	$EXP_{22} = \dfrac{\Sigma r_2 \Sigma c_2}{\Sigma x}$	$EXP_{23} = \dfrac{\Sigma r_2 \Sigma c_3}{\Sigma x}$	Σr_2
	Σc_1	Σc_2	Σc_3	Σx

For Example 9–18, expected frequencies are:

Expected Values	0	1-2	3+
Boys	$\dfrac{(110)(80)}{200} = 44.0$	$\dfrac{(110)(90)}{200} = 49.5$	$\dfrac{(110)(30)}{200} = 16.5$
Girls	$\dfrac{(90)(80)}{200} = 36.0$	$\dfrac{(90)(90)}{200} = 40.5$	$\dfrac{(90)(30)}{200} = 13.5$

4. Compute the chi square as follows:

$$\text{Chi Square} = \chi^2 = \Sigma \left(\frac{(OBS - EXP)^2}{EXP} \right)$$

That is, square the difference between the observed frequency and the expected frequency for each cell, divide by the expected frequency and add up the results for all cells to find the chi square.

For Example 9–18:

$$
\begin{aligned}
\chi^2 &= \frac{(50 - 44.0)^2}{44.0} + \frac{(50 - 49.5)^2}{49.5} + \frac{(10 - 16.5)^2}{16.5} \\
&\quad + \frac{(30 - 36.0)^2}{36.0} + \frac{(40 - 40.5)^2}{40.5} + \frac{(20 - 13.5)^2}{13.5} \\
&= .82 + .01 + 2.56 + 1.00 + .01 + 3.13 \\
&= 7.53
\end{aligned}
$$

5. Degrees of freedom for chi square are:

d.f. $= (r - 1)(c - 1)$.

For Example 9–18:

d.f. $= (2 - 1)(3 - 1) = 2$

6. Use Appendix 4 to find the critical value for a chi square with the given degrees of freedom. For d.f. $= 2$, the critical value for $p < .05$ is 6.0; for $p < .01$ it is 9.2. Since the obtained chi square is 7.53, we can reject the null hypothesis and conclude that sex is significantly related to counselor visits, $\chi^2_{(2)} = 7.53$, $p < .05$.

Two-by-Two Chi Squares

If there are two rows and two columns (that is, there is only one degree of freedom) in a chi square table, a slightly different formula should be used:

$$
\chi^2_{(1)} = \Sigma \left[\frac{(|OBS - EXP| - .5)^2}{EXP} \right]
$$

Where $|OBS - EXP| =$ The absolute value of the difference between each observed value and its corresponding expected value. "Absolute value" means that the sign is made positive whether it is positive or negative.

For example, let's say we wanted to know whether boys differ from girls in the degree to which they *ever* visit the counselor for a personal problem. We could collapse the "1–2" and "3+" cells in Example 9–18 and produce observed and expected frequencies as follows:

EXAMPLE 9–19

		Visits to Counselor						
		0	1+			0	1+	
Sex of Student	Boy	50	60	$\Sigma r_1 = 110$		44	66	110
	Girl	30	60	$\Sigma r_2 = 90$		36	54	90
		$\Sigma c_1 = 80$	$\Sigma c_2 = 120$	$\Sigma x = 200$		80	120	200
		Observed				Expected		

$$\chi^2 = \frac{(|50 - 44| - .5)^2}{44} + \frac{(|60 - 66| - .5)^2}{66} + \frac{(|30 - 36| - .5)^2}{36} + \frac{(|60 - 54| - .5)^2}{54}$$

$$= \frac{(6 - .5)^2}{44} + \frac{(6 - .5)^2}{66} + \frac{(6 - .5)^2}{36} + \frac{(6 - .5)^2}{54}$$

$$= .69 + .46 + .84 + .56$$

$$= 2.55$$

For d.f. = 1, the critical value for $p < .05$ is 3.8. Since the computed value does not exceed 3.8, we cannot reject the null hypothesis. There is no statistically significant difference between boys and girls in use or nonuse of counselors. Incidently, comparing the results of Examples 9–19 and 9–19, it might be suggested that the difference between boys and girls in Example 9–18 was substantially due to the higher proportion of girls who visit their counselor frequently (three times or more per year).

Chi square is an optional statistic in the SPSS computer program CROSSTABS, described in Chapter 10.

STATISTICS FOR RELIABILITY

As noted in Chapter 5, there are five primary measures of scale reliability; test-retest, parallel forms, split-half, KR 20, and coefficient alpha. Test-retest and parallel-forms methods employ correlations, described earlier in this chapter. This section presents methods for computing three internal consistency measures: KR-20, coefficient alpha, and split-half.

KR-20

KR-20 (named after the originators, Kuder and Richardson) is used to compute reliability when there are only two possible responses to each question (for example, right-wrong, agree-disagree). Let's say we gave a 10-item math test to 20 students. We would begin by listing the students' scores item by item with 1 representing a correct answer and 0 an incorrect answer. We would then list the total scores for each student as in Example 9–20.

EXAMPLE 9-20

Student	Item Number										Total x	x^2
	1	2	3	4	5	6	7	8	9	10		
1	1	0	1	1	0	1	0	1	1	0	6	36
2	1	1	1	1	1	1	1	1	0	1	9	81
3	1	1	1	1	1	1	1	1	1	1	10	100
4	0	1	0	1	0	1	0	0	0	0	3	9
5	1	1	0	1	0	0	0	1	0	0	4	16
6	1	1	1	1	1	1	1	1	1	1	10	100
7	1	1	1	1	0	1	1	1	1	0	8	64
8	1	1	1	1	1	1	0	1	1	0	8	64
9	0	1	0	1	0	1	0	0	0	0	3	9
10	1	1	1	1	0	1	1	1	1	0	8	64
11	1	0	0	1	0	0	0	0	0	0	2	4
12	1	1	1	1	1	1	1	1	1	1	10	100
13	1	1	1	1	1	1	1	1	1	1	10	100
14	1	1	1	1	1	1	1	1	0	1	9	81
15	0	1	1	1	0	1	1	1	1	0	7	49
16	0	1	1	1	0	1	0	0	0	0	4	16
17	1	1	1	1	1	1	1	1	1	0	9	81
18	0	1	1	0	0	0	0	1	0	0	3	9
19	1	1	1	1	1	1	1	1	0	0	8	64
20	1	1	1	1	1	1	1	1	1	1	10	100
Number of Correct Answers (C)	15	18	16	19	10	17	12	16	11	7	$\Sigma x = 141$	$\Sigma x^2 = 1147$

$$\bar{x} = 7.05 \quad s^2 = 8.05$$

$$N = 20$$

To compute KR-20, follow these steps:

1. Compute the sum of the total scores ($\Sigma x = 141$).
2. Square each score and sum the squares ($\Sigma x^2 = 1147$).
3. Count the number of scores ($N = 20$).
4. Compute the mean of the total scores:

$$\bar{x} = \frac{\Sigma x}{N} = \frac{141}{20} = 7.05$$

5. Compute the variance of the total scores:

$$s_x^2 = \frac{\Sigma x^2 - \dfrac{(\Sigma x)^2}{N}}{N - 1}$$

$$= \frac{1147 - \frac{(141)^2}{20}}{20 - 1}$$
$$= 8.05$$

6. For each item, count the number of individuals who got that item correct (C_1, C_2, etc.).
7. Square each C and sum the squares ($\Sigma C^2 = 2125$).
8. Count the number of items on the test ($I = 10$).
9. Compute KR-20 as follows:

$$KR\text{-}20 = \left(\frac{I}{I-1}\right)\left(1 - \frac{\overline{x} - \frac{\Sigma C^2}{N^2}}{s_x^2}\right)$$

$$= \left(\frac{10}{9}\right)\left[1 - \frac{7.05 - \frac{2125}{(20)^2}}{8.05}\right]$$

$$= (1.11)\left(1 - \frac{1.74}{8.05}\right)$$
$$= (1.11)\,(.784)$$
$$KR\text{-}20 = .870$$

A reliability coefficient of .870 would be considered adequate for research on achievement.

Coefficient Alpha

KR-20 is a simplification of *coefficient alpha*, which applies to reliabilities on scales where more than two responses are possible. For example, we might have a scale that uses responses "strongly agree," "agree," "disagree," and "strongly disagree." We might code "strongly agree" as 4, "agree" as 3, "disagree" as 2, and "strongly disagree" as 1, assuming that all items are phrased positively (in a "liking of school" scale, the statement "I *don't* like school" would be scored in reverse, with "strongly agree" coded as 1, "agree" as 2, etc.).

Computing coefficient alpha by hand is very tedious, but it can be done relatively easily with a calculator that computes variances. The formula is as follows:

$$\text{Coefficient Alpha} = \left(\frac{I}{I-1}\right)\left(1 - \frac{\Sigma s_I^2}{s_x^2}\right)$$

Where I = number of items in the scale
Σs_I^2 = sum of the variances of individuals' scores on each item in the scale
s_x^2 = variance of the individuals' scores on the total scale.

Split-half

Split-half reliability requires that half of the items on a scale be correlated with the other half. For example, scores could be computed on all even items and then for all odd items on a test for many subjects. Then a correlation between the two miniscales could be computed. Odd-even is not the only possible split; other methods, such as making matched pairs of items and then randomly assigning them (by coin flip) to one or another miniscale, are also permissible. Once the correlation between the two miniscales is determined, the following formula is computed:

$$\text{Split-half reliability} = \frac{2r_{xy}}{1 + r_{xy}}$$

Where r_{xy} = correlation between the two miniscales (for example odd items and even items)

For example, if the correlation between scores on odd-numbered items and even-numbered items is .70, split-half reliability would be as follows:

$$\text{Split-half reliability} = \frac{2r_{xy}}{1 + r_{xy}} = \frac{2 \, (.70)}{1 + (.70)} = \frac{1.40}{1.70} = .824$$

For more on statistics for reliability, see Cronbach (1970), Guilford and Fruchter (1978), or Stanley (1971).

STATISTICS TEXTS

This chapter only touches on the bare outlines of statistics for social science research. For additional information on statistics, see any of the following:

Cohen and Cohen (1975)
Edwards (1973)
Glass and Stanley (1970)
Guilford and Fruchter (1978)
Hopkins and Glass (1978)
Keppel (1982)
Pedhazur (1982)
Popham (1973)
Shavelson (1981)
Spence and others (1982)
Winer (1971)

EXERCISES

1) Indicate for each of the following scales whether the scale is likely to be a nominal, ordinal, interval, or ratio scale.
—achievement test scores
—scores on a self-esteem measure
—frequency counts of number of fights
—ranking of priorities for change within a school
—categorization of teachers by college or university where degree was granted.

2) The following data are from two 20-item science achievement tests.

Student	Test 1	Test 2	Student	Test 1	Test 2
1	10	19	11	9	17
2	13	14	12	8	18
3	9	18	13	10	17
4	11	19	14	6	20
5	9	18	15	12	12
6	11	16	16	12	16
7	10	20	17	14	20
8	8	19	18	10	11
9	7	19	19	11	19
10	10	20	20	11	16

  a) Calculate mean, mode, and median for both tests. What is the most appropriate measure of central tendency for each?
  b) Find the range for both tests.
  c) Use a graph to determine whether the scores are normally distributed for each test. Are they negatively or positively skewed?
  d) Find the standard deviation and variance for test 1.
  e) Convert students' scores on test 1 to z-scores.
  f) Assume that these 20 students are a sample drawn from a population of 2,000 students. Find the standard error of the mean for test 1, and identify the range of scores in which the "true mean" is likely to fall 95.4% of the time.

3) A teacher wishes to evaluate the effect on student absences of giving two different rewards (higher grades or weekly parties) for perfect attendance. She divides her class randomly into two groups, stratifying on number of absences to date. At the end of 8 months, she has the following data:

Group 1 (Grades)

(Student)	Absences
1	5
2	8
3	7

Group 2 (Parties)

(Student)	Absences
1	2
2	1
3	5

Group 1 (Grades)		Group 2 (Parties)	
(Student)	Absences	(Student)	Absences
4	4	4	0
5	6	5	4
6	8	6	0
7	9	7	3
8	4	8	4
9	5	9	1
10	7	10	2

The researcher uses a t-test to determine whether there are differences between the groups.

a) Should she use a t-test for matched or independent groups?

b) Should she use a one-tailed or two-tailed test of significance?

c) Determine whether the variances of the two groups are homogeneous.

d) Calculate the t-test and determine whether the groups are different at the .05 level of significance.

e) Describe the findings of the study.

4) A researcher wishes to determine the importance of individualization in math. He randomly assigns 30 students to one of three treatments. Scores on a math achievement test after 12 weeks are given below.

Whole Class Instruction	Ability Grouping	Individualized Instruction
13	22	22
19	24	20
18	23	21
17	25	19
15	20	20
17	22	18
18	23	21
16	21	17
16	23	20
17	19	19

a) Calculate the 3 × 1 ANOVA for these data, including degrees of freedom, and determine whether there are significant differences between the groups.

b) Describe the findings of the study.

5) An experiment was designed to determine whether the use of a microcomputer helps develop problem-solving skills. Pretests and posttests are presented for two randomly assigned groups. Use analysis of covariance (ANCOVA) to determine whether differences at $p < .05$ exist between the groups, controlling for pretests.

Problem-Solving Curriculum without Microcomputer		Problem-Solving Curriculum with Microcomputer	
Pre	Post	Pre	Post
15	19	14	19
14	18	12	15
15	20	15	17
17	21	16	22
16	19	14	18
19	22	15	19
13	17	18	21
15	20	13	16
14	17	14	18
16	19	13	17

6) A researcher wanted to find out whether there was a correlation between participation in sports activities and cross-race friendships. She asked students two questions: (1) Are you a member of a sports team? (2) Name your friends. Friendship choices were then classified as cross-race or same-race. The findings are presented below.

Student	Sports Team 1 = yes 0 = no	Number of Cross-Race Friends
1	1	2
2	1	3
3	0	2
4	1	4
5	0	1
6	0	0
7	1	2
8	1	3
9	1	1
10	0	1
11	1	3
12	0	1
13	0	0
14	1	4
15	0	2

a) What kind of correlation coefficient should be used to calculate the correlation?

b) Calculate the correlation and test it for significance.

c) Describe the results of the study.

7) A researcher wants to determine whether a home-visit follow-up program is effective in increasing attendance of very truant high school students. Sixty students were randomly assigned to home-visit follow-up or in-school follow-up groups. Because the distribution of number of absences was far from normal, she determined that a nonparametric statistic must be used. Number of unexcused

absences were reduced to three categories: 0 to 2, 3 to 6, 7 or more. The data are presented below:

	0-2	3-6	7+
Home-visit follow-up	16	8	6
In-school follow-up	8	10	12

    a) Compute the chi square.

    b) Recompute the chi square after collapsing the 0–2 and 3–6 categories into a single 0–6 category.

8) Compute KR-20 for the following 15-item self-esteem scale, which was given to ten students. Is the reliability adequate?

Item #

Student	1	2	3	4	5	6	7	8	9	10	11	12	13	14	15
1	1	1	1	1	0	1	0	1	1	1	0	0	1	1	1
2	1	0	1	1	1	0	1	1	1	0	1	0	0	0	0
3	1	1	0	1	0	1	0	0	0	1	1	0	0	1	0
4	1	1	1	1	1	1	0	1	1	0	1	1	1	0	1
5	0	1	0	0	0	1	0	0	1	1	0	0	0	1	0
6	0	1	1	0	0	1	0	1	1	0	1	0	0	0	0
7	1	1	1	1	1	1	1	1	1	1	1	1	0	0	1
8	0	1	1	0	0	0	0	0	1	0	0	0	0	0	0
9	1	1	0	0	1	1	0	1	0	0	1	1	1	1	1
10	1	1	1	1	1	1	1	0	1	1	1	0	0	1	1

chapter 10

Statistics by Computer

As noted in Chapter 9, the computer is the appropriate tool for all but the simplest analyses of data. Calculating statistics using the computer is faster and more accurate than computing statistics by hand or with a hand calculator. Use of the computer enables you to decide which statistics to use irrespective of computational difficulty. For example, analysis of covariance (ANCOVA) and multiple regression analyses have probably been underused in educational research in the past because they are difficult to calculate by hand, even though they are otherwise powerful statistical methods.

Using the computer for statistical calculations does not require knowledge of computers or computer programming. Virtually all colleges and universities have computers with "statistical package" software that facilitates the computation of most statistics. Dozens of such statistical packages exist; see Francis (1981) for descriptions of various statistical packages.

However, the great majority of computing facilities have access to SPSS (Statistical Package for the Social Sciences). SPSS is a comprehensive package of statistical programs, including all the statistics described in Chapter 9 (t-test, ANOVA, correlation, chi square, etc.) and many more. Although statistical packages, such as BMDP (Dixon and others 1981) and SAS (SAS Institute, Inc., 1982), are also widely used and may have advantages over SPSS for certain applications, this chapter is limited to consideration of using SPSS to analyze data from educational research.

This chapter provides an introduction to data analysis using SPSS. There are clearly written user's guides for SPSS (NIE 1975; Hull and Nie 1981) as well as special manuals for beginners (Klecka, Nie, and Hull

1975; Norusis 1982). This chapter is not intended to replace these manuals, but rather to supplement them by focusing on the most critical tasks involved in setting up data for analysis, preparing SPSS control cards, and conducting statistical analyses using SPSS.

The approach taken in this chapter is to focus on the easiest procedures that will work. There may be more efficient or more elegant ways of accomplishing certain tasks using SPSS; these are described in the SPSS user's guides.* However, by following the procedures outlined in this chapter in addition to the procedures clearly laid out in the SPSS user's guides for particular statistical analyses, you will be able to conduct almost every type of analysis available on SPSS.

Learning To Use Your Computing Facility

Your first task before beginning any computer analysis is to learn how your computing facility works. At some universities you are expected to submit your data and control cards (which instruct the computer as to what to do with the data) to a central computing facility. This is called a "batch" system. Your data and control cards may be on punched computer cards or on magnetic tape. In a batch system, you submit your cards or tape and wait for computer operators to process them. Other systems use terminals connected to a central processing unit. With terminals, you submit your job on the terminal, and you may either type in your data directly on the terminal or submit a tape or cards containing your data to the computing facility and enter the control cards or other instructions on the terminal. Every computing facility has some system of passwords, log-on procedures, job submittal forms, or other procedures to insure that only authorized individuals use the computer and to arrange for billing of users. You will need to learn how to enter, edit, and modify data and control cards in your particular system before you try to use a statistical package. Most computing facilities have manuals explaining these procedures and introductory classes in computer operation. The basic procedures can usually be learned in a couple of afternoons.

Data Preparation

Most data begin as a stack of tests, questionnaires, coding sheets, and so on. However, the computer needs to have data in special forms to be able to use it.

---

*For those who are familiar with SPSS, the most important omissions concern methods of creating system files (FILE NAME and SAVE FILE), creating subfiles, WRITE CASES, LIST CASES, and SORT CASES, formats other than fixed, format statements other than DATA LIST, file modifications, and EDIT.

Data are usually entered in one of two ways: punched on cards or entered on a terminal. If your data are to be punched on cards using a keypunch machine, you may do the keypunching yourself, or you may find a keypunching company to do it for you. Most university towns and many universities have commercial data services that will take data from coding sheets or questionnaires and put the data on cards or on magnetic tape. If you have a commercial service punch your cards, be sure to ask them to verify them. Verification involves punching the data twice and comparing the two sets to be sure there are no inaccuracies. This is expensive but essential, unless you are planning to check the data item by item yourself—a time-consuming, tedious, and error-prone process. If you keypunch cards yourself, you should verify them. Your university may have special equipment for verification, or you may need to punch the cards twice and have the two sets compared. Ask your computing facility staff for help with all aspects of data preparation.

You may be able to enter your data on terminals connected to a large computer. The process for this is similar to data entry using a keypunch machine; again, you will probably want to enter the data twice and have the computer compare the two sets of data as a means of detecting errors.

Procedures for data setup are presented in the following section.

Data Setup

Data for analysis using SPSS is usually organized in a "fixed" format, which means that the same variables always appear in the same columns. A "row" represents all variables for one subject. If data are on computer cards, up to 80 columns can be used on each card, so more than one card may be needed for each subject. Each variable may take up more than one column. Example 10–1 shows what a fixed-format data set would look like if there were fewer than 80 columns of data. Each line in Example 10–1 represents one physical card.

Example 10–1 illustrates the data setup for a study of mathematics achievement among eighth and ninth graders. The contents of each column are explained in the table at the bottom of the example. Note that a certain number of columns has been allocated to each variable—four for ID, one for grade level, three for grade equivalent, and two for each math test. The number of columns to reserve for each variable depends on the largest number of digits possible for that variable. For example, if we had an integer variable ranging from 1 to 99, we would reserve two columns; if it ranged from 1 to 100 we would need three columns.

Getting the numbers in the proper columns is critical. Unless instructed otherwise, SPSS reads blanks as zeros. If an integer variable is defined on a DATA LIST card (see below) as having two columns (that

EXAMPLE 10–1

Column	5	10	15	20	

Card 1	1101	9	08.5	12	19	B
Card 2	1102	8	10.3	07	16	C
Card 3	1103	8	11.1	18	25	A
Card 4	1104	9	07.6	09	15	C
Card 5	1105	8	09.0	11	23	A

.

.

.

Card N	6231	8	10.8	14	21	B

Columns	Contents
1-4	ID (number identifying each subject)
6	Grade level
8-11	Grade equivalent score, California Achievement Test—Mathematics Computations
13-14	Pretest (experimenter-made math test)
16-17	Posttest (experimenter-made math test)
19	Letter grade in math

is, two digits), the computer will consider the first column as the ten's place and the second as the one's place. Example 10–2 illustrates this. A variable has been defined as a two-digit integer in columns 1 and 2.

Cards 1 and 2 would be read as the value 1. However, Card 3 would be read as 10 (one ten, no ones). If the experimenter intended to put in a "1," he or she would have made an error by putting the "1" in the first column. For this reason, it is usually a good idea to put in leading zeros (for example, 08 rather than 8, 010 rather than 10, 003 rather than 3) to avoid making this common error. Looking back at Example 10–1, note that leading zeros have been included in the grade equivalent scores (columns 8–11, a four-column variable), and in the two-column math test scores. Grade level (column 6) is a one-column variable, so it does not need leading zeros. However, if tenth graders had been included in the study,

EXAMPLE 10–2

	Column				Computer
	1	2	3	4	Reads:
Card 1	0	1			1
Card 2		1			1
Card 3	1				10

grade level might have been defined as a two-column variable with possible values 08, 09, and 10.

Incidentally, the blanks between the variables indicated in Example 10–1 are not necessary for the computer; they simply make the data easier for you to read, an important consideration for punching or proofreading data cards.

The first four columns in Example 10–1 identify each subject. This identification is not absolutely necessary for all purposes, but it is almost always used as a way to link the computer file to the experimenter's stack of student tests, which would be marked with the same numbers. It is a good idea to assign ID numbers in a logical manner—the first number might indicate school, the second teacher, and the third and fourth the individual student in that teacher's class, with each of these factors listed in alphabetical order. For example, Arnold Aaron, a student in School 1 (Abington High School) with Teacher 1 at that school (Mr. Ackroyd) would be listed as 1101. Note that one digit is assigned to school and teacher, and two to student. This would work only if there are fewer than ten schools, fewer than ten teachers in each school, and fewer than 100 students in the same school with the same teacher. If we had 15 schools, as many as 53 teachers in the largest school, and as many as 123 students with the same teacher, we would have to allocate two columns for school, two for teacher, and three for student, so Arnold Aaron might be given an ID number as follows: 0101001, indicating School 01, Teacher 01, and Student 001. In allocating columns to decimal variables, you need to consider the largest number of total place values to be used, plus a column for the decimal points. For example, let's say your data included the following values: 12.1, 4.32, .621. Even though each of these would require four columns by itself, six place values are used (tens, ones, the decimal point, tenths, hundredths, and thousandths), so six columns would be needed. These values would be punched as in Example 10–3.

Again, the placement of the digits in the appropriate column is critical. A DATA LIST card (see below) would define column one as the ten's place, two as the one's place, and so on, so a value entered in the wrong column might be wrong by a factor of ten or more.

You need not actually punch in decimal points. The DATA LIST card (see below) can define some number of places in a particular variable as

EXAMPLE 10–3

	Column						
	1	2	3	4	5	6	...
Card 1	1	2	.	1	0	0	
Card 2	0	4	.	3	2	0	
Card 3	0	0	.	6	2	1	

lying to the right of the decimal point. For example, 19.73 and 7.42 could be entered as 1973 and 0742, and the DATA LIST card could indicate that two of the four digits are to the right of the decimal point.

Note that numbers are not the only information you may put on your data cards. Letters, symbols, and punctuation marks may also be used. For example, you might code the variable "sex" as "M" or "F." Variables in which letters and symbols are possible values are called "alphanumeric" variables. However, if you use alphanumeric variables in any analyses, you will have to recode them as numeric values later on. Hence, it is usually a good idea to code everything as numbers at the outset (for example, code male as "2," female as "1").

If you need more than one card for each subject, each card should begin with the subject's ID, followed by card number. In Example 10–4, card number is in column 5.

If your data are on tape or are input at a terminal, you need not use successive cards, as the record length (the number of columns for each subject) can be greater than 80.

In SPSS, you may define up to 500 variables. Up to 5,000 may be defined by use of special procedures explained in the SPSS manual. The SPSS program will read variables containing as many as six digits (not including decimal points and leading zeros).

As you code, set up, and keypunch your data, it is critical to document every decision you make. For example, you should record the columns each variable appears in, the kind of variable it is (for example, alphanumeric or numeric), the maximum and minimum possible values, whether you are using a decimal point or plan to have the DATA LIST card insert one, and so on. If you have decided on any arbitrary codes, you should record them (for example, male = 2, female = 1; Treatment A = 1, Treatment B = 2, control = 3). If you have established any decision rules to deal with certain problems, record these. For example, you might decide that if a subject gives two different answers to the same question, you will code the response as a missing value and leave it blank. You might decide to use a numeric code to indicate missing responses (for example, 1 = yes, 2 = no, 9 = missing). If so, you should record this. There is no way to be too organized when preparing data for a computer; careful organization and documentation at the outset will save time and errors in the long run.

EXAMPLE 10–4

```
           0 0 0 0 0 0 0 0 0 1 1 1 1 1 1 1 1 1 1 2 2 2 2 2 2 2 2 2 2 3
           1 2 3 4 5 6 7 8 9 0 1 2 3 4 5 6 7 8 9 0 1 2 3 4 5 6 7 8 9 0 . . .
Card 1   Subject 1   3 3 0 1 1 AL VAR E Z , MARI A      8 . 7      1 4
Card 2               3 3 0 1 2   1 8 . 3   9 8   4 2   7 1 1
Card 3   Subject 2   3 3 0 2 1 AXE L ROD , GE RAL D      9 . 4      0 7
Card 4               3 3 0 2 2   2 1 . 7   4 2   3 2   6 1 4
```

SPSS CONTROL CARDS

The control cards tell the SPSS program how to read your data, where the variables are and what they are called, how to modify the variables or select certain cases for various analyses, and which statistical procedures to use to analyze your data.

SPSS control cards consist of a control word or words in columns 1–15, and specifications in columns 16–80 or beyond.

Data Definition Cards

A series of control cards tell the computer how to read and label your variables. Example 10–5 presents data definition cards that would accompany the data presented in Example 10–1. Each control card is then discussed in detail.

EXAMPLE 10–5

1	16
RUN NAME	JUNIOR HIGH MATH STUDY
DATA LIST	FIXED(1)/1 ID 1-4, GRADE 6, CAT 8-11, PRE 13-14, POST 16-17, LETGR 19 (A)
INPUT MEDIUM	CARD
N OF CASES	177
RECODE	LETGR ('A'=5) ('B'=4) ('C'=3) ('D'=2) ('F'=1) (ELSE=−99)
RECODE	GRADE TO LETGR (BLANK=−99)
MISSING VALUES	GRADE TO LETGR (−99)

RUN NAME. The RUN NAME simply identifies the SPSS control card file. Whatever you list as the RUN NAME will be printed on each page of output.

DATA LIST. The DATA LIST card tells the computer the names of your variables and where they are located. Before you prepare the DATA LIST card, you must choose names for your variables. These are up to you, but the names must follow certain rules:

1. They may be no more than eight characters.
2. They must start with a letter, not a number or other character.
3. They must not contain a blank or punctuation mark (only letters and numbers are permissible).

It is a good idea to choose names that have some meaning to you, so that you can remember what they mean. Example 10–6 lists several correct and incorrect variable names.

EXAMPLE 10-6

Illegal Variable Name	Permissable Variable Name	Reason for Illegality
Names	Names	
MATH TEST	MATHTEST	Blank in name
SELF-RATE	SELFRATE	Dash in name
8DAY	DAY8	Begins with number
BIRTHWEIGHT	BIRTHWT	Too long
TRIAL (4)	TRIAL4	Punctuation mark in name

Start the DATA LIST card as follows:

```
1           16
DATA LIST   FIXED (N)/1
```

where N is the number of cards for each subject. In this example, there is only one card per subject. The "1" after the slash indicates that the list of variables to follow pertains to Card 1. For this example, the DATA LIST card would begin as follows:

```
1           16
DATA LIST   FIXED(1)/1
```

After this, simply list the variable names, followed by the beginning and ending columns for each variable, separated by a dash (for example, 1-4, 6-8, etc.). If there are any one-column variables, just indicate the column (for example, GRADE 6). If the variable is alphanumeric (a letter or symbol rather than a number*), the variable name must be followed by the column number(s) and then the letter A in parentheses:

LETGR 19 (A)

Example 10-5 illustrates the completed DATA LIST card for the data in Example 10-1.

If there were more than one data card, the last variable on Card 1 would be followed by a slash and a 2 (/2), indicating that the next set of variables appears on Card 2. For example, the DATA LIST for the data presented in Example 10-4 might be as follows:

EXAMPLE 10-7

```
1           16
DATA LIST   FIXED(2)/1 ID 1-4, AGE 23-25, PRETEST 28-29/2
            QUIZAV 7-10, READ 12-13, POSTTEST 15-16,
            TOTAL 18-20
```

*If a variable can have both letters and numbers as values, it is also considered alphanumeric.

Note that not all the variables on the data cards must be identified on the DATA LIST card; you list only the variables you intend to use. In Example 10–4, students' names were listed on the data cards, but since names cannot be directly used in statistical analyses, "name" was not defined as a variable in Example 10–6. The computer simply skips over any undefined columns as if they were blank.

It is not actually necessary to punch decimal points on decimal variables. The values 12.2, 9.8, and 8.75 could be punched in Columns 1–4 as follows:

```
Column
1 2 3 4 5 . . .

1 2 2 0
0 9 8 0
0 8 7 5
```

To indicate where the decimal point should be placed, you may use a number in parentheses to indicate how many numerals are to the right of the decimal point. In the above example, the decimal point would go between Columns 2 and 3, so there are two numerals to the right of the decimal point. The DATA LIST for this variable (which we will call QUIZAV) would be as follows:

```
1              16
DATA LIST      FIXED(1)/1 QUIZAV 1–4 (2),. . . .
```

It is often the case that you will have a long string of single column or two-column variables punched together. For example, let's say you gave a 50-item questionnaire consisting of statements with which students might agree (coded 2) or disagree (coded 1). We might call the 50 variables corresponding to responses to the 50 questions Q1, Q2, Q3, etc., up to Q50. The 1's and 2's are punched in columns 11 to 60. The DATA LIST card for this could be as follows:

```
1              16
DATA LIST      FIXED(1)/1 Q1 11, Q2 12, . . . Q49 59, Q50 60
```

However, there is a shortcut. If a string of variables all fill exactly the same number of columns and are not separated by blanks, you may simply list the variables (without commas) and indicate the columns in which the entire string appears, as follows:

```
1              16
DATA LIST      FIXED(1)/1 Q1 Q2 Q3. . . . . . . . . . . .Q49 Q50 11–60
```

The above notation could be used in any case where you have many variables that occupy the same number of columns punched together. The computer takes the total number of columns you defined (for example, 11-60 defines 50 columns) and divides by the number of variables you named to determine how many columns each variable occupies. However, in this particular case, an even shorter shortcut is possible. Because the end of each variable name is a number (Q1, Q2, etc.), the computer will fill in the variable names in sequence for you if you use a DATA LIST card of the following type:

```
1              16
DATA LIST    FIXED(1)/1 Q1 TO Q50 11-60
```

Use of the keyword TO in this case causes the computer to define variables Q1, Q2, Q3, and so on, just as in the above examples.

Figure 10-1 summarizes the major features of the DATA LIST card.

INPUT MEDIUM

The INPUT MEDIUM card indicates where the data are located. If the data are on physical cards *or* if the data are together with the SPSS control cards (even if they are typed in on a terminal or submitted on a tape), INPUT MEDIUM is CARD. If the data are on a tape separate from the SPSS control cards, INPUT MEDIUM is TAPE. In most cases when you are using a terminal rather than batch processing, your data will be on a disk, in which case INPUT MEDIUM is DISK. If you are not submitting a stack of cards containing the SPSS control cards and your data or submitting the SPSS control cards and data together on a tape or terminal,

FIGURE 10-1   SPSS Control Cards: DATA LIST

1 16	Interpretation
DATA LIST FIXED(1)	All data are on one card
DATA LIST FIXED(2)	Data occupy 2 cards
DATA LIST FIXED(2)/1	Data occupy 2 cards; variables following /1 are on Card 1
DATA LIST FIXED(2)/1 ABC 1-5 DEF 6-10, . . . /2 XYZ 1-8. .	Data occupy 2 cards, variables following /2 are on Card 2
DATA LIST FIXED(1)/1 ID 1-4	Numeric variable ID is in Columns 1-4 on Card 1
DATA LIST FIXED(1)/1 ID 1-4, LETGR 19 (A)	Alphanumeric (letter or symbol) variable LETGR is in Column 19 on Card 1
DATA LIST FIXED(1)/1 ID 1-4, Q1 Q2 Q3 Q4 11-14	Numeric variables Q1, Q2, Q3, Q4 each occupy one column in Columns 11-14
DATA LIST FIXED(1)/1 ID 1-4, Q1 TO Q4 11-14	Same meaning as above; computer infers Q2 and Q3 from use of keyword TO
DATA LIST FIXED(1)/1 ABC 1-3(1), . . .	Variable ABC is punched in Columns 1-3 without a decimal point, but a decimal point is implied between Columns 2 and 3 (for example, 378 is read as 37.8)

you will need to check with your computing facility to find out how to link the control cards with the data.

The possibilities for INPUT MEDIUM cards are summarized in Figure 10–2.

N OF CASES

The N OF CASES card informs the computer how many *cases* (subjects) to expect. Note that this is cases, not cards. If you had two cards for each of 134 subjects, N OF CASES would be 134, not 268.

If your data are on tape or disk (anything other than cards), you may enter N OF CASES as UNKNOWN. Figure 10–3 summarizes the possibilities for the N OF CASES card.

RECODE: Alphanumeric Variables and Blanks

RECODE is described in the SPSS user's guide not as a data definition card, but as a data modification card (see below). However, one or more recodes are usually needed as part of the initial data definition setup, so basic RECODE procedures are described here.

Recoding alphanumeric variables as numbers.   One common use of RECODE is to convert alphanumeric variables (letters and symbols) to numbers. The computer cannot, of course, do arithmetic with letters, so it is necessary to recode all alphanumeric variables you plan to use in analyses as numbers.

In SPSS, whenever you refer to an alphanumeric value, it must be surrounded by apostrophes (for example, 'X,' 'Y,' '%,' etc.).*

To recode a single alphanumeric variable as a numeric variable, make a RECODE card that indicates the name of the variable, followed

---

*If you have an alphanumeric variable that may take on number and letter values, the numbers must also be surrounded by apostrophes (for example, '3').

FIGURE10–2   SPSS Control Cards: INPUT MEDIUM

1	16	Application
INPUT MEDIUM	CARD	SPSS control cards and data are submitted *together* on cards, terminal, or tape.
INPUT MEDIUM	TAPE	SPSS control cards are submitted on cards or terminal, but data are on a separate tape; ask your computing facility staff for assistance.
INPUT MEDIUM	DISK	SPSS control cards are submitted on cards or terminal, but data are on disk; ask your computing facility for assistance.
INPUT MEDIUM	OTHER	Ask your computing facility staff for assistance if your data are on any medium other than cards, tape, or disk.

FIGURE 10–3   SPSS Control Cards: N OF CASES

1	16	
N OF CASES	NNN	If data are on cards, indicate exact number of cases (subjects).
N OF CASES	UNKNOWN	If data are on tape or disk, you need not know in advance how many cases you have.

by the letter code surrounded by apostrophes, an equal sign, and its numeric equivalent, all in parentheses. For example, let's say we have a variable SEX, which is listed on our data cards as F or M. We decide to code F as "2" and M as "1" (the choice of numbers is arbitrary). The necessary card for this conversion is shown below.

```
1          16
RECODE     SEX('F'=2)('M'=1)
```

The keyword ELSE.   The above RECODE would work if every subject were coded as F or M. However, if we suspect that there might be blanks or mispunches, we can prepare for this by defining anything other than F or M as a missing value (see below). Let's say we decide to assign a value of −99 to all missing values (this number is arbitrary, and can be any number that is not a possible value of a variable; see MISSING VALUES, below). We could do this using the keyword ELSE, as follows:

```
1          16
RECODE     SEX('F'=2)('M'=1)(ELSE=−99)
```

ELSE can also be used for other purposes. Let's say we had an alphanumeric variable RACE with subjects coded W, B, H, A, etc. If our only interest in the analyses were to contrast white (W) with nonwhite, we could recode RACE as follows:

```
1          16
RECODE     RACE('W'=2)(ELSE=1)
```

Recoding multiple variables.   If we have several alphanumeric variables to recode, we may simply include one RECODE card for each. However, if the recodes to be done are the same for several variables, we can combine them in a single card. For example, let's say we have students' grades in math (MATHGR), reading (READGR), science (SCIGR), and social studies (SSGR). We want to recode the letter grades as numbers, with A equal to 5, B equal to 4, and so on. This could be done by listing the variables (separated by commas) on one RECODE card, followed by the recode specifications common to all of the variables, as follows:

```
1          16
RECODE     MATHGR,READGR,SCIGR,SSGR('A'=5)('B'=4)('C'=3)
           ('D'=2)('F'=1)(ELSE=-99)
```

The keyword TO. The SPSS program remembers the variables you defined on the DATA LIST card in the order you defined them. When you must do the same thing to many variables defined together on the DATA LIST card, you can save time and trouble by using the keyword TO between the first variable defined the last one, instead of listing each variable. For example, the recode of various grades illustrated above could have been done as follows (assuming that MATHGR, READGR, SCIGR, and SSGR were defined in that order on the DATA LIST card with no other variable intervening):

```
1          16
RECODE     MATHGR TO SSGR ('A'=5)('B'=4)('C'=3)
           ('D'=2)('F'=1)(ELSE=-99)
```

Recoding blanks as missing values. One very important use of the RECODE card is to define blanks as missing values. If there are blanks in any of your variables, they will be read by the computer as zeros. Unless you intend blanks to be zeros, you must recode them as missing values. As noted previously, you will designate a number that is not a possible value of your variables (for example, −99) as a missing value indicator. You may then define blanks as missing values as follows:

```
1          16
RECODE     GRADE TO POST (BLANK=-99)
```

This would recode any blank on variables listed on the DATA LIST card between GRADE and POST (inclusive) as a −99. The MISSING VALUES card will then inform the computer that −99 indicates a missing value.

As described in the above section on the DATA LIST card, the computer will infer variable names ending with numbers if you use the keyword TO, as in Q1 TO Q50. RECODE may also use this keyword, as follows:

```
1          16
RECODE     Q1 TO Q50 (BLANK=-99)
```

MISSING VALUES

In social science research (particularly educational research), it is common to have problems getting complete data from every subject involved in your study. For example, if your study involves a reading test, an aptitude test, and an attitude scale, some subjects will typically complete one or two of these but not all three, due to absence or other factors. In preparing your data, you may leave the space for such missing values blank. However, the computer will read blank values as zeros and include them as such in all calculations unless you instruct it otherwise. The way to do this is first to use a RECODE card to give blanks some numeric value that is not a legitimate value of your variables (for example, −99), and then to use a MISSING VALUES card to inform the computer that whenever it sees that number, it indicates a missing value. The computer will then delete that case from its computations. The MISSING VALUES cards corresponding to the recodes discussed earlier are shown in Example 10.8.

```
EXAMPLE 10–8
1                    16
MISSING VALUES    SEX (–99)
MISSING VALUES    MATHGR TO SSGR (–99)
MISSING VALUES    GRADE TO POST (–99)
MISSING VALUES    Q1 TO Q50 (–99)
```

Note that the keyword TO is used in three of the above examples to indicate that for all variables listed on the DATA LIST card from MATHGR to SSGR, from GRADE to POST, and from Q1 to Q50 (inclusive), the missing value indicator is −99.

It is also possible to punch missing value indicators on the data cards when they are first made. For example, you might code responses to questions in an interview as follows:

Do you intend to stay in teaching until you reach retirement age?

Responses	Code
Yes	1
No	2
Not sure	3
No response	4

In this case, you might decide to define values of 3 or 4 ("Not sure" or "No response") for the variable STAYTCH as missing values, as follows:

```
1                    16
MISSING VALUES    STAYTCH (3,4)
```

This would cause the computer to exclude any cases containing codes 3 or 4 from calculations involving STAYTCH.

If a set of 50 questionnaire items were coded 2 (agree), 1 (disagree), or 9 (no response), the following MISSING VALUES card might be used:

```
1                    16
MISSING VALUES       Q1 TO Q50 (9)
```

Figure 10–4 summarizes the use of the MISSING VALUES card, including combinations of RECODE and MISSING VALUES.

FIGURE 10–4   SPSS Control Cards: RECODE and MISSING VALUES

1	16	Interpretation
MISSING VALUES	STAYTCH (3,4)	For the variable STAYTCH, values 3 and 4 are to be considered missing.
MISSING VALUES	Q1 TO Q50 (9)	For variables Q1, Q2, . . . Q50, the value 9 is to be considered missing.
RECODE	GRADE (BLANK=−99)	For the variable GRADE, blanks are
MISSING VALUES	GRADE (−99)	to be recoded as −99 and then considered missing.
RECODE	SEX ('M'=2) ('F'=1) (ELSE=−99)	The alphanumeric (letter) variable
MISSING VALUES	SEX (−99)	SEX is to be recoded M=2, F=1; any other letter, number, or blank is to be recoded −99 and considered missing.

Data Modification Cards

After the variables are defined, missing values identified, and alphanumeric variables recoded as numeric ones, you may need to make modifications in your variables, such as further recoding, forming scales by adding up values, deleting certain cases, and so on. These data modifications are discussed in this section.

RECODE. The RECODE card was discussed earlier as a means of handling alphanumeric variables and blanks. However, RECODE can be used for other purposes as well. For example, RECODE is often used to recode a continuous variable as a discrete one. Let's say we wished to recode the variable AGE (a continuous variable, because it can take on an infinite number of values) as a discrete variable with only three values: 0–12 (children), 13–19 (teenagers), and 20–99 (adults). We might do this using a RECODE card as follows:

```
1         16
RECODE    AGE (0 THRU 12=1) (13 THRU 19=2) (20 THRU 99=3)
```

Note that the keyword THRU was used in each case to indicate that all values between the two endpoints (and including the endpoints themselves) are to be recoded as indicated. The same recode could have been done using the keywords LOWEST and HIGHEST, as follows:

```
1               16
RECODE          AGE (LOWEST THRU 12=1)(13 THRU 19=2)
                (20 THRU HIGHEST=3)
```

RECODE is also often used to "collapse" some number of categories into a smaller number of categories. For example, suppose we had an interview item as follows:

When you leave school at 3:00, where do you go on most days?

Code

1. Straight home.
2. To a babysitter's house
3. To a day-care program
4. To a relative's house
5. To an after-school instructional program
   (such as music lessons, religious
   studies, or gymnastics)
6. To an organized activity (such as
   Boy Scouts, Girl Scouts, or
   school clubs)

The responses to this question could be recorded in six categories, but the researcher might only be interested in three possibilities: students who go home, students who go to some kind of child care, and students who go to an organized activity of some sort. To reduce the data to those three categories, the researcher might use the following RECODE card:

```
1               16
RECODE          AFTSCH (1=1)(2,3,4=2)(5,6=3)
```

The recodes described above are permanent data modifications, and apply to all operations following the recode card. Temporary re-codes(*RECODE) are discussed later in this chapter.

COMPUTE. It is often useful to modify variables numerically or to form scales out of several variables. This is the purpose of the COMPUTE card. For example, let's say we had a 20-item questionnaire, and we wished to form a scale, SCALE1, by summing the first five questionnaire items, Q1 to Q5. This would be done as follows:

```
1               16
COMPUTE         SCALE1=Q1+Q2+Q3+Q4+Q5
```

The new variable, SCALE1, would simply be the sum of the five indicated items (previously defined on the DATA LIST card). However, this would be insufficient if any of the variables being added had blank or missing values. If blanks have not been recoded as missing values, blanks will be treated as zeros; if they have been recoded, the missing value indicator will be added in. To avert this, you should almost always use an ASSIGN MISSING card along with a COMPUTE. This instructs the computer that if any of the variables that go into a sum, product, etc., are missing, the sum or product itself should also be given the missing value indicator defined previously on the MISSING VALUES card. For example, let's assume that the MISSING VALUES card had defined the missing values indicator for all questionnaire items as -99:

```
1                16
MISSING VALUES   Q1 TO Q20 (-99)
```

The COMPUTE and ASSIGN MISSING cards would then appear together as follows:

```
1                16
COMPUTE          SCALE1=Q1+Q2+Q3+Q4+Q5
ASSIGN MISSING   SCALE1(-99)
```

Variables may also be modified by a number rather than another variable. For example, if we wanted to create a new variable, PLUS5, by adding five to TESTSCOR, the COMPUTE card would be as follows:

```
1                16
COMPUTE          PLUS5=TESTSCOR+5
ASSIGN MISSING   PLUS5(-99)
```

Other commonly used COMPUTE operations are listed in Figure 10–5.

IF. The IF card is used to perform operations or calculations if certain conditions are satisfied. For example, let's say we have done an

FIGURE 10–5 SPSS Control Cards: Operations with COMPUTE

Symbol	Meaning	Example
+	Addition	SUM=Q1+Q2
−	Subtraction	DIFF=Q1−Q2
*	Multiplication	PROD=Q1*Q2
/	Division	DIV=Q1/Q2
**	Exponent	CUBE=Q1**3 (i.e., Q1 cubed)
SQRT	Square Root	ROOT=SQRT(Q1)
LN	Natural Logorithm	LOGN=LN(Q1)
LG10	Log Base 10	LOG=LG10(Q1)
RND	Round to nearest whole number	ROUND=RND(Q1)
TRUNC	Truncate (delete numbers after decimal point)	WHOLEND=TRUNC(Q1)

experiment in which some teachers have been in the experimental group and others in the control group. We gave the teachers ID numbers from 01 to 12 if they were in the experimental group and 13 to 24 if they were in the control group. The following IF statements would create a new variable, TRT (treatment) depending on values of TCHID (Teacher ID):

```
1     16
IF    (TCHID LE 12) TRT=1
IF    (TCHID GE 13) TRT=2
```

The keywords LE and GE mean "less than or equal to" and "greater than or equal to," respectively. The two IF cards would give the value 1 to TRT if the teacher ID number were less than or equal to 12, and 2 if the teacher ID number were greater than or equal to 13. A complete list of these keywords appears in Figure 10–6.

The computer reads the logical statements in each IF statement and decides whether or not they're true. If so, it performs the indicated operation; if not, it does nothing. For example, let's say we have student ages and birthdays and want to update the ages three months later. We have coded BMONTH (birthmonth) as 01=JAN., 02=FEB., etc. Since the initial study was done on September 30, all students who have their birthdays in October, November, or December will be a year older three months later. We will create a new variable, DECAGE (age at the end of December) from BMONTH and SEPTAGE (age at end of September) as follows:

```
1     16
IF    (BMONTH EQ 10 OR 11 OR 12) DECAGE=SEPTAGE+1
IF    (NOT(BMONTH EQ 10 OR 11 OR 12)) DECAGE=SEPTAGE
```

Note that more than one possible value is permitted by the use of

FIGURE 10–6   SPSS Control Cards: Keywords with IF and SELECT IF

Relation	Keyword	Example
Equal to	EQ	(AGE EQ 9)
Not equal to	NE	(AGE NE 9)
Greater than	GT	(AGE GT 9)
Greater than or equal to	GE	(AGE GE 9)
Less than	LT	(AGE LT 9)
Less than or equal to	LE	(AGE LE 9)
AND (two statements must be true)	AND	(AGE LT 9 AND SEX EQ 2)
OR (either of two statements must be true)	OR	(AGE LT 9 OR SEX EQ 2)
NOT (the following statement must not be true)	NOT	(NOT (AGE EQ 9 or 10))

the keyword OR. The use of the keyword NOT simply says that the indicated operation should be performed only if the following statement is *false*.

The same transformation could have been made with either of the following pairs of IF cards:

```
1    16
IF   (BMONTH GT 9)DECAGE=SEPTAGE+1
IF   (BMONTH LT 10)DECAGE=SEPTAGE

IF   (BMONTH GE 10)DECAGE=SEPTAGE+1
IF   (BMONTH LE 9)DECAGE=SEPTAGE
```

As with COMPUTE, it is usually a good idea to include an ASSIGN MISSING card with any IF statements. This will avert errors that might come about if missing values were taken at face value in analyses. For the above example, the ASSIGN MISSING card might be as follows:

```
1                 16
ASSIGN MISSING    DECAGE(−99)
```

Complex IF statements can be used with careful placement of parentheses. For example, let's say we wished to create a variable RELHT (relative height) depending on students' heights (HT) and sex. Boys (SEX=2) taller than 66 inches and girls (SEX=1) taller than 62 inches are to be coded RELHT=2, and shorter boys and girls are to be coded RELHT=1. The following cards would accomplish this:

```
1                 16
IF                (((SEX EQ 2) AND (HT GT 66)) OR
                  ((SEX EQ 1) AND (HT GT 62)))RELHT=2
IF                (((SEX EQ 2) AND (HT LE 66)) OR
                  ((SEX EQ 1) AND (HT LE 62))) RELHT=1
ASSIGN MISSING    RELHT (−99)
```

Note that the number of left and right parentheses must be the same.

Data Selection Cards

SELECT IF. It is often important to be able to select certain cases for separate analysis. This selection is usually accomplished by means of a SELECT IF card. SELECT IF uses the same keywords as IF (see Figure 10–6). Only those cases for which the statement on the SELECT IF card is true will be included in subsequent analyses. For example, let's say we wanted to perform a separate analysis on boys (SEX=2). We might do this as follows:

```
1          16
SELECT IF  (SEX EQ 2)
```

In an earlier example, experimental teachers were given codes from 1 to 12, while control teachers were given code numbers 13 to 24. If we wished to perform analyses on the control teachers *only*, we might use the following card:

```
1            16
SELECT IF    (TCHID GE 13)
```

If you wish to exclude certain cases, it is often easiest to use the keyword NOT. For example, if we wanted to exclude students who had Teacher 14 and Teacher 15, we might use the following:

```
1            16
SELECT IF    (NOT(TCHID EQ 14 or 15))
```

As with IF, SELECT IF statements may be quite complex. It is critical that the number of left and right parentheses balance.

SELECT IF is a permanant data selection card, applying to all operations following it. Temporary data selection (*SELECT IF) is discussed later in this chapter.

Task Definition Cards

After you have defined your variables, made any necessary modifications, and selected the cases to include in analyses, you are finally ready for the analyses themselves. Actually, the task definition cards are the easiest part of SPSS for most beginners; new SPSS users usually have more problems with the initial data definition, modification, and selection cards than with the task definition cards. For this reason, and because there are too many SPSS task definition cards to present in limited space, this chapter presents only a few examples of task definition cards, and directs the reader to the SPSS user's guide (Nie and others 1975) and the *SPSS Update 7-9* manual (Hull and Nie 1981) for more on these procedures.

STATISTICS and OPTIONS.   Most SPSS procedures have a variety of statistics available in addition to or instead of statistics ordinarily printed out as output. Also, most procedures have options concerning how data are to be read and processed, how results are to be presented, and so on. These are different for each procedure, and are clearly listed at the end of each section of the SPSS manuals referring to the procedure. To use optional STATISTICS and OPTIONS, place these cards immediately after the procedure described. Examples of STATISTICS and OPTIONS cards appear in Example 10–9 and in the descriptions of procedures that follow. Note that the keyword ALL may be used to request all statistics or options.

EXAMPLE 10–9

```
1             16
STATISTICS    1
STATISTICS    3,5,8
STATISTICS    ALL
OPTIONS       7
OPTIONS       1,2,4
OPTIONS       ALL
```

FREQUENCIES.   FREQUENCIES is a procedure that gives the number of cases taking on a particular value for a specified variable. Optional statistics available with FREQUENCIES include the mean, standard deviation, and median. FREQUENCIES can be run in the GENERAL mode or the INTEGER mode. The INTEGER mode takes less computer time, but is somewhat more difficult to set up and definitely more difficult to describe. Therefore, this chapter presents only the GENERAL mode. In GENERAL mode, the control cards for FREQUENCIES on a single variable, NSIBS (number of siblings) would be as follows:

```
1             16
FREQUENCIES   GENERAL=NSIBS
STATISTICS    1,3,5,6
```

Note that the STATISTICS card is not required, but it is commonly used with FREQUENCIES. The statistics requested are the mean, median, standard deviation, and variance (see Nie and others 1975, 201). These control cards would produce a listing of the number of students categorized as having no brothers or sisters, one sibling, two siblings, and so on. To run FREQUENCIES on more than one variable at a time, you may use a list of variables as follows:

```
1             16
FREQUENCIES   GENERAL=SEX,RACE,NSIBS
```

If the variables are together in order on the DATA LIST card, the keyword TO can be used:

```
1             16
FREQUENCIES   GENERAL=SEX TO NSIBS
```

BREAKDOWN.   This procedure constructs tables breaking down one variable by other variables. For example, we might want a table of INCOME broken down by SEX, RACE and years of education (YRED). BREAKDOWN, like FREQUENCIES, can be run in GENERAL or INTEGER mode. In GENERAL mode, the BREAKDOWN card might be as follows:

```
1                16
BREAKDOWN       TABLES=INCOME BY SEX BY RACE BY YRED
```

This procedure would produce a table showing the average income for every combination of sex, race, and years of education (YRED), such as for white men with 1-8 years of education, Hispanic women with 12-15 years of education, and so on. Again, a variable list can be used instead of a variable name. For example, we might have wanted separate breakdowns of INCOME and YRED by sex and race. These tables could have been produced with the following card:

```
1                16
BREAKDOWN       TABLES=INCOME,YRED BY SEX BY RACE
```

T-TEST. Let's say we wished to compare the means of two independent samples to see if the difference between them is statistically significant. As indicated in Chapter 9, we would use a t-test to do this. If we were comparing an experimental group (TRT=2) to a control group (TRT=1) on a measure of mathematics achievement (MATHACH) and a measure of mathematics attitudes (MATHATT) the T-TEST card would look like this:

```
1         16
T-TEST    GROUPS=TRT/VARIABLES=MATHACH,MATHATT
```

Following the word GROUPS appears the grouping variable (experimental versus control, male versus female, etc.), and following the word VARIABLES appear the variables on which the groups are to be compared.

If we wished to conduct a paired t-test, the procedure card might be as follows:

```
1         16
T-TEST    PAIRS=POST WITH PRE
```

This would compare each student's posttest with his or her own pretest. The keyword WITH would appear between each pair of variables being compared on the same subjects.

ANOVA. Analyses of variance and analyses of covariance are easily done in SPSS. Let's say we were comparing three experimental treatments in terms of their effects on language arts posttest achievement (LANGPOST), self-concept (SELFCON), and attitudes toward English class (ENGATT). The three treatments are coded 1, 2, and 3. The ANOVA comparing all three treatments on all variables might use the following card:

```
1          16
ANOVA      LANGPOST,SELFCON, ENGATT BY TRT (1,3)
```

Note that the range of values for the independent variable, treatment (TRT), must be specified in parentheses after the variable name.

Analysis of covariance is also done with ANOVA, using the keyword WITH. For example, if we wished to compare the language arts posttests (LANGPOST) across the three treatments controlling for language arts pretest (LANGPRE), the ANOVA card might be as follows:

```
1          16
ANOVA      LANGPOST BY TRT(1,3) WITH LANGPRE
```

Factorial designs are also easily analyzed in ANOVA. For example, a factorial analysis of covariance with factors treatment (TRT) and SEX might be done as follows:

```
1          16
ANOVA      LANGPOST BY TRT(1,3), SEX(1,2) WITH LANGPRE
```

This card would conduct a 3 × 2 (treatment × sex) analysis of covariance. The analysis would automatically include TRT and SEX main effects, as well as a TRT by SEX interaction term (see Chapter 9 for more on analysis of variance and covariance).

PEARSON CORRelation. Computing a simple Pearson product-moment correlation (see Chapter 9), or even a correlation table showing many individual correlations, is easy using SPSS. A correlation between two variables, reading score (READ) and math score (MATH), would be set up using the following card:

```
1               16
PEARSON CORR    READ WITH MATH
```

If we had several variables from which we wished to make a correlation matrix, we would list the variables, write WITH, and list the variables again, as follows:

```
1               16
PEARSON CORR    READ,MATH,LANG,SS,SCI WITH READ,
                MATH,LANG,SS,SCI
```

This would produce a 5 × 5 correlation matrix showing the correlations between every possible pair of variables.

As before, if these variables were located together on the DATA LIST card, we might produce the same table of correlations as follows:

```
1               16
PEARSON CORR    READ TO SCI WITH READ TO SCI
```

Other Procedures

Figure 10–7 lists the names and functions of the statistical procedures available in SPSS and described in the SPSS user's guide (Nie and others 1975). The figure also lists the page numbers on which the procedures are explained. Figure 10–8 lists the names and functions of additional procedures introduced in *SPSS Update 7-9* (Hull and Nie 1981), which are currently available on most computing facilities that have SPSS. In Figures 10–7 and 10–8, statistical procedures beyond the scope of this book (such as REGRESSION, DISCRIMINANT, FACTOR, and GUTTMAN SCALE) are listed but not extensively described. See any of the statistics books listed at the end of Chapter 9 or the SPSS user's guides themselves for descriptions of these statistical procedures.

FIGURE 10–7   Descriptive List of SPSS Statistical Procedures Described in Nie and others (1975)

Procedure	Pages in Nie and others	Description
AGGREGATE	203-217	Computes descriptive statistics for collections of individuals, such as students in classrooms and schools; forms new aggregated variables, such as class or school means
ANOVA	398-433	Computes analyses of variance and analyses of covariance (see Chapter 9).
BREAKDOWN	249-266	Computes means, standard deviations, and other statistics on variables broken down by other categorical variables (for example, academic achievement broken down by student sex and grade level).
CANCORR	515-527	Computes canonical correlations and outputs canonical variate scores.
CONDESCRIPTIVE	181-193	Computes descriptive statistics (mean, standard deviation, skewness, etc.).
CROSSTABS	218-248	Shows numbers of cases falling into certain categories. For example, a 2 x 2 crosstab might be treatment (experimental versus control) and sex (boy versus girl); this would produce four cells. CROSSTAB also computes chi square and related statistics (see Chapter 9).
DISCRIMINANT	434-467	Computes discriminant analyses.
FACTOR	468-514	Computes factor analyses.
FREQUENCIES	194-202	Shows number of cases having each value of a discrete (categorical) variable. Also computes mean,

(continued)

FIGURE 10–7   Descriptive List of SPSS Statistical Procedures Described in Nie and others (1975) (Cont.)

Procedure	Pages in Nie and others	Description
		median, mode, standard deviation, and other statistics (see Chapter 9).
GUTTMAN SCALE	528-539	Builds and evaluates Guttman Scales.
NONPAR CORR	288-292	Computes Spearman and Kendall rank-order (nonparametric) correlation coefficients.
ONEWAY	422-433	Computes one-way analyses of variance, tests for trends, a posteriori contrasts, and homogeneity of variance statistics.
PARTIAL CORR	305-319	Computes partial correlations (see Chapter 9).
PEARSON CORR	276-288	Computes Pearson (parametric) correlation coefficients (see Chapter 9).
REGRESSION	320-367	Computes multiple regression analyses, where the effects of many independent variables on one dependent variable may be assessed.
SCATTERGRAM	293-300	Prints a graph showing relationship between two variables (see Chapter 9).
T-TEST	267-275	Computes t-tests (see Chapter 9).

FIGURE 10–8   Descriptive List of Statistical Procedures Described in Hull and Nie (1981) (SPSS Update 7–9)

Procedure	Pages in Hull and Nie	Description
BOX-JENKINS	80-93	Analyzes time series data (see Chapter 3 of this book).
MANOVA	1-79	Computes analyses of variance, analyses of covariance, and multivariate analyses of variance. Allows for many analyses not available on ANOVA, such as repeated measures, hierarchical designs, multiple dependent variables, and other designs relating to analysis of variance and analysis of covariance.
MULT RESPONSE	240-247	Facilitates handling of questionnaire data where multiple responses are possible for each question (for example, "What do you feel are the most important problems facing this school district?").

(continued)

FIGURE 10–8   Descriptive List of Statistical Procedures Described in Hull and Nie (1981) (SPSS Update 7–9) (Cont.)

Procedure	Pages in Hull and Nie	Description
NPAR	220-239	Computes a variety of nonparametric statistics (for example, sign test, Wilcoxin test, Mann-Whitney U, Kruskal-Wallis test).
RELIABILITY	248-267	Computes coefficient alpha and KR-20, as well as other reliability estimates. Also computes repeated measures analyses of variance (but MANOVA is better for this).
SURVIVAL	205-219	Facilitates survival analysis, such as considerations of various factors affecting the length of time a student will stay in school before dropping out.
New SPSS Graphics Procedures:	122-165	
BARCHART		Draws bar charts.
LINECHART		Draws line charts.
PIECHART		Draws pie charts.

SPSS Update 7–9

SPSS is continually being updated to respond to user needs and suggestions. The primary SPSS user's guide (Nie and others 1975) was Release 6 in a series of versions of SPSS. As of this writing, three additional releases are available, numbers 7 to 9. Not all computing facilities have the new programs installed; check to be sure before using features in the updated versions.

Most of the procedures listed in Figure 10–7 were modified to some degree in the updated version of SPSS. In most cases, one or two additional options or statistics were added, minor changes in formulas or computational procedures were made, and so on. See Hull and Nie (1981) for descriptions of these changes. Figure 10–8 lists completely new procedures available on facilities that have the SPSS updated programs, and gives the page numbers in Hull and Nie (1981) on which the procedures are explained.

Temporary Data Modification and Data Selection

Most of the data modification and data selection cards can be used in two ways: as permanent modifications (changes apply to all operations that follow the data modification or data selection card) or as temprorary modifications (changes apply only to the next procedure). Temporary data modification and selection cards are preceded by an asterisk (*) as follows:

```
1
*RECODE
*COMPUTE
*IF
*SELECT IF
```

For example, let's say we gave a questionnaire consisting of statements with responses "strongly agree" (coded 4), "agree" (coded 3), "disagree" (coded 2), and "strongly disagree" (coded 1). We might wish to analyze the effect of treatment (TRT) on responses to the statement, "I like this class" (LIKECL), using a *t*-test. We might also wish to conduct the same analysis, recoding "strongly agree" and "agree" as 2, and "disagree" and "strongly disagree" as 1. This could be done with the following control cards:

```
1              16
*RECODE        LIKECL (3,4=2)(1,2=1)
T-TEST         GROUPS=TRT/VARIABLES=LIKECL
T-TEST         GROUPS=TRT/VARIABLES=LIKECL
```

Because the *RECODE applies only to the next operation (the first T-TEST), this set of control cards would produce a *t*-test assessing the effect of TRT on the *recoded* LIKECL, and then a second *t*-test on the unaltered LIKECL.

Probably the most common use of temporary data modification and selection cards is *SELECT IF. For example, let's say we wished to compute correlations between reading achievement (READ) and mathematics achievement (MATH) separately for boys (SEX=2) and girls (SEX=1), and then we wanted the correlation between READ and MATH for all children in our sample taken together. The following cards would produce these correlations:

```
1              16
*SELECT IF     (SEX EQ 2)
PEARSON CORR   READ WITH MATH
*SELECT IF     (SEX EQ 1)
PEARSON CORR   READ WITH MATH
PEARSON CORR   READ WITH MATH
```

Again, note that the *SELECT IF applies only to the next procedure. The final PEARSON CORR would not be influenced by either *SELECT IF, so it would include all subjects.

READ INPUT DATA and FINISH Cards

A READ INPUT DATA card must appear immediately after the first procedure you request, including any STATISTICS and OPTIONS cards. If your data are together with your control cards (that is, INPUT MEDIUM is CARD), the data are stacked (or typed) immediately following the READ INPUT DATA card. If your data are on tape or disk separately from your control cards (that is, INPUT MEDIUM is TAPE or DISK), the READ INPUT DATA card must still be included after the first procedure card(s).

Any additional procedure cards after the first one are placed after the data (or after the READ INPUT DATA card if the data are in a separate location). At the end of all procedures, a FINISH card indicates that your job is complete. If there is only one procedure, the FINISH card goes at the end of the data cards.

Example 10–10 illustrates several uses of the READ INPUT DATA and FINISH cards.

EXAMPLE 10–10

For data on cards or typed with control cards:

```
1                    16
ANOVA                POST BY TRT (1,2) WITH PRE
STATISTICS           1
READ INPUT DATA
1101  12  14
1102  09  16
. . . .   . .   . .
. . . .   . .   . .
. . . .   . .   . .
FINISH


T-TEST               GROUPS=TRT/VARIABLES=LIKECL,LIKESCH
READ INPUT DATA
1101  3.2  5.3
1102  2.6  3.4
. . . .   . . .   . . .
. . . .   . . .   . . .
. . . .   . . .   . . .
FREQUENCIES          GENERAL=TRT,GRADE,LIKECL,LIKESCH
STATISTICS           ALL
FINISH
```

For data in separate location (tape or disk):

```
PEARSON CORR         Q1 TO Q5 WITH Q1 TO Q5
STATISTICS           1
OPTIONS              3
READ INPUT DATA
BREAKDOWN            TABLES=Q1 TO Q5 BY SEX BY GRADE
STATISTICS           1
FINISH
```

Elaborated Example of SPSS Control Cards

Example 10–11 shows the complete set of control cards that might have been used in an experiment testing the effects of three treatments (peer tutoring, individualized instruction, and control) on the mathematics achievement of eighth and ninth graders. Posttest mathematics achievement was measured in three ways. Students took the California Achievement Test (CAT) and an experimenter-made math test (POST) at the end of the study, and students' letter grades in math (LETGR) were used as an indication of mathematics performance. The experimenter-made math test was also given at the beginning of the study (PRE), and scores on this test were used as covariates to control for initial student ability and knowledge.

EXAMPLE 10–11

Card #	1	16
1	RUN NAME	JUNIOR HIGH MATH STUDY
2	DATA LIST	FIXED(1)/1 ID 1-4, GRADE 6, CAT 8-11, PRE 13-14, POST 16-17,
3		LETGR 19 (A)
4	INPUT MEDIUM	CARD
5	N OF CASES	177
6	RECODE	LETGR ('A'=5) ('B'=4) ('C'=3) ('D'=2) ('F'=1) (ELSE= −99)
7	RECODE	GRADE TO LETGR (BLANK= −99)
8	MISSING VALUES	GRADE TO LETGR (−99)
9	IF	(ID LT 4000) TRT=1
10	IF	((ID GT 4000) AND (ID LT 7000)) TRT=2
11	IF	(ID GT 7000) TRT=3
12	COMPUTE	GAIN=POST−PRE
13	ASSIGN MISSING	TRT,GAIN (−99)
14	ANOVA	CAT,POST,LETGR BY TRT (1,3) WITH PRE
15	STATISTICS	1
16	READ INPUT DATA	
17	1101 9 08.5 12 19 B	
18	1102 8 10.3 07 16 C	
19	1103 8 11.1 18 25 A	
..	....	
..	....	
193	9924 8 10.8 14 21 B	
194	*SELECT IF	(GRADE EQ 8)
195	ANOVA	CAT,POST,LETGR BY TRT (1,3) WITH PRE
196	STATISTICS	1
197	*SELECT IF	(GRADE EQ 9)
198	ANOVA	CAT,POST,LETGR BY TRT (1,3) WITH PRE
199	STATISTICS	1
200	*SELECT IF	((PRE NE −99) AND (CAT NE −99) AND (POST NE −99)
201		AND (LETGR NE −99))
202	BREAKDOWN	TABLES=PRE,CAT,POST,LETGR,GAIN BY GRADE BY TRT
203	FINISH	

The meanings of the control cards shown in Figure 10–12 are explained in the following section.

1. RUN NAME. This card simply identifies the study. This label will be printed on each page of the output.

2–3. DATA LIST. These cards identify the locations of the variables on the data cards, gives them names, and identifies any alphanumeric (letter) variables. For example, LETGR 19(A) indicates that LETGR is an alphanumeric variable in column 19.

4. INPUT MEDIUM. This card indicates that the data are located on the same medium (cards, tape, disk) as the SPSS control cards.

5. N OF CASES. This card indicates that there are 177 cases.

6. RECODE. This card recodes the letter values of LETGR as numeric values.

7. RECODE. This card recodes blanks as −99. The following MISSING VALUES card will inform the computer that −99 indicates a missing value.

8. MISSING VALUES. This card defines −99 as a missing value indicator.

9–11. IF. These three IF statements define a new variable indicating which treatment (TRT) students received. Students in the peer tutoring group were given ID numbers from 1101 to 3999; those in the individualized instruction group from 4101 to 6999; and those in the control group from 7101 to 9999. The IF statements use GT (greater than) and LT (less than) operators to identify the students in each treatment group.

12. COMPUTE. This card creates a new variable (GAIN) by subtracting PRE from POST.

13. ASSIGN MISSING. This card gives a value of −99 (the missing value indicator) to TRT if ID is missing, and to GAIN if either PRE or POST is missing.

14. ANOVA. This card calls for three analyses of covariance; CAT controlling for PRE, POST controlling for PRE, and LETGR controlling for PRE.

15. STATISTICS. This card asks that a multiple classification analysis be printed along with the usual ANOVA statistics. This shows deviations of each treatment mean from the overall mean after adjustment for the covariate(s) and other independent variables. Use of this card is optional.

16. READ INPUT DATA. This card goes after the first procedure (including any STATISTICS or OPTIONS). It tells the computer that the following cards will be data cards. If the data were on tape or disk, the READ INPUT DATA card would go in the same location, but the data would not actually appear among the control cards.

17– 193. Data cards. Since the data in this example are on cards, these cards are stacked immediately after the READ INPUT DATA card.

194. *SELECT IF. This card informs the computer that the next procedure to follow will use only subjects for whom GRADE is 8. This is a temporary data selection card, so it applies to only one procedure (the ANOVA).

195– 196. ANOVA-STATISTICS. These cards repeat the analyses of covariance, but for the eighth graders only.

197– 199. *SELECT IF-ANOVA-STATISTICS. These cards perform the same analyses of covariance, but for ninth graders only.

200–
201. *SELECT IF. These cards select only cases without any missing values for PRE, CAT, POST or LETGR. This ensures that for the BREAKDOWN (Card 202), the number of cases for each variable is the same, and is the same as the number of cases in the analysis of variance (which includes only cases with no missing values on any of the variables listed on the ANOVA card).

202. BREAKDOWN. This card calls for computation of the mean and standard deviation of each of the indicated variables (PRE, CAT, POST, LETGR, and GAIN), broken down by GRADE and by TRT.

203. FINISH. This card informs the computer that your job is complete.

EXERCISES

1) Complete the following exercises using this data set, which comes from an experiment evaluating a new curriculum. Treatment 1 was the control group; Treatment 2 was the new curriculum. Variable names are in parentheses.

Col. 1-3	Col. 5	Col. 7	Col. 9	Col. 11-14	Col. 16-19
ID	Treatment	Sex	Grade	Pretest	Posttest
(ID)	(TRT)	(SEX)	(GRADE)	(PRETEST)	(POSTTEST)
101	1	M	4	(missing)	06.1
102	1	F	4	05.3	08.7
103	1	F	4	05.2	07.4
104	1	M	4	07.8	10.6
105	1	M	3	04.9	07.5
106	1	F	4	05.4	08.9
107	1	M	4	06.7	09.5
108	1	F	3	03.6	06.8
109	1	M	3	04.4	08.8
110	1	M	4	06.9	10.3
201	2	M	4	06.0	09.2
202	2	M	3	04.5	10.2
203	2	F	4	05.0	(missing)
204	2	M	4	07.5	11.9
205	2	F	4	05.1	09.4
206	2	F	3	04.7	09.6
207	2	F	4	06.6	10.0
208	2	M	4	07.8	12.1
209	2	F	3	03.2	07.3
210	2	M	4	05.3	08.7

a) Set up the basic data description cards: RUN NAME, DATA LIST, INPUT MEDIUM, and N OF CASES. Assume that the data are on cards.

b) Modify the sex codes so that males are coded as 0, females as 1.

c) Change blanks (missing data) to a numeric code (−99) and designate that code as a missing value.

d) Using SPSS, compute the number of males and females in each treatment group. Compute the number of students in each grade within each treatment group as well. Use FREQUENCIES and at least one *SELECT IF card.

e) Find the mean and standard deviation for the pretest and posttest for each treatment group. Use BREAKDOWN.

f) Conduct a *t*-test to determine whether differences exist between the groups at posttest.

g) Use analysis of covariance, using pretest as the covariate, to determine whether differences exist at posttest.

h) Describe the findings of the experiment.

2) Complete the following exercises on these data, which simulate a study of teacher evaluations. Assume that the data are on cards. Variable names are in parentheses.

Col. 1-2 Teacher	Col. 4 Urban or Rural School	Col. 6-7 Years of Experience Teaching	Col. 9 Principal's Evaluation	Col. 11-12 Other Teacher's Evaluation	Col. 14 Student Evaluation
(ID)	(LOCATION)	(EXPERNCE)	(EVALPRIN)	(EVALTCH)	(EVALSTU)
1	R	12	7	14	3
2	R	2	4	8	2
3	R	3	5	8	2
4	U	5	5	4	3
5	U	6	8	15	2
6	U	4	(missing)	9	3
7	R	10	9	15	2
8	U	(missing)	6	10	3
9	R	3	2	3	1
10	U	9	6	7	2
11	U	4	5	9	1
12	U	7	5	16	2
13	U	1	6	11	3
14	R	5	3	2	1
15	R	8	6	(missing)	3
16	R	3	4	10	(missing)
17	U	19	9	12	2
18	R	4	6	9	2
19	U	22	9	17	3
20	R	5	4	11	1

a) Complete the data definition cards using −99 to indicate missing data. Compute a correlation matrix showing the correlations between the three evaluation methods. Use OPTIONS 3 to request a two-tailed test of significance. Describe the pattern of correlations.

b) Add all three evaluations together to form one scale (call it OVERALL), and compute the correlation between years of experience in teaching and the overall evaluation scale you have constructed. Use OPTIONS 3 to request a two-tailed test of significance.

c) Compute the correlation between years of experience and overall evaluation score for urban and rural teachers separately. Evaluate the significance of the correlation. Use OPTIONS 3 for a two-tailed test.

d) Collapse years of experience in teaching into three categories: 1–3 years, 4–6 years, and more than 6 years. (Use GE and LE only.) Call this variable LONGEVTY. Compute the correlation between the collapsed years of experience variable and the overall evaluation scale. Use OPTIONS 3. Evaluate the statistical significance of the correlation. Describe the findings.

chapter 11

Writing Up the Project:

Dissertations and Articles

CLARITY AND COMPLETENESS

The last stage in conducting a research project is writing the report. This is one of the most critical steps in the research process, and it is the most difficult for many.

Writing a dissertation or an article requires adherence to a well-defined set of guidelines concerning format and style. However, within these constraints, your goal as a writer of a research report is like that of any writer of nonfiction: to make the information you present as clear, complete, and convincing as possible. This means emphasizing main points, writing in a plain-spoken manner, and avoiding unnecessary detail, jargon, and overly technical or scientific-sounding language. In a word, your task is to write something from which readers will learn and which readers will enjoy. You will also want to adopt a scientific writing style of modesty, moderation, and objectivity. You want to convince your readers that you set out to learn about your topic, not to "prove" one theory or another.

WRITING A DISSERTATION

Format and Style

Every university has its own rules concerning dissertation format and other elements of style. Of course, you will want to obtain a copy of these rules. In addition, you should locate several recent dissertations from your department and look them over as examples of format and style. You might ask your adviser to suggest one or two recent dissertations that he or she thought was outstanding. As to fine points on preparing the manuscript, your department will probably direct you to a style manual, such as Turabian (1973), *The Chicago Manual of Style* (1982), or the *Publication Manual of the American Psychological Association* (1983). The style manuals and the university guidelines cover all details concerning typing of the manuscript, references and citations, figures, headings, footnotes, and so on; hence these topics are not discussed here.

The parts of a dissertation are mostly standard from university to university. A representative outline is presented below:

Title Page
Acknowledgements
Table of Contents
List of Tables
List of Figures
Chapter 1: Introduction
  The Problem
  Hypotheses
  Significance of the Problem
  Definitions of Terms
Chapter 2: Review of Literature
Chapter 3: Methods
Chapter 4: Results
Chapter 5: Discussion
References
Appendixes

Title page.   Choosing an appropriate title for the dissertation is a very important task, as it is the primary indication of the contents for others who might use it. The title should be short but should communicate what the study was about, avoiding unfamiliar terms or excessive detail. Look through journals and other dissertations for examples of good titles. A few are listed below:

"Effects of Effort Attributional Feedback on Children's Perceived Self-Efficacy and Achievement." (Schunk 1982)

"Relationship between Academic Tracking and Degree of Interracial Acceptance." (Schwartzward and Cohen 1982)

"Teacher-Pupil Relationships in the Elementary School: Teacher-Gender and Pupil-Gender Differences." (Stake and Katz 1982)

The title should be limited to what was actually done in the study. For example, let's say a study of the relationship between third graders' average grades and their scores on a questionnaire scale measuring achievement motivation found no relationship between these measures after IQ was partialled out (see Chapter 4). Titles such as "Are Grades Really Necessary?" or "Grades and Motivation" would both communicate too little and claim too much. A more appropriate title might be "The Relationship between Grades and Achievement Motivation among Suburban Third Graders."

Again, details of how to prepare the title page vary from university to university. An example of a title page from one recent dissertation is presented in Figure 11–1.

FIGURE 11–1   Example of a Title Page for a Dissertation

EFFECTS OF COOPERATIVE LEARNING ON THE SOCIAL

ACCEPTANCE OF MAINSTREAMED ACADEMICALLY

HANDICAPPED STUDENTS

by

Nancy A. Madden

Submitted to the

Faculty of the College of Arts and Sciences

of The American University

in Partial Fulfillment of

the Requirements for the Degree

of

Doctor of Philosophy

Signatures of Committee:

Chair:_____

_____   _____

Dean of the College   _____

_____

Date

1980

The American University

Washington, DC 20016

Acknowledgements.   On this page, you may acknowledge everyone who helped you get to this point in your educational career. This might include teachers, administrators, or others who helped you collect your data; your dissertation adviser and other faculty members who gave you important advice; and any personal acknowledgements you might want to make—to your parents, spouse, children, or even the sixth-grade teacher who believed in you. There is no need to list everyone who had any involvement in the project, but there is no reason not to list everyone to whom you are truly grateful.

Table of contents and lists of tables and figures.   The Table of Contents lists the preliminary matter (for example, acknowledgements, list of tables, list of figures), the chapters, and the references and appendixes. Under the chapter listings should be listed the subheadings that appear in the chapter, as shown in Figure 11–2. Headings, titles, tables, and figures must all be exactly as listed in the text.

FIGURE 11–2   Example of a Table of Contents

LIST OF TABLES

LIST OF FIGURES

Chapter 1: Introduction

The purpose of Chapter 1 is to introduce the reader to the reasons you undertook the study, what you expected to find, and why the study is important.

The problem. This section should contain a brief statement of the problem to be solved, usually including the critical pieces of earlier research that led up to this particular investigation. A well-written problem statement should state why the past literature demands the current study (for example, "Based on the findings of X, Y, and Z, we now know such-and-such. However, there is still one unresolved and very important problem: 'How would the QRS Treatment affect student achievement in science, a subject quite different from those studied by X, Y, and Z?' This is the problem addressed by the present investigation.") However, Chapter 1 should not contain a complete literature review, only citations of articles directly related to the problem at hand.

Hypotheses. In this section, you should formally state your hypotheses concerning the results of the study, as in the example in Figure 11–3.

FIGURE 11–3   Example of Hypotheses

Hypothesis 1:   The posttest mathematics achievement of students who are assigned daily homework will exceed that of students who are not assigned homework, controlling for pretest mathematics achievement.

Hypothesis 2:   Among students who are assigned daily homework there will be a positive correlation between the percent of days students do their homework assignments and their posttest mathematics achievement, controlling for pretest mathematics achievement.

Some universities perfer that you state your hypotheses in null form, as in Figure 11–4. As noted in Chapters 1 and 9, your actual expectation is that the data will allow you to *reject* the null hypothesis.

Significance of the problem. In this section, you should clearly state the importance of the problem you have chosen for a particular body of educational, psychological, or sociological theory and for the practice of education. Essentially, you should say why the world should be waiting with bated breath for your findings.

FIGURE 11–4   Example of Hypotheses Stated in Null Form

Hypothesis 1:   The posttest mathematics achievement of students who are assigned daily homework will not differ from that of students who are not assigned homework, controlling for pretest mathematics achievement.

Hypothesis 2:   Among students who are assigned daily homework, there will be no relationship between the percent of days students do their homework and their posttest mathematics achievement, controlling for pretest mathematics achievement.

Definitions of terms.   Even if your university does not demand it, it is often a good idea to include a list of important terms that might not be familiar to many readers.

Chapter 2: Review of the Literature

In introducing the problem in Chapter 1, you should cite only the most critical articles or other writings that led up to your investigation. In Chapter 2, you should conduct a *complete* review of literature in the area or areas which are involved in your study. This review should be quite extensive. It should *not* be simply a listing of articles and findings (for example, "Smith (1970) found A; Jones (1971) found B; Wilson (1972) replicated A but not B"). Instead, it should intelligently discuss the literature with an eye toward illuminating critical issues (for example, "Smith (1970) and Wilson (1972) both found A in studies of urban tenth graders, but Jones (1971) found B in a study involving suburban fifth graders. Since Wilson's (1972) study failed to replicate B, it might be assumed that differences in settings and grade levels could account for the different findings. Support for this is also provided by Gonzales (1974), who found. . .").

For examples of literature reviews, look at recent volumes of the *Review of Educational Research.* Some of these reviews began as literature reviews for dissertations. Also, ask your adviser to suggest an outstanding literature review from a recent dissertation in your own department.

Chapter 3: Methods

Chapter 3 presents a detailed description of the methods you used (see Chapter 5 of this book). The particular subheadings under the methods section depend on the kind of study. A methods section for an experimental study would ordinarily have subsections dealing with subjects, design, treatments, measures, and analyses.

Subjects.   This section should list the number, location, and major characteristics of the individuals who served as subjects in your study.

This might include the average ages of the subjects; the number of blacks, whites, and orientals; the number of males and females; the kind of school(s) involved (for example, "an open-space elementary school in an upper-middle-class neighborhood"), and so on. In a study of teachers, you might include data on the teachers' average years of experience and years of postgraduate education. The purpose of this section is to describe the characteristics of your sample that might be important to the results, so the readers can infer to what other settings your findings might apply.

Design.   In this section, you should name the treatments and describe how subjects were assigned to the treatments (for example, random assignment of individuals; random assignment of classes, teachers, or schools; matching; etc.). If you are using a factorial design or anything other than a simple two-treatment comparison, you should include a diagram depicting the design (see, for example, Figure 2–5 in Chapter 2).

Treatments.   Here you may describe the various treatments in detail. Be sure to make clear what the different treatments have in common and exactly how they differ.

Measures.   In this section, describe each measure, presenting any information you can on the reliability and validity of each measures (see Chapter 5). You may want to put copies of any questionnaires, interview schedules, or behavioral observation forms in an appendix.

Analyses.   This section should describe the statistical analyses you performed on the data collected in your study.

Chapter 4: Results

In this section, you should describe in detail the results you obtained in the analyses described under Methods (Chapter 3). Use tables and figures (such as graphs) to present the data in an understandable format. It is generally a good idea to present a graph depicting any important interactions (see Figure 2–6 in Chapter 2). The results section should list the means and standard deviations for every measure in each treatment group, as well as the results of the analyses. The text need not mention every single result (the tables will do this), but it should point out the important findings. Discussion of the findings should be limited, as this will be taken up in the next section.

Chapter 5: Discussion

The discussion section should summarize the results of the study in relation to the hypotheses presented at the beginning of the report and in relation to the past literature. The primary questions to be answered in the discussion section are, "How have the theory and/or practice of education been informed by the results of this study?" and "What further investigations are now needed to continue to shed light on these findings?"

In writing the discussion section, it is important not to wander too far from the data. It is not inappropriate to speculate about what the findings might imply, but this is not a place to launch into an extended critique of American education. As noted earlier in this chapter, your ideas and findings will be more positively received if you maintain a modest, objective, and scientific tone, especially in the Discussion section.

References

All articles, books, and other writings referred to in the text are listed in the references section in alphabetical order. The specific format for references will be identified in your university guidelines.

Appendixes

Appendixes are used at the end of the dissertation to present lengthy material that may be important in understanding the methods used in the study. Examples of materials that typically appear in appendixes are listed below:

1. Questionnaires, tests, interview schedules, and observation forms
2. Teacher's manuals or scripts
3. Examples of curriculum materials
4. Training manuals for observers
5. Diagrams of the physical arrangement of the classroom

WRITING A JOURNAL ARTICLE

Many graduate students conduct excellent research, but then fail to submit their research to academic journals for publication or present their research at a conference. This is a shame, because the impact of a journal article or conference presentation is far greater than that of a dissertation.

Writing a journal article or conference paper after writing a dissertation requires a major mental shift. The essence of a journal article is brevity. In as few as 15 to 20 double-spaced pages, the writer must cover the most critical information from a dissertation that is often more than 100 pages long.

Which Journal?   Every academic research journal has its own format and other requirements for articles. These are described in the journals, either in every issue or once per year, in a section usually entitled

"Instructions for Contributors." You should choose a journal before writing your article so that you can be sure you are following the appropriate guidelines.

In choosing a journal for your article, keep several factors in mind. One is that it generally takes 6 months or more for an article to be reviewed, and then another 6 to 12 months to appear in print. If it is important to you to have your article published quickly, you should send it to a specialized journal with a relatively high acceptance rate rather than to one of the major general readership journals (such as the *American Educational Research Journal* or the *Journal of Educational Psychology*). Of course, if your article will directly concern a special field, such as reading, mathematics, special education, and so on, you will want to choose a journal in the appropriate field.

Spend some time browsing through educational journals in the current periodicals section of your university library. You will want to choose a journal that has many articles on your area of interest, and you should be sure that the journal you choose publishes the kind of article you plan to submit. Some journals publish only formal research papers, others only reviews, others only practitioner-oriented narratives. Some journals devote each issue to a difficult special topic, while most publish a mix of articles within their area of interest in every issue.

Conference papers

Before submitting a manuscript to a journal, you may wish to consider presenting it at a national or regional conference. The acceptance rate for conferences is much higher than for most journals, and a conference presentation typically gives you good feedback. To obtain a schedule of upcoming conferences (with paper deadlines) and guidelines for submitting papers, contact one of the following organizations (or others in your area of interest). Be sure to ask for information on regional as well as national conferences.

American Educational Research Association
1230 17th St., NW
Washington, DC 20036

American Psychological Association
1200 17th St., NW
Washington, DC 20036

Council for Exceptional Children
1920 Association Drive
Reston, VA 22901

Format and style of journal articles and conference papers

The format and style of journal articles and conference papers are described in the particular journal's or conference's "call for papers," and can be inferred by looking at articles already published or presented. Most education-related journals use what is called APA format, described in the *Publication Manual of the American Psychological Association* (1983). In general, research articles consist of an abstract, an introduction, a methods section, a results section, a discussion section, references, and tables and figures.

Abstract.   Many journals require an abstract of 100 to 150 words, very briefly summarizing the purpose, methods, and results of the study.

Introduction.   This section reviews relevant literature leading up to the current investigation, describes the purpose and significance of the study, and presents the study hypotheses. The literature review should not be an exhaustive review of the area of investigation, but should review literature with a direct bearing on the current study, such as articles on the theory on which the study is based, previous studies attempting to answer the same questions, and so on. Similar to the problem statement in a dissertation, the introduction of an article should make it clear how the current investigation is a logical outgrowth of earlier research and how it addresses theoretical or practical points previously left unresolved.

Methods.   The methods section of an article has the same content as the methods chapter in a dissertation. However, nonessential details of the methods may be left out. Whenever possible, you should refer to other sources for descriptions of procedures or measures if they are widely known or if a detailed description of the procedure or method is not needed to understand the current study. For example, you might simply provide citations for such common measures as sociometric questions (Moreno 1934), the Coopersmith Self-Esteem Inventory (Coopersmith 1975), or the Learning Environment Inventory (Anderson 1969). Standardized achievement tests (for example, Comprehensive Test of Basic Skills, Iowa Test of Basic Skills, Wechsler Intelligence Scale for Children) are so familiar that they are usually neither described nor given special citations, but are simply named.

Results.   The results section of an article has essentially the same elements as the results section of a dissertation except that, again, nonessential detail should be excluded. Journal editors particularly appreciate keeping the number of tables and figures to a minimum, although tables and figures should definitely be used in place of long strings of numbers in the text.

Discussion.   The discussion section of an article is also like that of a dissertation. You should summarize the results concisely and show how they illuminate the theory and literature discussed in the Introduction. Many articles end with recommendations for further research, but this is not absolutely necessary.

References.   References appear immediately after the narrative part of the article. Only articles actually cited in the text should be listed in the references section.

Tables and figures.   If your article is published, the tables and figures will be printed in the body of the article. However, when you submit the manuscript to the journal or to a conference review committee, you should put the tables and figures on separate pages at the back of the paper and indicate where in the text they should go, as shown in Figure 11–5.

FIGURE 11–5   Placement of Figures

This sex by treatment interaction is illustrated in Figure 3.

Figure 3 About Here

As is clear in Figure 3, the interaction between sex and treatment is ordinal; females exceed males in both treatments, but the difference is especially large in Treatment 2 . . .

Tips on Getting an Article Published

1. Be sure to have several people whose opinions you trust read your manuscript before sending it to the journal. These readers are likely to find many of the flaws that might otherwise lead to rejection of the article.
2. Follow the format, style, and other journal requirements carefully. Send the required number of copies.
3. If your article is rejected, revise it according to reviewers' suggestions (if you feel they have merit) and then send it to another journal. Many outstanding and widely cited articles were rejected by the first journal to which they were sent. If the journal does not send you the reviewers' comments, write the editor to request a copy. Even if you don't agree with them, the reviewer's comments are helpful in indicating how others read your work.

Term Papers and Other Research Reports

In general, the description of the contents of a journal article or conference paper will apply to any research report or term paper reporting the results of research. However, check to see if your department requires any particular format.

For more information on writing dissertations and other research papers, see Allen (1973), Campbell (1969), or Riebel (1972).

Appendices

Percentage of Area Lying between the Mean and Successive Standard Deviation Units under the Normal Curve

$z\left(\dfrac{x}{\sigma}\right)$	.00	.01	.02	.03	.04	.05	.06	.07	.08	.09
.0	.0000	.0040	.0080	.0120	.0160	.0199	.0239	.0279	.0319	.0359
.1	.0398	.0438	.0478	.0517	.0557	.0596	.0636	.0675	.0714	.0753
.2	.0793	.0832	.0871	.0910	.0948	.0987	.1026	.1064	.1103	.1141
.3	.1179	.1217	.1255	.1293	.1331	.1368	.1406	.1443	.1480	.1517
.4	.1554	.1591	.1628	.1664	.1700	.1736	.1772	.1808	.1844	.1879
.5	.1915	.1950	.1985	.2019	.2054	.2088	.2123	.2157	.2190	.2224
.6	.2257	.2291	.2324	.2357	.2389	.2422	.2454	.2486	.2517	.2549
.7	.2580	.2611	.2642	.2673	.2704	.2734	.2764	.2794	.2823	.2852
.8	.2881	.2910	.2939	.2967	.2995	.3023	.3051	.3078	.3106	.3133
.9	.3159	.3186	.3212	.3238	.3264	.3290	.3315	.3340	.3365	.3389
1.0	.3413	.3438	.3461	.3485	.3508	.3531	.3554	.3577	.3599	.3621
1.1	.3643	.3665	.3686	.3708	.3729	.3749	.3770	.3790	.3810	.3830
1.2	.3849	.3869	.3888	.3907	.3925	.3944	.3962	.3980	.3997	.4015
1.3	.4032	.4049	.4066	.4082	.4099	.4115	.4131	.4147	.4162	.4177
1.4	.4192	.4207	.4222	.4236	.4251	.4265	.4279	.4292	.4306	.4319
1.5	.4332	.4345	.4357	.4370	.4383	.4394	.4406	.4418	.4429	.4441
1.6	.4452	.4463	.4474	.4484	.4495	.4505	.4515	.4525	.4535	.4545
1.7	.4554	.4564	.4573	.4582	.4591	.4599	.4608	.4616	.4625	.4633
1.8	.4641	.4649	.4656	.4664	.4671	.4678	.4686	.4693	.4699	.4706
1.9	.4713	.4719	.4726	.4732	.4738	.4744	.4750	.4756	.4761	.4767
2.0	.4772	.4778	.4783	.4788	.4793	.4798	.4803	.4808	.4812	.4817
2.1	.4821	.4826	.4830	.4834	.4838	.4842	.4846	.4850	.4854	.4857
2.2	.4861	.4864	.4868	.4871	.4875	.4878	.4881	.4884	.4887	.4890
2.3	.4893	.4896	.4898	.4901	.4904	.4906	.4909	.4911	.4913	.4916
2.4	.4918	.4920	.4922	.4925	.4927	.4929	.4931	.4932	.4934	.4936
2.5	.4938	.4940	.4941	.4943	.4945	.4946	.4948	.4949	.4951	.4952
2.6	.4953	.4955	.4956	.4957	.4959	.4960	.4961	.4962	.4963	.4964
2.7	.4965	.4966	.4967	.4968	.4969	.4970	.4971	.4972	.4973	.4974
2.8	.4974	.4975	.4976	.4977	.4977	.4978	.4979	.4979	.4980	.4981
2.9	.4981	.4982	.4982	.4983	.4984	.4984	.4985	.4985	.4986	.4986
3.0	.4987									

Example: Between the mean and $+1.00z$ is 34.13% of the area.
Between the mean and $-.50z$ is 19.15% of the area.

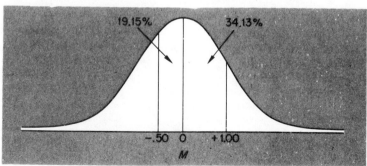

From John W. Best, **Research in Education**, *4th ed., © 1981, p. 411. Reprinted by permission of Prentice-Hall, Inc., Englewood Cliffs, N.J.*

APPENDIX 2

Critical values of *t*.

	Level of significance for one-tailed test			
	5%	2.5%	1%	.5%
	Level of significance for two-tailed test			
df	10%	5%	2%	1%
1	6.3138	12.7062	31.8207	63.6574
2	2.9200	4.3027	6.9646	9.9248
3	2.3534	3.1824	4.5407	5.8409
4	2.1318	2.7764	3.7469	4.6041
5	2.0150	2.5706	3.3649	4.0322
6	1.9432	2.4469	3.1427	3.7074
7	1.8946	2.3646	2.9980	3.4995
8	1.8595	2.3060	2.8965	3.3554
9	1.8331	2.2622	2.8214	3.2498
10	1.8125	2.2281	2.7638	3.1693
11	1.7959	2.2010	2.7181	3.1058
12	1.7823	2.1788	2.6810	3.0545
13	1.7709	2.1604	2.6503	3.0123
14	1.7613	2.1448	2.6245	2.9768
15	1.7531	2.1315	2.6025	2.9467
16	1.7459	2.1199	2.5835	2.9208
17	1.7396	2.1098	2.5669	2.8982
18	1.7341	2.1009	2.5524	2.8784
19	1.7291	2.0930	2.5395	2.8609
20	1.7247	2.0860	2.5280	2.8453
21	1.7207	2.0796	2.5177	2.8314
22	1.7171	2.0739	2.5083	2.8188
23	1.7139	2.0687	2.4999	2.8073
24	1.7109	2.0639	2.4922	2.7969
25	1.7081	2.0595	2.4851	2.7874
26	1.7056	2.0555	2.4786	2.7787
27	1.7033	2.0518	2.4727	2.7707
28	1.7011	2.0484	2.4671	2.7633
29	1.6991	2.0452	2.4620	2.7564
30	1.6973	2.0423	2.4573	2.7500

From Donald B. Owen, **Handbook of Statistical Tables**, © 1962. U.S. Department of Energy. Published by Addison-Wesley Publishing Co., Inc., Reading, MA. Reprinted with permission of the publisher.

APPENDIX 3

Values of F at the 5% and 1% significance levels.

(df associated with the denominator)		1	2	3	4	5	6	7	8	9
				(df associated with the numerator)						
1	5%	161	200	216	225	230	234	237	239	241
	1%	4052	5000	5403	5625	5764	5859	5928	5982	6022
2	5%	18.5	19.0	19.2	19.2	19.3	19.3	19.4	19.4	19.4
	1%	98.5	99.0	99.2	99.2	99.3	99.3	99.4	99.4	99.4
3	5%	10.1	9.55	9.28	9.12	9.01	8.94	8.89	8.85	8.81
	1%	34.1	30.8	29.5	28.7	28.2	27.9	27.7	27.5	27.3
4	5%	7.71	6.94	6.59	6.39	6.26	6.16	6.09	6.04	6.00
	1%	21.2	18.0	16.7	16.0	15.5	15.2	15.0	14.8	14.7
5	5%	6.61	5.79	5.41	5.19	5.05	4.95	4.88	4.82	4.77
	1%	16.3	13.3	12.1	11.4	11.0	10.7	10.5	10.3	10.2
6	5%	5.99	5.14	4.76	4.53	4.39	4.28	4.21	4.15	4.10
	1%	13.7	10.9	9.78	9.15	8.75	8.47	8.26	8.10	7.98
7	5%	5.59	4.74	4.35	4.12	3.97	3.87	3.79	3.73	3.68
	1%	12.2	9.55	8.45	7.85	7.46	7.19	6.99	6.84	6.72
8	5%	5.32	4.46	4.07	3.84	3.69	3.58	3.50	3.44	3.39
	1%	11.3	8.65	7.59	7.01	6.63	6.37	6.18	6.03	5.91
9	5%	5.12	4.26	3.86	3.63	3.48	3.37	3.29	3.23	3.18
	1%	10.6	8.02	6.99	6.42	6.06	5.80	5.61	5.47	5.35
10	5%	4.96	4.10	3.71	3.48	3.33	3.22	3.14	3.07	3.02
	1%	10.0	7.56	6.55	5.99	5.64	5.39	5.20	5.06	4.94
11	5%	4.84	3.98	3.59	3.36	3.20	3.09	3.01	2.95	2.90
	1%	9.65	7.21	6.22	5.67	5.32	5.07	4.89	4.74	4.63
12	5%	4.75	3.89	3.49	3.26	3.11	3.00	2.91	2.85	2.80
	1%	9.33	6.93	5.95	5.41	5.06	4.82	4.64	4.50	4.39
13	5%	4.67	3.81	3.41	3.18	3.03	2.92	2.83	2.77	2.71
	1%	9.07	6.70	5.74	5.21	4.86	4.62	4.44	4.30	4.19
14	5%	4.60	3.74	3.34	3.11	2.96	2.85	2.76	2.70	2.65
	1%	8.86	6.51	5.56	5.04	4.70	4.46	4.28	4.14	4.03
15	5%	4.54	3.68	3.29	3.06	2.90	2.79	2.71	2.64	2.59
	1%	8.68	6.36	5.42	4.89	4.56	4.32	4.14	4.00	3.89
16	5%	4.49	3.63	3.24	3.01	2.85	2.74	2.66	2.59	2.54
	1%	8.53	6.23	5.29	4.77	4.44	4.20	4.03	3.89	3.78
17	5%	4.45	3.59	3.20	2.96	2.81	2.70	2.61	2.55	2.49
	1%	8.40	6.11	5.18	4.67	4.34	4.10	3.93	3.79	3.68

Merrington, M., and Thompson, C. M. Tables of percentage points of the inverted beta (F) distribution, **Biometrika**, 1943, 33, 73–88, by permission of the editor.

Values of F at the 5% and 1% significance levels, *continued*.

(*df associated with the denominator*)		\(df associated with the numerator\)								
		1	2	3	4	5	6	7	8	9
18	5%	4.41	3.55	3.16	2.93	2.77	2.66	2.58	2.51	2.46
	1%	8.29	6.01	5.09	4.58	4.25	4.01	3.84	3.71	3.60
19	5%	4.38	3.52	3.13	2.90	2.74	2.63	2.54	2.48	2.42
	1%	8.18	5.93	5.01	4.50	4.17	3.94	3.77	3.63	3.52
20	5%	4.35	3.49	3.10	2.87	2.71	2.60	2.51	2.45	2.39
	1%	8.10	5.85	4.94	4.43	4.10	3.87	3.70	3.56	3.46
21	5%	4.32	3.47	3.07	2.84	2.68	2.57	2.49	2.42	2.37
	1%	8.02	5.78	4.87	4.37	4.04	3.81	3.64	3.51	3.40
22	5%	4.30	3.44	3.05	2.82	2.66	2.55	2.46	2.40	2.34
	1%	7.95	5.72	4.82	4.31	3.99	3.76	3.59	3.45	3.35
23	5%	4.28	3.42	3.03	2.80	2.64	2.53	2.44	2.37	2.32
	1%	7.88	5.66	4.76	4.26	3.94	3.71	3.54	3.41	3.30
24	·5%	4.26	3.40	3.01	2.78	2.62	2.51	2.42	2.36	2.30
	1%	7.82	5.61	4.72	4.22	3.90	3.67	3.50	3.36	3.26
25	5%	4.24	3.39	2.29	2.76	2.60	2.49	2.40	2.34	2.28
	1%	7.77	5.57	4.68	4.18	3.86	3.63	3.46	3.32	3.22
26	5%	4.23	3.37	2.98	2.74	2.59	2.47	2.39	2.32	2.27
	1%	7.72	5.53	4.64	4.14	3.82	3.59	3.42	3.29	3.18
27	5%	4.21	3.35	2.96	2.73	2.57	2.46	2.37	2.31	2.25
	1%	7.68	5.49	4.60	4.11	3.78	3.56	3.39	3.26	3.15
28	5%	4.20	3.34	2.95	2.71	2.56	2.45	2.36	2.29	2.24
	1%	7.64	5.45	4.57	4.07	3.75	3.53	3.36	3.23	3.12
29	5%	4.18	3.33	2.93	2.70	2.55	2.43	2.35	2.28	2.22
	1%	7.60	5.42	4.54	4.04	3.73	3.50	3.33	3.20	3.09
30	5%	4.17	3.32	2.92	2.69	2.53	2.42	2.33	2.27	2.21
	1%	7.56	5.39	4.51	4.02	3.70	3.47	3.30	3.17	3.07
40	5%	4.08	3.23	2.84	2.61	2.45	2.34	2.25	2.18	2.12
	1%	7.31	5.18	4.31	3.83	3.51	3.29	3.12	2.99	2.89
60	5%	4.00	3.15	2.76	2.53	2.37	2.25	2.17	2.10	2.04
	1%	7.08	4.98	4.13	3.65	3.34	3.12	2.95	2.82	2.72
120	5%	3.92	3.07	2.68	2.45	2.29	2.18	2.09	2.02	1.96
	1%	6.85	4.79	3.95	3.48	3.17	2.96	2.79	2.66	2.56

APPENDIX 4

Abridged Table of Critical Values for CHI Square

df	Level of significance	
	.05	.01
1	3.84	6.64
2	5.99	9.21
3	7.82	11.34
4	9.49	13.28
5	11.07	15.09
6	12.59	16.81
7	14.07	18.48
8	15.51	20.09
9	16.92	21.67
10	18.31	23.21
11	19.68	24.72
12	21.03	26.22
13	22.36	27.69
14	23.68	29.14
15	25.00	30.58
16	26.30	32.00
17	27.59	33.41
18	28.87	34.80
19	30.14	36.19
20	31.41	37.57
21	32.67	38.93
22	33.92	40.29
23	35.17	41.64
24	36.42	42.98
25	37.65	44.31
26	38.88	45.64
27	40.11	46.96
28	41.34	48.28
29	42.56	49.59
30	43.77	50.89

*From John W. Best, **Research in Education**, 4th edition, © 1981, p. 413. Reprinted by permission of Prentice-Hall, Inc., Englewood Cliffs, N.J.*

APPENDIX 5: ANSWERS TO EXERCISES

Chapter 9

1) Ratio, interval, ratio, ordinal, nominal
2) a) Test 1: mean = 10.05, mode = 10, median = 10; mean most appropriate measure
   Test 2: mean = 17.40, mode = 19, median = 18; median most appropriate measure
   b) Test 1: range is 8
      Test 2: range is 9

   c) Test 1

   Normally distributed

```
                                x
                                x     x
                          x     x     x
                    x     x     x     x     x
        x     x     x     x     x     x     x     x     x
        +-----+-----+-----+-----+-----+-----+-----+-----+
        6     7     8     9    10    11    12    13    14
```

   Test 2

   Negatively skewed

```
                                                  x
                                                  x     x
                                x           x     x     x
                                x     x     x     x     x
        x     x           x     x     x     x     x     x
        +-----+-----+-----+-----+-----+-----+-----+-----+-----+
       11    12    13    14    15    16    17    18    19    20
```

   d) Standard deviation: 1.96   Variance: 3.84
   e) z-scores are: −.03, 1.51, −.54, .48, −.54, .48, −.03, −1.05, −1.56, −.03, −.54, −1.05, −.03, −2.07, 1.00, 1.00, 2.02, −.03, .48, .48
   f) Standard error of the mean: .438. The true population mean will fall in the range of 9.17 to 10.93.
3) a) Independent groups
   b) Two-tailed. Either group may be higher.
   c) $F = 1.00$, d.f. = 9, 9; nonsignificant. Variances are homogeneous.
   d) $t = 5.21$, d.f. = 18; two-tailed probability $< .001$

e) The null hypothesis, that there were no differences between the groups, can be rejected. This study indicates that students are absent less frequently when weekly parties are held to reward attendance than when higher grades are given to reward attendance.

4) a) $F = 27.922$, d.f. $= 2,27$; probability $< .001$.

b) The ANOVA indicates that there are significant differences among the means. Ability grouping produced the greatest achievement. Individualized instruction produced a moderate amount of achievement, and whole class instruction produced the least achievement. However, differences between each pair would have to be tested using t-tests or other individual comparison statistics before conclusions could be made about differences between methods.

5) $F = .10$ d.f. $= 1,17$; no significant differences between the groups.

6) a) Point biserial

b) $r = .706$, $t(13) = 3.59$, $p < .01$.

c) There is a strong relationship between participation on a sports team and cross-racial friendships in this study.

7) a) $\chi^2 = 4.89$, d.f. $= 2$, nonsignificant (criterion is 6.0).

b) $\chi^2 = 1.98$, d.f. $= 1$, nonsignificant (criterion is 3.8).

8) KR20 $= .780$. This would be considered adequate for a self-esteem scale.

Chapter 10

1) a)

```
1                    16
RUN NAME             EXERCISES, CHAPTER 10, QUESTION 1
DATA LIST            FIXED(1)/1 ID 1–3,TRT 5, SEX 7(A), GRADE 9,
                     PRETEST 11–14, POSTTEST 16–19
INPUT MEDIUM         CARD
N OF CASES           20
```

b)

```
1                16
RECODE           SEX ('M'=0) ('F'=1)
```

c) 1

```
              16
RECODE             ID TO POSTTEST (BLANK=–99)
MISSING VALUES     ID TO POSTTEST (–99)
```

d) (Use the data definition cards above; RUN NAME to MISSING VALUES)

```
1                16
*SELECT IF       (TRT EQ 1)
FREQUENCIES      GENERAL=SEX,GRADE
READ INPUT DATA
(Data cards go here)
```

```
*SELECT IF            (TRT EQ 2)
FREQUENCIES           GENERAL=SEX,GRADE
FINISH
```

Answers

	Treatment 1	Treatment 2
Males	6	5
Females	4	5
Grade 3	3	3
Grade 4	7	7

e) (Use the data definition cards above; RUN NAME to MISSING
VALUES)

```
1                 16
BREAKDOWN         TABLES=PRETEST, POSTTEST BY TRT
READ INPUT DATA
(Data cards go here)
FINISH
```

Answers

	Pretest Mean	(Standard Deviation)	Posttest Mean	(Standard Deviation)
Treatment 1	5.58	1.32	8.46	1.48
Treatment 2	5.57	1.42	9.82	1.50

f) (Use the data definition cards above; RUN NAME to MISSING
VALUES)

```
1                 16
T-TEST            GROUPS=TRT/VARIABLES=POSTTEST
READ INPUT DATA
(Data cards go here)
FINISH
```
Answers
    $t=1.99$, $df=17$, $p<.06$ two-tailed, non-significant

g) (Use the data definition cards above; RUN NAME to MISSING
VALUES)

```
1                 16
ANOVA             POSTTEST BY TRT(1,2) WITH PRETEST
READ INPUT DATA
(Data cards go here)
FINISH
```
Answers
    $F=9.597$, $df=1,15$, $p<.007$

h) Assuming adequate experimental design, it can be concluded
that the new curriculum produces greater achievement than
the control curriculum, controlling for pretest scores.

2) a)

```
1                              16
RUN NAME                       EXERCISES, CHAPTER 10, QUESTION 2
DATA LIST                      FIXED(1)/2 ID 1–2, LOCATION 4(A),
                               EXPERNCE 6–7, EVALPRIN 9, EVALTCH
                               11–12, EVALSTU 14
INPUT MEDIUM                   CARD
N OF CASES                     20
RECODE                         LOCATION ('U'=1) ('R'=2)
RECODE                         ID TO EVALSTU (BLANK= –99)
MISSING VALUES                 ID TO EVALSTU (–99)
PEARSON CORR                   EVALPRIN, EVALTCH, EVALSTU WITH
                               EVALPRIN, EVALTCH, EVALSTU
OPTIONS                        3
READ INPUT DATA
(Data cards go here)
FINISH
```

Correlation Matrix

	EVALPRIN	EVALTCH	EVALSTU
EVALPRIN	—	.74**	.52*
EVALTCH		—	.35
EVALSTU			—

* p<.05 two-tailed
** p<.001 two-tailed

Principal and teacher evaluations are very highly correlated. Principal and student evaluations are also correlated. The correlation between teacher and student evaluations does not reach statistical significance at the .05 level.

b) (Use the data definition cards above; RUN NAME to MISSING VALUES)

```
1                16
COMPUTE          OVERALL=EVALPRIN+EVALTCH+EVALSTU
ASSIGN MISSING   OVERALL(–99)
PEARSON CORR     EXPERNCE,OVERALL WITH EXPERNCE,OVERALL
OPTIONS          3
READ INPUT DATA
(Data cards go here)
FINISH
```

Answers
The correlation between years of experience teaching and the sum of all of the evaluations is .64, p=.008, two-tailed.

c) (Use the data definition cards above; RUN NAME to MISSING VALUES)

```
1                16
*SELECT IF       (LOCATION EQ 1)
PEARSON CORR     EXPERNCE,OVERALL WITH EXPERNCE, OVERAL
OPTIONS          3
READ INPUT DATA
(Data cards go here)
```

```
*SELECT IF            (LOCATION EQ 2)
PEARSON CORR          EXPERNCE,OVERALL WITH EXPERNCE, OVERALL
OPTIONS               3
FINISH
```

Answers

For rural teachers, the correlation between experience and the overall evaluation score is .74, $p = .035$, two-tailed.
For urban teachers, the correlation between experience and the overall evaluation score is .60, nonsignificant.

d) (Use the data definition cards above; RUN NAME to MISSING VALUES)

```
1                     16
IF                    (EXPERNCE LE 3) LONGEVTY=1
IF                    (EXPERNCE GE 4 AND LE 6) LONGEVTY=2
IF                    (EXPERNCE GE 7) LONGEVTY=3
ASSIGN MISSING        LONGEVTY (−99)
PEARSON CORR          LONGEVTY,OVERALL WITH LONGEVTY,
                      OVERALL
OPTIONS               3
READ INPUT DATA
(Data cards go here)
FINISH
```

Answers

The correlation between the experience categories chosen and the overall evaluation score is .60, $p = .014$, two-tailed.

ABA Design. *See* **Reversal Design.**

Achievement Test. A test designed to assess how much individuals have actually learned from a course of study or other activity. *Compare* **Aptitude Test.**

Alpha Error. *See* **Type I Error.**

Alpha Level. A number set in advance of an experiment or correlational study to indicate the probability that the researcher is willing to accept of mistakenly rejecting the null hypothesis. For example, an alpha level of .05 (written p < .05) indicates that the researcher is willing to accept a 5% chance that a statistically significant finding will be in error. *See* **False Positive Error** and **Type I Error.**

Alphanumeric Variable. A variable that can take on letter, symbol, or number values.

Analysis of Covariance (ANCOVA). A statistical method that compares two or more group means after adjustment for some control variable or covariate (such as pretest) to see if any differences between the adjusted means are statistically significant. *Compare* **Analysis of Variance.**

Analysis of Variance (ANOVA). A statistical method that compares two or more group means to see if any differences between the means are statistically significant. *Compare* **Analysis of Covariance** and **t-Test.**

Aptitude Test. A test designed to predict an individual's ability to perform or learn to perform one or more tasks or ability to succeed in one or more performance settings. For example, an IQ test is designed to predict school performance, among other things; a mechanical aptitude test is designed to predict ability to perform mechanical tasks. *Compare* **Achievement Test.**

Assessment Research. Descriptive research conducted to determine to what degree individuals (such as students) have certain capabilities or characteristics. Assessment research typically uses criterion-referenced tests.

Attrition. Loss of subjects over the course of a study, due to dropping out, absenteeism on the day of the test, and so on. Attrition may be a source of bias in experimental comparison studies if different treatments have different effects on attrition.

Background Factors. Variables that may cause other variables but are not caused by them, and are typically unchangeable attributes of individuals. Examples are sex, race, parents' education and income, number of siblings, and so on. *See* **Path Analysis** and **Mediating Factors.**

Baseline. An average level of some variable over a period of time before or after a treatment is applied. A baseline is meant to be the "natural" level of a variable in the absence of treatment. *See* **Single-Case Experiment** and **Reversal Design.**

Beta Error. *See* **Type II Error.**

Bias. Any factor that introduces systematic, unwanted prejudice or error to a finding. Any uncontrolled factor other than variables formally hypothesized to be part of a cause-and-effect relationship is a potential source of bias.

Case. The smallest unit from which data are collected. A case is usually a single individual ("subject"), but may be a class, school, or large group.

Categorical Variable. A variable (such as sex, race, or treatment) that can take on a limited number of values. *Compare* **Continuous Variable.** Also called a "Discrete Variable."

Causal Model. A theoretical ordering of variables in terms of their effects on other variables. Correlations between several pairs of variables may be used to evaluate a particular causal model, as in the technique of path analysis.

Causation. The degree to which one variable causes or affects another. Note that a correlation between two variables does not necessarily imply that one causes the other. *See* **Mutual Causation, Spurious Correlation,** and **Causal Model.**

Ceiling Effect. A characteristic of a distribution of scores in which many scores are near the maximum possible value. For example, a distribution of test scores on which half of all students received scores from 90% to 100% correct would probably exhibit a ceiling effect. *Compare* **Floor Effect.**

Chi Square (χ^2). A statistic used to compare observed frequencies of scores on categorical variables to expected frequencies (based on the total frequencies in each column and row). A chi square test assesses the relationship between two or more categorical variables.

Class Effects. The effects on students of being in a certain class (such as the effects of students in the same class on one another).

Closed Form Question. A question on a questionnaire or interview for which a limited number of possible responses are specified in advance, such as Do you expect to go to college?

a) yes

b) no

c) not sure

Compare **Open Form Question.**

Cluster Sampling. A sampling method in which clusters of individuals (such as teachers in selected schools) are randomly chosen from among a much larger population of such clusters (such as all schools in the U.S.). *See* **Sampling.**

Coefficient Alpha. An internal consistency measure of scale reliability for scales in which more than two answers (such as "agree," "not sure," "disagree") are coded for each question. *Compare* **KR-20.**

Concurrent Validity.   The degree to which a scale or test correlates with another scale, test, or other variable of known validity measured at the same time.

Confounding.   A situation in which the independent effects of two or more variables cannot be determined because the variables cannot be studied separately. For example, if Teacher A teaches Method 1 and Teacher B teaches Method 2, there is no way to separate the effects on students of experiencing the different methods from the effects of having the different teachers; method and teacher are completely confounded.

Construct Validity.   The degree to which a scale or test has a pattern of correlations with other variables that would be predicted by a sound theory. A construct valid scale would correlate with other measures of the same concept, but would fail to correlate well with scales believed to measure different concepts.

Construct.   A theoretically existing (but unobservable) variable. For example, intelligence is a construct, because it cannot be directly observed but its existence and effects can be inferred from a variety of observable variables.

Content Validity.   The degree to which test items correspond to the content of a course, training program, or some other important criterion. For example, a content valid scale measuring teachers' knowledge of laws related to their work would have items determined (by authorities on law, pupil personnel policies, student rights, and so on) to actually measure knowledge about laws that are likely to be important in teachers' day-to-day activities and decisions.

Content-Specific Test.   An achievement test designed to measure concepts taught in a specific course or text. *See* **Criterion-Referenced Test** and **Content Validity.** *Compare* **Standardized Test.**

Continuous Variable.   A variable (such as age, test score, or height) that can take on a wide or infinite number of values. *Compare* **Categorical Variable.**

Control Cards.   Instructions (which may be on computer cards, tapes, or terminals) that tell a computer what to do with data.

Control Group.   A group assigned (usually randomly) to be untreated, or to receive a treatment other than the experimental treatment. Data collected on individuals in the control group are contrasted with data collected on members of one or more experimental group(s) in many experimental comparison designs. *Compare* **Experimental Group.**

Control Variable.   A variable used to remove the effect of some factor on the relationship between two or more other variables. For example, in examining a correlation between participation in class and achievement, ability might be controlled out, using partial correlation, analysis of covariance, or multiple regression. Variables may also be controlled for by separate analyses; for example, sex might be controlled for by conducting separate analyses for boys and girls. When used in analysis of covariance (and sometimes multiple regression), a control variable is called a covariate.

Correlation Coefficient.   A statistic, usually designated r, indicating the degree to which two variables are correlated. May take on values from -1.0 (perfect negative correlation; when variable A is high, variable B is low, and vice versa) to $+1.0$ (perfect positive correlation; when variable A is high, variable B is high, and vice versa). A correlation coefficient of 0 indicates that variables A and B are unrelated. *See* **Correlation Matrix** and **Partial Correlation.**

Correlation Matrix.   A table of correlation coefficients showing all possible pairwise correlations between a set of variables.

Correlation. The degree to which two variables tend to vary in the same direction (positive correlation) or in opposite directions (negative correlation). *See* **Correlation Coefficient.**

Correlational Design. A nonexperimental research design in which the researcher collects data on two or more variables to determine if they are related (that is, if they consistently vary in the same or opposite directions).

Covariate. A control variable (such as pretest) used in analysis of covariance or multiple regression analysis to adjust other values. Use of covariates may help make groups that are somewhat dissimilar more statistically equivalent (as when posttest scores of two groups that differ on a pretest are adjusted for the pretest). Use of covariates may also increase statistical power (the ability of a statistic to avoid false negative errors).

Criterion-Referenced Test. A test designed to indicate how any individual performs in comparison to a preestablished criterion. For example, it may be decided that 14-year-olds should know how to find 27% of 132; a criterion-referenced test would be designed to indicate how many 14-year-olds can do this correctly. *Compare* **Norm-Referenced Test.**

Curvilinear Relationship. A relationship between two variables that changes in form depending on the values of the variables. For example, there might be a positive correlation between age and appetite up to age 16, but a negative or zero correlation afterwards. *Compare* **Linear Relationship.** Also, *see* **Correlation.**

Data. Information systematically collected in research. Data are usually information about individuals or groups.

Delayed Treatment Control Group. A control group that will later receive the experimental treatment (after the study is over). Use of delayed treatment control groups helps insure that individuals who participate in the control group are, like those in the experimental group, willing to have the experimental treatment(s) applied to them.

Dependent Variable. An outcome variable hypothesized to be affected by one or more causes (independent variables).

Descriptive Research. Research conducted to describe some phenomenon as it exists, rather than finding relationships between variables (correlational research) or varying treatments to observe the outcomes (experimental research). Examples of descriptive research are surveys, assessment and evaluation research, ethnography, and historical research.

Dichotomous Variable. A categorical variable (such as sex, on-off task, experimental-control) that can take on only two values.

Discrete Variable. *See* **Categorical Variable.**

Distribution. A pattern of scores on some variable. For example, a normal distribution of scores is one in which most scores are near the mean of the set of scores and other scores cluster around the mean in a bell-shaped pattern. *See* **Normal Curve, Skewed Distribution,** and **Kurtosis.**

Ethnography. Descriptive research in which social or instructional situations are observed and described in great detail.

Evaluation Research. Descriptive research directed at evaluating a certain policy or program, using such means as comparing relevant data to preestablished criteria of success.

Experimental Comparison Design. An experimental design in which subjects are assigned by the experimenter (usually randomly) to two or more groups, different treatments are applied to the different groups, and the effects of the treatments on one or more outcomes (dependent variables) are measured.

Experimental Designs. Research designs in which the experimenter decides how and when subjects will receive certain treatments and observes the effect of the treatments on one or more dependent variables. Includes experimental comparison and single-case designs.

Experimental Condition, Experimental Treatment. A treatment applied to some subjects in an experimental comparison design whose effects on one or more dependent (outcome) variable(s) are to be contrasted with the effects of other treatments or control (untreated) conditions.

Experimental Group. A group assigned (usually randomly) to receive some experimental treatment. Data collected on individuals in one or more experimental group(s) are contrasted with data collected in other experimental groups or in untreated control groups in experimental comparison designs. *Compare* **Control Group.**

External Validity. The degree to which the results of a study can be applied to other subjects, settings, or situations. Same as "generalizability."

Face Validity. The degree to which scale items look as though they measure what the scale is supposed to measure. That is, the items "make sense" as measures of the concept the scale is meant to measure.

Factor. A variable hypothesized to affect or cause another variable or variables; an independent variable.

Factorial Analysis of Variance (or Covariance). Analysis of variance (or covariance) with two or more factors.

Factorial Design. An experimental comparison design in which treatments or other variables are analyzed as levels of one or more factors. For example, a factorial experiment might contrast three levels of the factor "treatment" (individualized instruction, peer tutoring, or traditional instruction), and two levels of student sex (male versus female). This would be a 3 × 2 factorial experiment.

False Negative Error. Incorrectly deciding that two variables are not related (that is, incorrectly accepting the null hypothesis). Related to Type II or Beta Error.

False Positive Error. Incorrectly deciding that two variables are related (that is, incorrectly rejecting the null hypothesis). Related to Type I or Alpha Error.

Fan Spread. The tendency of some variables to increase in variability over time, with individuals who had relatively high scores on an initial test gaining more on a subsequent test than individuals who initially had low scores.

Floor Effect. A characteristic of a distribution of scores in which many scores are near the minimum possible value. For example, a distribution of test scores on which half of all students received scores from 0% to 10% correct would probably exhibit a floor effect. *Compare* **Ceiling Effect.**

Generalizability. The degree to which results of a study apply to a larger population. Same as **External Validity.**

Grade Equivalent. A score on a norm-referenced, standardized test that indicates the approximate average grade level of students who made a raw score of a certain level. For example, a grade equivalent of 3.5 indicates that a test-taker has scored about where the average student in the fifth month of third grade would score.

Hawthorne Effect. A tendency of subjects in an experimental group to exert outstanding efforts because they are conscious of being in an experiment rather than because of the experimental treatments themselves. *Compare* **John Henry Effect.** *Also see* **Reactivity** and **Social Desirability Bias.**

Historical Research. Research directed at describing or explaining events in the past.

Homogeneity of Variance. The degree to which the variances of two or more samples can be considered equivalent.

Human Subjects Review. Procedures established in universities and other institutions engaged in research activities to protect the rights of human subjects in research. A human subjects review committee routinely reviews research proposals involving human subjects to be sure that the subjects will not experience physical or psychological pain, risk, or deception out of proportion to benefits to be derived by the subjects themselves or society at large.

Hypothesis. A statement concerning supposed relationships among variables on which research will shed light.

High-Inference Behaviors. Behaviors observed by a behavioral observer that require a good deal of judgment to code correctly. Examples are "teacher enthusiasm," "friendly interaction," and so on. *Compare* **Low-Inference Behaviors.**

Independent Variable. A variable (such as treatment) hypothesized to cause one or more outcomes (dependent variables).

Interaction. An effect on a dependent (outcome) variable of a combination of two or more factors or independent variables that is not simply the sum of the separate effects of the variables. For example, giving a rat either food or water would have a small positive effect on his survival, but giving him both food and water would have an interactive positive effect beyond the sum of the effects of food and water alone.

Internal Consistency. The degree to which scores on items in a scale correlate with one another. Several measures of scale reliability, such as coefficient alpha, KR-20, and split-half reliability, are internal consistency measures.

Internal Validity. The degree to which the results of a study can be attributed to the treatments or other independent variables identified in the hypothesis, as opposed to bias or uncontrolled factors.

Interval Scale. A scale of measurement in which any two adjacent values are the same distance apart, but in which there is no meaningful zero point. For example, in Fahrenheit and centigrade temperature scales, the difference between 32 degrees and 33 degrees is the same as that between −5 degrees and −4 degrees, but there is no zero point, so 32 degrees is not "twice" 16 degrees. *Compare* **Nominal Scale, Ordinal Scale,** and **Ratio Scale.**

Interview Protocol. A carefully laid out set of questions and instructions used by an interviewer to conduct an interview.

Interview. A structured series of questions given by an interviewer to which respondents make verbal responses. *Compare* **Questionnaire.**

John Henry Effect. A tendency of subjects in a control group to exert outstanding efforts because they are conscious of being in an experiment and do not want to come out worse than the experimental group. *Compare* "Hawthorne Effect." *Also see* **Reactivity** and **Social Desirability Bias.**

Kurtosis. The degree to which the shape of distribution departs from the bell shape characteristic of a normal curve. Examples of distributions with non-normal kurtosis are distributions more clustered around the mean than a normal distribution (producing a "peaked" curve) and distributions more spread out than a normal curve (producing a "flat-topped" curve). *Compare* **Skewed Distribution.**

KR-20. An internal consistency measure of scale reliability for scales in which only two possible answers (for example, right-wrong, agree-disagree, yes-no) are coded. *Compare* **Coefficient Alpha.**

Linear Relationship. A correlational relationship between two variables that is the same at every value of the variables. For example, there is a positive correlation between height and weight at every value of these variables. *Compare* **Curvilinear Relationship.** *Also see* **Correlation.**

Low-Inference Behaviors. Behaviors observed by a behavioral observer that require minimal judgement to code correctly. Examples are "teacher is talking," "student in seat," and so on. *Compare* **High-Inference Behaviors.**

Main Effect. A simple effect of a factor or independent variable on a dependent (outcome) variable. *Compare* **Interaction.**

Mean. The average of a set of numbers (that is, the sum of a set of scores divided by the number of scores).

Median. The middle number in a set of ranked scores, or (if the number of scores is even) the number halfway between the two scores closest to the middle of a ranked list of scores.

Mediating Factors. Variables that may be caused by some variables (such as background factors) and in turn cause other variables. *See* **Path Analysis.**

Mode. The most frequent score in a set of scores.

Multiple Baseline Design. A single-case experimental design in which a baseline is established on some variable, a treatment is applied, and then the treatment is applied to the same subject in a different setting, to a different behavior, or a different subject. If an abrupt change in the variable occurs at the time the treatment is introduced for two or more behaviors, settings, or subjects, the variable is assumed to be under the control of the treatment. *Compare* **Reversal Design.**

Multiple Regression. A statistical method that evaluates the effects of one or more independent variable(s) on a dependent (outcome) variable.

Mutual Causation. A situation in which each of two variables affects the other. For example, achievement level affects student self-esteem, which in turn affects achievement.

Nominal Scale. A scale of measurement in which numbers simply identify individuals but have no order or value (for example, School 215, Bus 12). *Compare* **Ordinal Scale, Interval Scale** and **Ratio Scale.**

Nonexperimental Designs. Research designs in which the researcher measures or observes subjects without attempting to alter any aspect of the situation. Includes correlational and descriptive designs.

Nonparametric Statistics. Statistics designed for use with distributions that do not meet the assumptions required for use of parametric statistics.

Norm-Referenced Test. A test designed to indicate how any individual performs in comparison to others (such as others of the same grade level or age). *Compare* **Criterion-Referenced Test.**

Normal Curve, Normal Distribution. A distribution of scores on some variable in which most scores are near the mean and other scores cluster around the mean in a symmetrical bell-shaped pattern. A normal distribution is a mathematically defined theoretical distribution of scores, but many variables (such as height, weight, and intelligence) have distributions that closely resemble a normal distribution. *Compare* **Skewed Distribution** and **Kurtosis.**

Norms. Standards for performance of some kind. On a standardized test, the norms would indicate how any score would compare with the scores of a large group of individuals (such as students at a particular grade level or age).

Null Hypothesis (H_o). A hypothesis that two or more variables are *not* related, or that the means of two or more treatment groups on some variable are not different. The task of research is to provide overwhelming evidence that the null hypothesis is untenable. *See* **One-Tailed Test of Significance** and **Two-Tailed Test of Significance.**

Occurrence Reliability.   A measure of reliability used in behavioral observation that compares the number of observation intervals in which each of two observers agreed that they saw a particular behavior divided by the number of intervals in which either observer reported seeing that behavior. Occurrence reliability is computed on each category in a behavioral observation scheme, in contrast to overall reliability, which is computed on the entire scheme. Occurrence reliability may also be used to compute reliability in coding of interview responses.

One-Tailed Test of Significance.   A test of a directional hypothesis (for example, $H_0: \mu_1 > \mu_2$), in which the possibility that the results will come out in a direction opposite to that hypothesized is ignored. *Compare* **Two-Tailed Test of Significance.** *Also see* **Null Hypothesis.**

One-Way Analysis of Variance (or Covariance).   Analysis of variance (or covariance) with a single factor.

Open-Form Question.   A question on a questionnaire or interview to which subjects may give any answer, as "Why did you choose this college?" *Compare* **Closed-Form Question.**

Opinion Polling.   Surveys of the opinions of some group of people on one or more topics. Usually involves sampling of a relatively small but representative group from among a much larger population. *See* **Survey, Sampling.**

Ordinal Scale.   A scale of measurement in which numbers indicate rank (for example, 5 is higher than 6), but differences between ranks may not be equal (for example, the difference between ranks 1 and 2 may not be the same as that between ranks 9 and 10). Finishing positions in a race is an ordinal scale. *Compare* **Nominal Scale, Interval Scale** and **Ratio Scale.**

Outcome Variable.   Same as **Dependent Variable.**

Overall Reliability.   A measure of reliability used in behavioral observation that compares the number of observation intervals in which each of two observers agreed to the total number of intervals. Overall reliability is computed on an entire observation scheme, in contrast to occurrence reliability, which is computed on each observation category. Overall reliability may also be used to compute reliability in coding of interview responses.

Parallel Forms Reliability.   A measure of scale reliability that is the correlation between the scores of two closely related ("parallel") forms of the same scale.

Parameter.   Any statistic (such as the mean, standard deviation, skewness, kurtosis) describing a distribution of scores. *See* **Parametric Statistics** and **Nonparametric Statistics.**

Parametric Statistics.   Statistics designed for use with distributions that meet certain assumptions, such as interval or ratio scales approximating a normal distribution. *Compare* **Nonparametric Statistics.**

Partial Correlation.   A correlation in which the relationship between two variables has the effect of a third variable removed. *See* **Control Variable.**

Path Analysis.   A method of evaluating components of a theoretically derived causal model by computing correlations between pairs of variables, controlling for other variables presumed to be earlier in a chain of causality. For example, a path analysis might be conducted to construct a causal model showing how ultimate occupational success is a product of background factors (for example, sex, race, parents' education and income), and mediating factors, such as the individual's education, abilities, peer relationships, attitudes, and life experiences.

Percentile Score, Percentile Rank. A score that indicates what percent of some category of test-takers were exceeded by a certain raw score. For example, if a fifth grader scores in the 58th percentile for his or her grade level, this means that the student's score exceeded that of 58% of all fifth graders on whom the test was normed (standardized).

Pilot Study. A preliminary study conducted to try out experimental procedures for the purpose of working out potential problems before the main study begins.

Pilot Test. Administration of a test or scale to individuals like those who will ultimately be in a study for the purpose of working out potential problems in the test or test administration procedures before the main study begins.

Population. A large group to which the results of a study involving a subgroup ("Sample") are meant to apply (for example, all third graders, all high school teachers, etc.). *Compare* **Sample.** *Also see* **Sampling.**

Posttest. A test or questionnaire given at the end of some treatment period.

Power Test. A test without a time limit or with such a generous time limit that few test takers will run out of time. *Compare* **Speeded Test.**

Predictive Validity. The degree to which scores on a scale or test predict later behavior or scores.

Pretest. A test or questionnaire given before some treatment begins.

Pretest Effects. The effects on a subject's posttest score of the subject's having taken a pretest. For example, taking a pretest may increase a posttest score by giving subjects practice or by alerting them to the topics to be covered on the posttest.

Privacy Act. A law (PL93-579) establishing who may have access to educational records of various kinds, and when parents' consent must be obtained for release of information to individuals other than school district employees.

Programmed Instruction. Any of several instructional methods in which students proceed through individualized curriculum materials at their own rate.

Questionnaire. A set of written questions usually consisting of one or more scales, to which respondents make written responses. *Compare* **Interview.**

Random Assignment. Selection into one or another treatment (or control) group in an experimental comparison design by chance, in such a way that all individuals to be assigned have a known and equal probability of being assigned to any given group. *Also see* **Stratified Random Assignment.**

Random Variation. Chance differences in variables not due to any systematic cause. Successive die rolls exhibit random variation.

Range. The difference between the highest and lowest values in a set of scores.

Ratio Scale. A scale of measurement in which any two adjacent values are the same distance apart and there is a true zero point. Examples are age, height, percent correct on a test, and so on. *Compare* **Nominal Scale, Ordinal Scale,** and **Interval Scale.**

Reactivity. The tendency of observation or experimentation to change the phenomenon being studied. For example, students may act differently when an observer is watching them than when the observer is not there; individuals may act differently when they know that they are in an experiment rather than in usual circumstances. *See* **Hawthorne Effect, John Henry Effect, Social Desirability Bias.**

Reliability. Consistency of a measure over time, across subjects, tests, or observers, or within a test or scale. Reliability may also refer to consistency of a difference or relationship between variables. *Compare* **Validity.** *Also see* **Reliability Coefficient.**

Reliability Coefficient.   A statistic indicating the reliability of a scale, observation system, or interview coding system. Reliability coefficients may range from 0 (complete unreliability) to 1.0 (complete reliability). *See* **Coefficient Alpha, KR-20, Internal Consistency, Split-Half Reliability, Test-Retest Reliability,** and **Parallel Forms Reliability.**

Representativeness.   The degree to which a sample resembles in important aspects the population from which it was drawn.

Research Design.   Selecting samples, assigning individuals to treatments, measuring outcomes, analyzing data, and so on, for the purpose of answering a well-defined research question.

Research.   Organized inquiry directed at answering questions. *Compare* **Study.**

Reversal Design.   A single-case experimental design in which a baseline is established on some variable, a treatment is applied, and then the treatment is removed. If changes in the variable correspond to changes in the treatment, the variable is assumed to be under the control of the treatment. Often designated ABA, ABAB, ABABA designs, where A is baseline, B is treatment.

Sample.   A group of subjects chosen from a larger group ("Population") to which research findings are assumed to apply. *See* **Sampling.**

Sampling.   Systematic procedures for choosing a group to be in a study that is similar in its characteristics to a larger population. Usually involves random selection of subjects or groups from among a much larger population. *See* **Cluster Sampling, Representativeness.**

Sampling Error.   A statistic that indicates the range of scale units around a sample mean within which there is a 95% chance that the population mean falls. For example, a questionnaire might indicate that 27% of teachers agree that they are adequately paid, with a sampling error of 5%. This means that there is a 95% chance that the population mean on this question would lie between 22% and 32%. Sampling error is twice the standard error of the mean. *See* **Sampling.**

Scale.   A variable composed of the sum of a set of items (as on a questionnaire or test).

School Effects.   The effects on students or teachers of being in a particular school.

Scientific Method.   Systematic inquiry directed at discovering cause-and-effect relationships.

Selection Bias.   Any nonrandom factor that might influence the selection of individuals into one or another treatment. For example, meaningfully comparing private schools and public schools is difficult because there are many nonrandom (systematic) reasons that some students would find themselves in one or the other type of school.

Self-Selection.   A form of selection bias in which individuals' own desires, interests, or abilities cause them to appear in one or another group. For example, it is difficult to compare the effects on students of having teachers who check homework every day to those of having teachers who do not check homework, since teachers who select themselves into the "check homework" group might be different in many other ways from teachers who select themselves into the "don't check homework" group.

Semi-Randomized Experimental Comparisons.   Experimental comparisons in which groups (such as classes or schools) are randomly assigned to treatments, as opposed to random assignment of individuals.

Single-Case Experiment.   An experimental design in which one or more subjects are observed under a succession of treatments. If changes in the subjects' levels on one or more outcomes (dependent variables) accompany changes in introduction and withdrawal of various treatments, the outcomes are demonstrated to be affected by the treatment(s).

Skewed Distribution. An asymmetrical distribution of scores on some variable, with scores clustering toward the high end of the possible range of values (negative skew, as in a ceiling effect) or clustering toward the low end of the possible range of values (positive skew, as in a floor effect). *Compare* **Kurtosis.**

Social Desirability Bias. A tendency of individuals responding to a questionnaire or interview to say what they think the researcher wants to hear, or to give answers that put themselves in the best possible light, rather than to give true but potentially embarrassing information or opinions.

Sociometric Questionnaire. A question or questions (such as "Who are your friends in this class?") directed at finding out about relationships between individuals.

Speeded Test. A test in which a time limit is given. Many students fail to complete such tests because of the time limit. *Compare* **Power Test.**

Split-Half Reliability. An internal consistency measure of scale reliability that is derived from the correlation of scores on half of the items on a scale (such as odd-numbered items) with the other half of the items (such as even-numbered items).

Spurious Correlation. A situation in which two variables are correlated, but neither causes the other, as when both are caused by a third variable. For example, average daily temperature is related to the proportion of students in a country who will go to college. Temperature has no effect on college chances, but underdeveloped countries happen to be located in hotter climates, producing a spurious correlation between temperature and college attendance.

Standard Deviation. A statistic indicating the degree of dispersion or scatter of a set of numbers. The standard deviation is the square root of the variance.

Standard Error of the Mean (S_m). A statistic indicating the degree of potential error with which a sample mean might estimate a population mean. *See* **Sampling Error** and **Sampling.**

Standardized Test. A norm-referenced test designed to determine broad knowledge and skills in a particular area rather than specific knowledge from a particular course or text. Standardized tests are typically given to hundreds or thousands of students to derive norms for certain grade levels or age levels, making it possible to translate a given score into a grade equivalent or percentile rank among a large group of students of a given age or grade.

Statistic. A number that describes some characteristic of a variable such as its mean (average) and variance (dispersion).

Statistical Regression. The tendency of individuals with extremely high scores on one variable to have somewhat lower scores on other similar variables (including the same variable measured a different way or at a different time), or of individuals with extremely low scores to have somewhat higher scores on related variables.

Statistical Significance. A condition in which two or more statistics (such as means) are found to be more different than would be expected by random variation.

Stratified Random Assignment. Random assignment of subjects to one or more groups done in such a way as to insure that each group will have certain characteristics. For example, we might wish to have two groups with equal proportions of boys and girls. To do this, we would randomly assign boys to the two groups, and then randomly assign the girls to the two groups. This would be random assignment stratifying on sex.

Study. Systematic collection of data to answer one or more questions. Examples are experiments, correlational inquiries, ethnographies, and so on. The term "study" usually refers to a single project or closely related set of projects, while "research" is a broader term implying organized inquiry into a problem or problems that may involve many individual studies and many investigators.

Subjects. Individuals whose responses serve as the principal information ("data") in a study.

Survey. Research directed at determining the level of some variable for a particular population, usually by sampling a relatively small but representative group from among a much larger population. For example, we might survey a sample from among all U.S. elementary school principals to see how many elementary schools have microcomputers. An opinion poll is a survey. Surveys may also be used to gather information that will be used in correlational or experimental comparison research. *See* **Sampling** and **Descriptive Research.**

Systematic Bias. *See* **Bias.**

t-Test. A statistic used to test the difference between two means for statistical significance. Also used to test correlation coefficients and regression coefficients for statistical significance.

Teacher Effects. The effects on students of having a particular teacher.

Test-Retest Reliability. A measure of scale reliability that is the correlation between scale scores obtained at one test administration and scores on the same scale taken at a different time.

Theory. A set of propositions linking known or hypothesized facts and relationships to predict one or more outcomes. A theory seeks to explain observed phenomena in a cause-and-effect fashion.

Time Series Analysis. Statistical procedures designed to determine whether an abrupt change in a frequently measured variable occurring at the same time as a treatment is introduced is likely to be related to the introduction of the treatment, rather than coincidence. *Compare* **Reversal Design.**

Treatment. A systematic set of instructions or conditions applied to experimental (but not control) groups in experimental designs.

Two-Tailed Test of Significance. A test of a non-directional hypothesis (for example, H_0: $\mu_1 = \mu_2$) in which it is possible that there will be statistically significant findings in either direction (for example, $\mu_1 > \mu_2$ or $\mu_1 < \mu_2$).

Type I Error. Incorrectly rejecting the null hypothesis. Also called alpha error. *See* **False Positive Error.**

Type II Error. Incorrectly accepting the null hypothesis. Also called Beta Error. *See* **False Negative Error.**

Validity. The degree to which an instrument (such as a test or questionnaire) actually measures the concept or construct it is supposed to measure. Also, the degree to which the results of a study can be attributed to treatments, rather than to flaws in the research design (internal validity), or the degree to which the results of a study have relevance to subjects and settings other than the ones involved in the research (external validity). *Compare* **Reliability,** and *see* **Face Validity, Content Validity, Predictive Validity, Concurrent Validity,** and **Construct Validity.**

Variable. Anything that can take on more than one value (for example, age, sex, science achievement level).

Variance.   A statistic indicating the degree of dispersion or scatter of a set of numbers. The variance is the square of the standard deviation.

z-Score.   A statistic indicating how many standard deviation units a score lies from a sample or population mean. For example, a z-score of -1.50 indicates a score that is $1\frac{1}{2}$ standard deviation units below the mean. The z distribution has a mean of zero and a standard deviation of one. *Compare* **Z-score.**

Z-Score.   A statistic that translates scores on some variable into a distribution with a mean of 50 and a standard deviation of 10. Related to the z-score as follows: $Z = 10z + 50$.

REFERENCES

ALLEN, G.R. *The Graduate Students' Guide to Theses and Dissertations.* San Francisco: Jossey-Bass, 1973.

ANASTASI, A. *Psychological Testing (5th ed.).* New York: Macmillan, 1982.

ANDERSON, G.J. *The Learning Environment Inventory Manual.* Montreal, Canada: Center for Learning and Development, McGill University, 1969.

BARZUN, J., and GRAFF, H. *The Modern Researcher (2nd ed.).* New York: Harcourt Brace Jovanovich, Inc., 1977.

BLAU, T. and DUNCAN, O.D. *The American Occupational Structure.* New York: John Wiley, 1967.

BLOCK, M. *The Historian's Craft.* New York: Knopf, 1953.

BORICH, G.C., and MADDEN, S.K. *Evaluating Classroom Instruction: A Sourcebook of Instruments.* Reading, Mass.: Addison-Wesley, 1977.

BRADBURN, N., and SUDMAN, S. *Improving Interview Method and Questionnaire Design.* San Francisco: Jossey-Bass, 1979.

BRICKMAN, W. *Guide to Research in Educational History.* Norwood, Pa.: Norwood Editions, 1973.

BRICKMAN, W., and CORDASCO, F. *A Bibliography of American Educational History.* New York: AMS Press, 1975.

BUROS, O. *Mental Measurements Yearbook (vol. 8).* Highland Park, N.J.: Gryphon, 1978.

CAMPBELL, W.C. *Form and Style in Thesis Writing.* Boston: Houghton Mifflin, 1969.

CAMPBELL, D.T., and STANLEY, J.C. *Experimental and Quasi-Experimental Designs for Research.* Skokie, Ill.: Rand McNally, 1963.

Chicago Manual of Style (13th ed.). Chicago: University of Chicago Press, 1982.

CHILDERS, P., and ROSS, J. The relationship between viewing television and student achievement. *Journal of Educational Research,* 1973, 66, 317–319.

COHEN, J., and COHEN, P. *Applied Multiple Regression/Correlation Analysis for the Behavioral Sciences.* Hillsdale, N.J.: Lawrence Erlbaum Associates, 1975.

COLEMAN, J.S., and others. *Equality of Educational Opportunity.* Washington, D.C.: U.S. Department of Health, Education, and Welfare, 1966.

COOK, T., and CAMPBELL, D. *Quasi-Experimentation: Design and Analysis Issues for Field Settings.* Chicago: Rand McNally, 1979.

COOPERSMITH, S.A. *Coopersmith Self-Esteem Inventory.* San Francisco: Self Esteem Institute, 1975.

CORNFIELD, J., and TUKEY, J. Average mean squares in factorials.. *Annals of Mathematical Statistics, 1956, 27, 907–949.*

CRONBACH, L. *Essentials of Psychological Testing)(3rd ed.).* New York: Harper & Row, Pub., 1970.

DILLMAN, D. *Mail and Telephone Surveys.* New York: John Wiley, 1978.

DIXON, W. and others. *BMDP Statistical Software (1981 ed.).* Berkeley, Calif.: University of California, 1981.

DUNCAN, O.D. *Introduction to Structural Equation Models.* New York: Academic Press, 1975.

EDWARDS, A. *Statistical Methods.* New York: Holt, Rinehart & Winstopn, 1973.

ESPOSITO, D. Homogeneous and heterogeneous ability grouping: Principal findings and implications for evaluating and designing more effective educational environments, *Review of Educational Research,* 1973, 43, 163–179.

FRANCIS, I.*Statistical Software: A Comparative Review.* New York: North Holland, 1981.

FRASER, B. and FISHER, D. Predicting students' outcomes from their perceptions of classroom psychological environment. *American Educational Research Journal,* 1982, *19,* 498–518.

GLASS, G., and STANLEY, J. *Statistical Methods in Education and Psychology.* Englewood Cliffs, N.J.: Prentice-Hall, 1970.

GOOD, T., and BROPHY, J. *Looking in Classrooms (2nd ed.).* New York: Harper & Row, Pub., 1978.

GUILFORD, J.P., and FRUCHTER, B. *Fundamental Statistics in Education and Psychology.* McGraw-Hill, 1978.

HELMSTADTER, G. *Research Concepts in Human Behavior.* New York: Prentice-Hall, Inc., 1970.

HERBST, J. *The History of American Education: A Bibliography.* Northbrook, Ill.: AHM Publishing, 1973.

HERSEN, M., and BARLOW, D. *Single Case Experimental Designs.* Elmsford, N.Y.: Pergamon Press, 1976.

HOPKINS, K. The unit of analysis: Group means versus individual observations. *American Educational Research Journal,* 1982, 19, 5–18.

HOPKINS, K., and GLASS, G. *Basic Statistics for the Behavioral Sciences.* Englewood Cliffs, N.J.: Prentice-Hall, 1978.

HULL, C.H., and NIE, N. *SPSS Update 7–9* New York: McGraw-Hill, 1981.

KAZDIN, A. Statistical analyses for single case experimental designs. In M. Hersen and D. Barlow, *Single Case Experimental Designs,* Elmsford, N.Y.: Pergamon Press, 1976.

KEITH, T. Time spent on homework and high school grades: A large sample path analysis. *Journal of Educational Psychology,* 1982, 74, 248–253.

KEPPEL, G. *Design and Analysis: A Researcher's Handbook (2nd ed.).* Englewood Cliffs, N.J.: Prentice-Hall, 1982.

KISH, L. *Survey Sampling.* New York: John Wiley, 1965.

KLECKA, W., NIE, N., and HULL, C.H. *SPSS Primer.* New York: McGraw-Hill, 1975.

LAZERWITZ, B. Sampling theory and procedures. In H. Blalock and A. Blalock (eds.), *Methodology in Social Research.* New York: McGraw-Hill, 1968.

LORD, F.   Large-sample covariance analysis when the control variable is fallible. *Journal of the American Statistical Association,* 1960, 55, 307–321.

MADDEN, N.   Effects of cooperative learning on the social acceptance of mainstreamed academically handicapped students. Unpublished Doctoral Dissertation, American University, 1980.

MARSH, H.   Validity of students' evaluations of college teaching: Multimethod analysis. *Journal of Educational Psychology,* 1982, 74, 264—279.

MCCLEARY, R., and HAY, R.   *Applied Time Series Analysis for the Social Sciences.* Beverly Hills, Calif.: Sage Publications, Inc., 1980.

MORENO, J.L.   *Who Shall Survive?* Washington, D.C.: Nervous and Mental Disease Publishing Company, 1934.

NIE, N., HULL, C.H., JENKINS, J., STEINBRENNER, K., and BENT, D.   *Statistical Package for the Social Sciences (2nd ed.).* New York: McGraw-Hill, 1975.

NORUSIS, M.   *SPSS Introductory Guide: Basic Statistics and Operations.* New York: McGraw-Hill, 1982.

OVERHOLT, G., and STALLINGS, W.   Ethnographic and experimental hypotheses in educational research. *Educational Researcher,* 1976, 5 (8), 12–14.

PAGE, E.   Statistically recapturing the richness within the classroom. *Psychology in the Schools,* 1975, 12, 339–344.

PAYNE, S.   *The Art of Asking Questions.* Princeton, N.J.: Princeton University Press, 1951.

PEDHAZUR, E.   *Multiple Regression in Behavioral Research.* New York: Holt, Rinehart & Winston, 1982.

PETERSON, P., SWING, S., BRAVERMAN, M., and BUSS, R.   Students' aptitudes and their reports of cognitive processes during direct instruction. *Journal of Educational Psychology,* 1982, 74, 535–547.

POPHAM, J.   *Educational Statistics: Use and Interpretation.* New York: Harper & Row, 1973.

Publication Manual of the American Psychological Association (3rd ed). Washington, D.C.: APA, 1983.

RIEBEL, J.   *How to Write Reports, Papers, Theses, and Articles.* New York: Arco, 1972.

ROETHLISBERGER, F., and DICKSON, W.   *Management and the Worker.* Cambridge, Mass.: Harvard University Press, 1939.

SAS User's Guide (1982 ed.).   Cary, N.C.: SAS Institute, Inc., 1982.

SCHUNK, D.   Effects of effort attributional feedback on children's perceived self-efficacy and achievement. *Journal of Educational Psychology,* 1982, 74, 548–556.

SCHWARTZWALD, J., and COHEN, S.   Relationship between academic tracking and degree of interracial acceptance. *Journal of Educational Psychology,* 1982, 74, 588–597.

SHAVELSON, R.   *Statistical Reasoning for the Behavioral Sciences.* Newton, Mass.: Allyn and Bacon, 1981.

SHAW, M.E., and WRIGHT, J.   *Scales for the Measurement of Attitudes.* New York: McGraw-Hill, 1967.

SIMON, A. and BOYER, E.G., eds.   *Mirrors for Behavior.* Philadelphia Research for Better Schools, 1967.

SLAVIN, R.E.   Student level analysis in experiments with random assignment of intact classes. Paper presented at the Annual Convention of the American Educational Research Association, Montreal, 1983.

SLAVIN, R.E.   Basic vs. applied research: A response. *Educational Researcher,* 1978, 7 (2), 15–17.

SPENCE, J., COTTON, J., UNDERWOOD, B., and DUNCAN, C. *Elementary Statistics (4th ed.)*. Englewood Cliffs, N.J.: Prentice-Hall, 1982.

STAKE, J., and KATZ, J. Teacher-pupil relationships in the elementary school classroom: teacher-gender and pupil-gender differences. *American Educational Research Journal,* 1982, 19, 465–471.

STANLEY, J. Reliability. In Thorndike, R.L., ed., *Educational Measurement (2nd ed.)*. Washington, D.C.: American Council on Education, 1971.

SUDMAN, S. *Applied Sampling*. New York: Academic Press, 1976.

TURABIAN, K. *A Manual for Writers of Term Papers, Theses, and Dissertations.* Chicago: University of Chicago Press, 1973.

WELCH, W., ANDERSON, R., and HARRIS, L. The effects of schooling on mathematics achievement. *American Educational Research Journal,* 1982, 19, 145–153.

WILSON, S. The use of ethnographic techniques in educational research. *Review of Educational Research,* 1977, 47, 245–265.

WINER, B.J. *Statistical Principles in Experimental Design*. New York: McGraw-Hill, 1971.

WOODBURY, M. *A Guide to Sources of Educational Information*. Washington, D.C.: Information Resources Press, 1976.

YARROW, L. Interviewing children. In P. Mussen, ed., *The Handbook of Research Methods in Child Development*. New York: John Wiley, 1960.

Author Index

Subject Index